Java™ Programming For Dummies
3rd Edition

 W9-CGY-231

Cheat Sheet

Responding to Java Events

To Handle This Event	Use This Listener	Use This Method
User moved mouse to object area	MouseListener	public void mouseEntered()
User moved mouse out of object area	MouseListener	public void mouseExited()
User pressed mouse button	MouseListener	public void mousePressed()
User released mouse button	MouseListener	public void mouseReleased()
User pressed and released mouse button	MouseListener	public void mouseClicked()
User moved mouse	MouseMotionListener	public void mouseMoved()
User dragged mouse	MouseMotionListener	public void mouseDragged()
User pressed key	KeyListener	public void keyPressed()
User released key	KeyListener	public void keyReleased()
User pressed and released key	KeyListener	public void keyTyped()
User pressed Return key in text area	ActionListener	public void actionPerformed()
User selected item	ItemListener	public void itemStateChanged()
User deselected item	ItemListener	public void itemStateChanged()
User clicked button	ActionListener	public void actionPerformed()
User clicked checkbox	ItemListener	public void itemStateChanged()
User selected item	ItemListener	public void itemStateChanged()
User double-clicked item on list	ActionListener	public void actionPerformed()
Object got focus	FocusListener	public void focusGained()
Object lost focus	FocusListener	public void focusLost()

Using Java Classes

If You Want to Make	Follow This Example
package declaration	package *MyPackage*
class declaration	public class *MyClass* extends *MyParentClass* {*variable declarations* *constructors* *methods*}
constructor	*MyClass* (*type parameter1, type parameter2, and so on*) { *setup statements*; }
method	public *returntype MyMethod* {*statements*; }

IDG BOOKS WORLDWIDE

For Dummies®: Bestselling Book Series for Beginners

Java Programming For Dummies, 3rd Edition

Cheat Sheet

Using Java Statements

To Use This Statement	Follow This Example (the elements that you must supply are shown in italics)
if	if (*expression*) {*contingent statements*}
if. . .else	if (*expression*) {*contingent statements*} else {*contingent statements*}

switch	switch (*expression*) {
	    case **val1**: *statements*; break;
	    case **val2**: *statements*; break;
	    ...
	    default: *statements*; break}

for	for (*initialization; expression; increment*) {*loop statements*}
while	while (*expression*) {*loop statements*}

Using Java GUI Components

If You Want to Make	Follow This Example
button	Button *okButton* = new Button ("*OK*");
checkbox	Checkbox *espresso* = new Checkbox ("*Espresso*"); Checkbox *cappuccino* = new Checkbox ("*Cappuccino*"); add (*espresso*); add (*cappuccino*);
checkbox group (radio buttons)	CheckboxGroup *Coffee* = new CheckboxGroup() Checkbox *esp* = new Checkbox ("*Espresso*",*Coffee, true*); Checkbox *cap* = new Checkbox ("*Cappuccino*",*Coffee, false*); add (*esp*); add (*cap*);
choice (drop-down list)	Choice *drinks* = new Choice(); *drinks*.addItem ("*Espresso*"); *drinks*.addItem ("*Cappuccino*");
list	List *coffee* = new List(); *coffee*.addItem ("*Espresso*"); *coffee*.addItem ("*Cappuccino*");
text field	TextField *textField* = new TextField("*TextField*"); add(*textField*);
text area (multiline)	TextArea *textArea* = new TextArea(*5,10*); add(*textArea*);
label	Label *coffeeLabel* = new Label ("*Coffee, anyone?*");

TM

References for the Rest of Us!®

BESTSELLING BOOK SERIES

Are you intimidated and confused by computers? Do you find that traditional manuals are overloaded with technical details you'll never use? Do your friends and family always call you to fix simple problems on their PCs? Then the *...For Dummies*® computer book series from IDG Books Worldwide is for you.

...For Dummies books are written for those frustrated computer users who know they aren't really dumb but find that PC hardware, software, and indeed the unique vocabulary of computing make them feel helpless. *...For Dummies* books use a lighthearted approach, a down-to-earth style, and even cartoons and humorous icons to dispel computer novices' fears and build their confidence. Lighthearted but not lightweight, these books are a perfect survival guide for anyone forced to use a computer.

Already, millions of satisfied readers agree. They have made *...For Dummies* books the #1 introductory level computer book series and have written asking for more. So, if you're looking for the most fun and easy way to learn about computers, look to *...For Dummies* books to give you a helping hand.

IDG BOOKS WORLDWIDE

JAVA™
PROGRAMMING
FOR
DUMMIES®
3RD EDITION

JAVA™ PROGRAMMING FOR DUMMIES®
3RD EDITION

by Donald Koosis
and David Koosis

IDG Books Worldwide, Inc.
An International Data Group Company

Foster City, CA ♦ Chicago, IL ♦ Indianapolis, IN ♦ New York, NY

Java™ Programming For Dummies,® 3rd Edition

Published by
IDG Books Worldwide, Inc.
An International Data Group Company
919 E. Hillsdale Blvd.
Suite 400
Foster City, CA 94404
www.idgbooks.com (IDG Books Worldwide Web site)
www.dummies.com (Dummies Press Web site)

Library of Congress Catalog Card No.: 98-87912

ISBN: 0-7645-0388-X

Printed in the United States of America

10 9 8 7 6

3O/RZ/QS/QQ/IN

Distributed in the United States by IDG Books Worldwide, Inc.

Distributed by CDG Books Canada Inc. for Canada; by Transworld Publishers Limited in the United Kingdom; by IDG Norge Books for Norway; by IDG Sweden Books for Sweden; by IDG Books Australia Publishing Corporation Pty. Ltd. for Australia and New Zealand; by TransQuest Publishers Pte Ltd. for Singapore, Malaysia, Thailand, Indonesia, and Hong Kong; by Gotop Information Inc. for Taiwan; by ICG Muse, Inc. for Japan; by Intersoft for South Africa; by Eyrolles for France; by International Thomson Publishing for Germany, Austria and Switzerland; by Distribuidora Cuspide for Argentina; by LR International for Brazil; by Galileo Libros for Chile; by Ediciones ZETA S.C.R. Ltda. for Peru; by WS Computer Publishing Corporation, Inc., for the Philippines; by Contemporanea de Ediciones for Venezuela; by Express Computer Distributors for the Caribbean and West Indies; by Micronesia Media Distributor, Inc. for Micronesia; by Chips Computadoras S.A. de C.V. for Mexico; by Editorial Norma de Panama S.A. for Panama; by American Bookshops for Finland.

For general information on IDG Books Worldwide's books in the U.S., please call our Consumer Customer Service department at 800-762-2974. For reseller information, including discounts and premium sales, please call our Reseller Customer Service department at 800-434-3422.

For information on where to purchase IDG Books Worldwide's books outside the U.S., please contact our International Sales department at 317-596-5530 or fax 317-572-4002.

For consumer information on foreign language translations, please contact our Customer Service department at 1-800-434-3422, fax 317-572-4002, or e-mail rights@idgbooks.com.

For information on licensing foreign or domestic rights, please phone +1-650-653-7098.

For sales inquiries and special prices for bulk quantities, please contact our Order Services department at 800-434-3422 or write to the address above.

For information on using IDG Books Worldwide's books in the classroom or for ordering examination copies, please contact our Educational Sales department at 800-434-2086 or fax 317-572-4005.

For press review copies, author interviews, or other publicity information, please contact our Public Relations department at 650-653-7000 or fax 650-653-7500.

For authorization to photocopy items for corporate, personal, or educational use, please contact Copyright Clearance Center, 222 Rosewood Drive, Danvers, MA 01923, or fax 978-750-4470.

is a registered trademark under exclusive license to IDG Books Worldwide, Inc. from International Data Group, Inc.

About the Authors

Donald Koosis has developed materials to help people understand computers for more than 20 years. He has worked for IBM, Bell Labs, Xerox, and now owns his own company, Instructional Systems Co., Inc. He is the author of best-selling self-instructional books on Statistics and Electricity/Electronics. He can be reached at donald@isc.com.

David Koosis is a native citizen of cyberspace. He writes programs to help computers understand people, working in Java, Delphi, C++, and other unspeakable tongues. David has developed software for a variety of Fortune 500 companies and Wall Street firms. He co-developed the 1994 edition of *PC Magazine*'s computer benchmarks and has contributed to several successful commercial software programs. He is head of software development for ISC Consultants, Inc., and can be reached at dkoosis@isc.com.

ABOUT IDG BOOKS WORLDWIDE

Welcome to the world of IDG Books Worldwide.

IDG Books Worldwide, Inc., is a subsidiary of International Data Group, the world's largest publisher of computer-related information and the leading global provider of information services on information technology. IDG was founded more than 30 years ago by Patrick J. McGovern and now employs more than 9,000 people worldwide. IDG publishes more than 290 computer publications in over 75 countries. More than 90 million people read one or more IDG publications each month.

Launched in 1990, IDG Books Worldwide is today the #1 publisher of best-selling computer books in the United States. We are proud to have received eight awards from the Computer Press Association in recognition of editorial excellence and three from Computer Currents' First Annual Readers' Choice Awards. Our best-selling ...For Dummies® series has more than 50 million copies in print with translations in 31 languages. IDG Books Worldwide, through a joint venture with IDG's Hi-Tech Beijing, became the first U.S. publisher to publish a computer book in the People's Republic of China. In record time, IDG Books Worldwide has become the first choice for millions of readers around the world who want to learn how to better manage their businesses.

Our mission is simple: Every one of our books is designed to bring extra value and skill-building instructions to the reader. Our books are written by experts who understand and care about our readers. The knowledge base of our editorial staff comes from years of experience in publishing, education, and journalism — experience we use to produce books to carry us into the new millennium. In short, we care about books, so we attract the best people. We devote special attention to details such as audience, interior design, use of icons, and illustrations. And because we use an efficient process of authoring, editing, and desktop publishing our books electronically, we can spend more time ensuring superior content and less time on the technicalities of making books.

You can count on our commitment to deliver high-quality books at competitive prices on topics you want to read about. At IDG Books Worldwide, we continue in the IDG tradition of delivering quality for more than 30 years. You'll find no better book on a subject than one from IDG Books Worldwide.

John Kilcullen
Chairman and CEO
IDG Books Worldwide, Inc.

Eighth Annual
Computer Press
Awards ≥1992

Ninth Annual
Computer Press
Awards ≥1993

Tenth Annual
Computer Press
Awards ≥1994

Eleventh Annual
Computer Press
Awards ≥1995

IDG is the world's leading IT media, research and exposition company. Founded in 1964, IDG had 1997 revenues of $2.05 billion and has more than 9,000 employees worldwide. IDG offers the widest range of media options that reach IT buyers in 75 countries representing 95% of worldwide IT spending. IDG's diverse product and services portfolio spans six key areas including print publishing, online publishing, expositions and conferences, market research, education and training, and global marketing services. More than 90 million people read one or more of IDG's 290 magazines and newspapers, including IDG's leading global brands — Computerworld, PC World, Network World, Macworld and the Channel World family of publications. IDG Books Worldwide is one of the fastest-growing computer book publishers in the world, with more than 700 titles in 36 languages. The "...For Dummies®" series alone has more than 50 million copies in print. IDG offers online users the largest network of technology-specific Web sites around the world through IDG.net (http://www.idg.net), which comprises more than 225 targeted Web sites in 55 countries worldwide. International Data Corporation (IDC) is the world's largest provider of information technology data, analysis and consulting, with research centers in over 41 countries and more than 400 research analysts worldwide. IDG World Expo is a leading producer of more than 168 globally branded conferences and expositions in 35 countries including E3 (Electronic Entertainment Expo), Macworld Expo, ComNet, Windows World Expo, ICE (Internet Commerce Expo), Agenda, DEMO, and Spotlight. IDG's training subsidiary, ExecuTrain, is the world's largest computer training company, with more than 230 locations worldwide and 785 training courses. IDG Marketing Services helps industry-leading IT companies build international brand recognition by developing global integrated marketing programs via IDG's print, online and exposition products worldwide. Further information about the company can be found at www.idg.com.
1/26/00

Dedication

To four generations of beautiful, bright, strong women:

Pauline   Irene   Rachel   Sarah and Emma

Authors' Acknowledgments

Our thanks to Pat O'Brien, project editor; Paula Lowell, copy editor; and the rest of the IDG Books staff that helped bring this new edition to birth. Thanks also to Irene Mungiu for her business judgment, moral support, and editorial suggestions, without which neither this edition nor its predecessor would have existed. And to the hundreds of readers of the first edition who asked questions, pointed out errors, and cheered us on — *thanks*.

For the previous edition, our thanks to Kathy Cox, Kelly Oliver, Constance Carlisle, Leah Cameron, and Susan Christophersen for their intelligent and sensitive editorial guidance and assistance. They were graceful partners under the pressures of a demanding schedule. And, similarly, thanks to our technical reviewer, Jesper Rasmussen, for keeping us honest with attentive but constructive feedback.

Thanks to Diane Steele, Mary Bednarek, and Gareth Hancock for recognizing the need for a book like this one and allowing us to be its authors.

Besides being a pleasure to work with, our colleague Anatoly Goroshnik contributed three of the applets in Part III, Sprites, JavaBots, and Fractals. Rachel Vigier provided valuable assistance in obtaining permissions for the applets that appear on the CD-ROM that comes with this book. Generous programmers from all over the world — members of the Java Internet community — consented to share their work on the CD that comes with this book. We thank them and encourage you to follow their example.

Thanks also to Raymond Mungiu for reviewing the manuscript and to Aron Koosis for reminding us not to take ourselves too seriously.

Publisher's Acknowledgments

We're proud of this book; please register your comments through our IDG Books Worldwide Online Registration Form located at http://my2cents.dummies.com.

Some of the people who helped bring this book to market include the following:

Acquisitions, Editorial, and Media Development

Project Editor: Pat O'Brien
(*Previous Editions: Kathy Cox, Kelly Oliver*)

Acquisitions Editor: Joyce Pepple

Copy Editor: Paula Lowell

Technical Editor: Jesper Rasmussen

Media Development Editor: Marita Ellixson

Associate Permissions Editor: Carmen Krikorian

Media Development Coordinator: Megan Roney

Editorial Manager: Mary C. Corder

Media Development Manager: Heather Heath Dismore

Editorial Assistant: Alison Walthall

Production

Project Coordinator: Regina Snyder

Layout and Graphics: Lou Boudreau, J. Tyler Connor, Angela F. Hunckler, Brent Savage, Jacque Schneider, Rashell Smith, Michael A. Sullivan, Brian Torwelle

Proofreaders: Christine Berman, Michelle Croninger

Indexer: Liz Cunningham

General and Administrative

IDG Books Worldwide, Inc.: John Kilcullen, CEO

IDG Books Technology Publishing Group: Richard Swadley, Senior Vice President and Publisher; Walter Bruce III, Vice President and Associate Publisher; Joseph Wikert, Associate Publisher; Mary Bednarek, Branded Product Development Director; Mary Corder, Editorial Director; Barry Pruett, Publishing Manager; Michelle Baxter, Publishing Manager

IDG Books Consumer Publishing Group: Roland Elgey, Senior Vice President and Publisher; Kathleen A. Welton, Vice President and Publisher; Kevin Thornton, Acquisitions Manager; Kristin A. Cocks, Editorial Director

IDG Books Internet Publishing Group: Brenda McLaughlin, Senior Vice President and Publisher; Diane Graves Steele, Vice President and Associate Publisher; Sofia Marchant, Online Marketing Manager

IDG Books Production for Dummies Press: Debbie Stailey, Associate Director of Production; Cindy L. Phipps, Manager of Project Coordination, Production Proofreading, and Indexing; Tony Augsburger, Manager of Prepress, Reprints, and Systems; Laura Carpenter, Production Control Manager; Shelley Lea, Supervisor of Graphics and Design; Debbie J. Gates, Production Systems Specialist; Robert Springer, Supervisor of Proofreading; Kathie Schutte, Production Supervisor

Dummies Packaging and Book Design: Patty Page, Manager, Promotions Marketing

◆

The publisher would like to give special thanks to Patrick J. McGovern, without whom this book would not have been possible.

◆

Contents at a Glance

Cartoons at a Glance

By Rich Tennant

page 291

page 323

page 7

page 301

page 71

page 177

Fax: 978-546-7747
E-mail: richtennant@the5thwave.com
World Wide Web: www.the5thwave.com

Table of Contents

Introduction

● ●

*W*elcome to *Java Programming For Dummies*, 3rd Edition! This book is the quickest way to start making your own Java applets to add to your World Wide Web pages or your corporate intranet. Java applets, short programs that add interactivity and computing power, can be distributed over the Internet or your intranet as part of a Web page and can run on almost any type of computer now manufactured.

Other books about Java assume that you have a black belt in computer science and a burning desire to know the details of synchronizing threads, throwing exceptions, and other Java beasties.

This book assumes you want to make applets.

Who Are You?

Because you're holding this book in your hands, we want to make a few more assumptions about you:

- You have access to a computer that can run Java. (Most common types of personal computers and workstations that connect to the Internet qualify.)
- You have surfed the World Wide Web.
- You know a bit of HTML and may have your own Web page.
- You've heard all the ruckus about Java and want to see what it's about.
- You may have written some macros or even programs in Visual Basic, C++, or Pascal.
- You do not invent your own computer languages as a form of relaxation.

About This Book

This book is intended to quickly get you writing your own Java applets. We don't intend for this book to turn you into an object-oriented programming guru, but we do want to give you the confidence to try your hand at putting interesting, fun, and useful Java applets on your Web pages.

We give you a firm foundation in the basic tools of a Java programmer without trying to explain every nook and cranny of the language. Sample topics you find in this book include the following:

Object-Oriented Programming: The Basic Elements

Inside the Programmer's Mind

The Java Interpreter

Writing the Code for Your Applet

Rules of Punctuation and Grammar for Class and Method Definitions

This book is based on the newest version of the Java language, Java 2. This new version of Java is a bit easier to master and a bit more powerful, but it is basically the same language as the original Java 1.0 and its earlier upgrade, Java 1.1. When you are comfortable with Java 2, you understand the earlier versions of Java as well.

How This Book Is Organized

There are six parts to this book. The book begins with a whirlwind tour, moves on to a more systematic treatment of the basics of the language, and then gives you sample applet code and a variety of additional, useful information.

Part I: Hello, Java

This part is an overview of Java, the Internet, and the whole kettle of fish. We explain the significance of Java and its place in cyberspace as succinctly as we can. We talk about the unique features of Java, applications of Java on the World Wide Web, and the importance of having a Java-enabled Web browser (that's how you look at the wonderful applets you create).

Next, we introduce you to a simple Java applet and the thought processes (the dreaded mind of a programmer) that bring it about. Of course, we must include a chapter on HTML, HyperText Markup Language, so that you know how to include your Java applets on your Web pages. Finally, we give you an introduction to the terms and concepts relating to the components of object-oriented programming (and, you know, Java is an object-oriented programming language).

Part II: Javanese

In Part II, we talk about Java language basics. We start with *yet another* "HelloWorld" program (with a New York twist) and explain how to embed applets in your Web pages. You discover the object of *objects* and *object-oriented programming*. You try using some Java building blocks such as *if, for,* and *while.* And you master *classes.*

Part III: Caffeinated Pages

This part is our cookbook of Java applet examples:

- ✔ **Calendar:** A `calendar` class for selecting dates
- ✔ **Ticker Tape:** A scrolling ticker tape
- ✔ **Sprite:** A simple `sprite` class for making stuff fly around the screen
- ✔ **JavaBots:** An animated game written in Java
- ✔ **Quizem:** An interactive quiz engine
- ✔ **Shopping Cart:** A simple database applet that uses CGI (that is, Common Gateway Interface)
- ✔ **Fractal:** Where mathematics meets art

Along the way, we show you a bit about animation, databases, and other useful programming tools.

Part IV: Only Java

Part IV gives you the word about the other kind of Java programs, the ones that don't run in a Web browser: Java applications. And this part's solitary chapter looks at the current and future status of Java as a programming language.

Part V: The Part of Tens

This part, familiar to *...For Dummies* readers, provides a home for several of the goodies we couldn't bear to give up telling you about, but had trouble finding a home for. We include "Ten Common Mistakes," and "Ten Facts about the Other Java." (Yes, the island!)

About the CD-ROM

The CD-ROM at the back of this book includes all the software you need to start writing Java applets, as well as some extra goodies:

- ✔ The Java Developer's Kit from Sun Microsystems Inc., for Windows 95, Windows NT, Macintosh System 7.5, and Solaris.
- ✔ Some nifty applets from the international online Java community including graphics effects, text effects, games, and more!
- ✔ Code excerpts from Part II of this book, to save you the effort of typing.
- ✔ The applets from Part III of this book.

See Appendix A for more about the CD-ROM.

Icons Used in This Book

When you see this icon, you know that the paragraph contains some technical details that may not be essential to your understanding or using Java, but they're interesting to know! (And if you read all the text next to these icons, you may find yourself developing a liking for pocket protectors.)

With this icon, we flag useful information, shortcuts, or any other hints we can think of to help you in your Java programming adventure.

Remember the text that's associated with this icon — the information may come in handy someday.

This icon is self-explanatory: Beware!

We use this icon to draw your attention to extra-special Java features or unique elements.

Use the text next to these icons to pattern your thinking; now all that unreadable code suddenly makes sense!

 This icon marks the terms that all good little programmers know.

What Now?

Now it's up to you. Read this book and meet us in cyberspace! You'll find us at the *Java Programming For Dummies* Resource page at this URL:

```
http://www.isc.com/jpfd
```

You can reach David and Don via e-mail at jpfd@isc.com.

Part I
Hello, Java

The 5th Wave   **By Rich Tennant**

"Finally! A programming language that lets us express
the nuance of our style on the Web."

In this part . . .

*B*ecause we believe in looking before we leap, we want to give you the vision to do the same. That's why Part I includes an introduction to the surroundings and characteristics of the Java programming language. We identify Java's place as a revolutionary addition of rapid animation and interactivity to the World Wide Web. Then we show you how to create your first simple Java applet to incorporate into your Web pages.

Web pages are designed using a language called *HyperText Markup Language* (HTML). We tell you the elements of HTML that you need to understand to include Java applets in your Web pages. We conclude Part I with an introduction to the basic elements of object-oriented programming (Java is an object-oriented programming language) in which you discover the classes, objects, methods, and other structures used to create programs in Java.

And then you're ready to leap!

Chapter 1

Java and the World Wide Web

• •

In This Chapter

▶ Understanding the Internet and the World Wide Web

▶ Understanding intranets

▶ Writing portable programs

▶ Keeping the user's system safe

▶ Making intelligent Web pages

▶ Appreciating open systems

• •

*J*ava has won acceptance as a major programming language in just a few years. The reason for this success is Java's acceptance as the programming language of the Internet and the World Wide Web. To understand the value and importance of Java, you need to know something about the Internet. In the beginning, the Internet was quite literally for rocket scientists. The Net began as a system of interconnected computers used by government and academic researchers in many parts of the world. By adhering to some standard ways of transferring data among varied computer systems, these researchers were able to trade raw data and to share computing resources.

When connected systems follow mutually agreed upon standards, the users know how to share data and computing resources among the systems. Consider the following scenario as an example of the sharing made possible by Internet standards.

A scientist at Upstate University connects through his university computing center to a statistical analysis program that's installed on a computer at the NASA data center. After analyzing his data, the scientist sends the results to the computer account of a colleague at Downstate University.

The Downstate colleague, in turn, can access the raw data at the Upstate computing center and perform her own analysis with a program that she developed on the Downstate computer. Or she can use the NASA program.

Because they're connected through the Internet, the three computers (at Upstate, NASA, and Downstate) work together. The Internet now connects most of the large public computing facilities in the world, and computing projects often use the combined resources of many computers in different locations.

The Internet: A Reality and an Idea

The Internet is both a *physical reality* and an *idea.*

The *physical reality* is that most large public computing centers in the world, such as university and government computing centers, are linked by a cross-connected web of data communications lines (see Figure 1-1). Although each center may be directly connected only to a few other centers, the interconnections enable any center to connect *indirectly* with any other center.

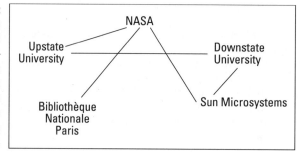

Figure 1-1: The physical reality — most large computing centers in the world are connected.

The *idea* is that after a number of computers are connected, passing information from any one computer to any other computer is easy, provided that users can agree on a single standard way to communicate. In the Internet community, as illustrated in Figure 1-2, all the participants have agreed to accept and forward messages by using mutually agreed-upon technical specifications and ways of addressing the messages. Believe it or not, Internet technical standards are set by a nongovernmental committee of volunteers!

At first, if you wanted an Internet address (the Internet equivalent of a telephone number), you had to claim some sort of connection with the government and the academic research community. But the attractions of the Internet were irresistible. College students discovered that being able to send e-mail to friends on other campuses was very convenient. Professors discovered that they could publish a research proposal or a simple request for information to the Internet community and receive valuable help from unexpected sources. As Internet users moved on to different places and other jobs, they found ways to maintain their Internet accounts.

Figure 1-2:
The idea —
users
can pass
information
from any
place to any
other place.

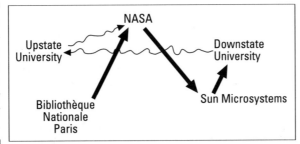

Eventually, the Internet was opened to the public. Now, millions of individuals in the general public have Internet accounts. The communications links of the Internet have extended and merged with telephone communications so that connecting any personal computer to the Internet is a simple matter.

As an individual consumer, you find that a variety of companies are competing for your Internet connection business. In many parts of the world, the cost of having an Internet address is only slightly more than the cost of having a telephone number. In fact, your telephone company is probably one of the companies offering you Internet service.

The World Wide Web: Narrowing the search

In the beginning, navigating the Internet was hard. You needed to memorize and type obscure commands and long, complicated addresses. But bright, lazy people are always looking for an easier way to do things. As a result, they developed many tools and ideas to make communicating over the Internet easier. One of the most exciting developments is the World Wide Web (WWW). And the World Wide Web is where Java has found its first major successes.

The World Wide Web was invented by a research group at the European Center for Nuclear Research (CERN). The group set out to automate the process of following cross-references among documents posted on the Internet.

The CERN researchers noticed that often a technical paper posted to the Internet at one location would refer to another paper or data posted elsewhere. To follow the cross-reference required locating a new Internet address and then completing a series of steps to access the data. The CERN researchers proposed a standard way to include, within a document, the necessary Internet addresses for its cross-references.

This method for including cross-references is called *Hypertext Markup Language* (HTML). The universe of interconnected documents on Internet computers throughout the world is called the *World Wide Web*. Programs called *Web browsers* enable users to display HTML documents on the screen of a personal computer and to move among interconnected documents almost as easily as turning the pages of a book. Figure 1-3 shows an example of a Web document viewed with a Web browser.

Like the Internet, the World Wide Web was too good to leave to the academics. Nonacademic users of the Internet discovered the WWW and turned it into a broad communications medium. Now, the World Wide Web is a public forum filled with consumer information, political communications, and personal whimsy, as well as research data. Organizations and businesses maintain special purpose computers — "Web servers" — to store and distribute HTML documents.

Figure 1-3:
Web browsers make it simple to find anything on the World Wide Web.

Intranets: Internal corporate Web sites

The computer network of a large corporation is often similar to the Internet:

✔ Computers of many types are in many locations.

✔ Networks provide webs of data connections among computers.

✔ Users share data and computing resources.

Although many technologies compete to meet the networking needs of large organizations, an increasing number of corporate networks use the technology of the Internet and the World Wide Web.

Corporations are using Internet technologies to provide for communications among computers in different locations and dedicated to different primary uses. In the same way that a scientist can access NASA's data on the orbit of a planet, a branch manager in Singapore can study the results of an advertising campaign in Costa Rica. A salesperson with a laptop computer can check corporate data on inventories and prices.

Just like their academic sisters and brothers, corporate employees now forward internal memos with Internet e-mail tools and publish documentation in HTML. When Internet technology is applied within a private organization's network, people refer to the resulting network as an *intranet*.

Internet technology enables the manager of the corporate network to control who has access to certain portions of the corporate intranet. Internet technology not only supports internal communications, but it also allows companies to give selected customers or business associates access to the corporate intranet. Dealers can access product and marketing data that isn't available to the general public. Software developers can access prerelease "beta" versions of new software products and trade notes with the product developers.

Java: The Magical Flying Program

Java does for programs what HTML does for documents. Java is a programming language that enables people to create *applets* — small programs that are attached to Web pages and move across the Internet to whatever computer views the page. The person viewing and using an applet can use this program without concern for the logistics of installing software, without concern for security, and without concern for the type of computer hardware in use.

May I borrow that program?

To understand the role of Java, think about what happens when you want to borrow a program that someone else has written so that you can run it on your computer. If you're a serious personal computer user, you have probably shared an experience like this:

- ✔ Your friend makes a copy of the program on a diskette (or perhaps you use a modem to connect to her computer and download the program).

- ✔ You check to make sure that your friend has the same type of computer you do. If you're fortunate, you both have the same type of computer. Otherwise, the program won't run on your computer.

- ✔ You scan the diskette for viruses to make sure that the code on the diskette won't do something nasty to your computer.

- ✔ You copy the program to your hard drive. You key in additional information needed to set up your system properly — a directory path, changes to operating system settings, and so on.

- ✔ If your friend completes a new, improved version the next day, you start the same process all over again.

If both you and your friend are programming in Java, you can bypass these problems when you want to borrow a program. Consider the following alternative experience:

- ✔ You connect to your friend's Web page. A program written in Java, as a Java applet, is posted on the Web page. The program automatically transfers itself to your computer over the Internet connection.

- ✔ You don't need to check what kind of computer your friend has. A program written in Java runs on any type of computer that has a Java-enabled Web browser. The fact that your friend has a UNIX workstation and you have a PC doesn't matter.

- ✔ You don't need to scan for viruses; the Java language locks the borrowed program out of all the areas of your computer where a virus may do harm.

- ✔ You don't need to copy the program or make setup adjustments to your computer — the program is designed to run on your computer with no installation or adjustments.

- ✔ If your friend develops a new, improved version of the program, you automatically receive the update when you next connect to her Web page.

Java effortlessly delivers the program over the Internet. Whether the program resides in your machine or your friend's machine makes no difference to you as a user.

It's portable

As you probably know, you can find programs specifically for Windows 95 and Windows NT, for Macintosh, for Solaris, for UNIX, and more. When a program is written in Java, however, you need only one version of the program — the Java version. The exact same program runs on all these operating systems and hardware platforms.

When you write programs in Java, you don't need to concern yourself about porting to different systems. This cross-platform capability extends even to mainframes, and it applies to large programs that aren't intended for distribution across the Internet as well as to applets that live on Web pages. For example, IBM has adopted Java as the language to unify applications across all the varied operating systems and platforms it manufactures. So Java runs on mainframes running MVS, RS/6000 and AS/400 minicomputers, and PCs running OS/2 and Windows. Every major operating system now supports Java. (See Chapter 18 for more about Java as an applications development language.)

Java is favored by developers of electronic commerce Web sites who find that they can develop and test new sites on small and inexpensive Windows NT systems and then move to large UNIX-based production servers with no need to revise the programs they have created.

Multiply by 300 — or 1,500

Java delivers the most current version of an applet to the user's machine at the moment it's needed. If the Java delivery model sounds appealing to you on an individual basis, imagine the position of a computer support manager in a company with 300 personal computers — or 1,500. With traditional software, the introduction of a new application or an upgrade requires the installation and configuration of new software on 300 or 1,500 separate machines. When different departments use different types of computers — engineers with UNIX workstations and marketers with personal computers, for example — the installation and support problems are even greater. Developers of corporate software are hard at work developing Java applet versions of their products to save some of this installation and support money.

In fact, Apple, IBM, Netscape, Oracle, and Sun have joined to design the Network Computer — a new type of computer workstation designed specifically to connect to the Internet and intranets. The Network Computer is intended to operate without disk drives and individual copies of programs. Instead, it will enable users to have instant access to the newest version of any program they need in the form of Java applets. The future of Network

Computer as a product is still uncertain; it's unlikely to replace the personal computer on most office workers' desktops anytime soon. But it offers an attractive alternative for workers like reservation agents who use only custom software. And the Network Computer is a low-cost way to provide access to the Internet in schools, libraries, and other public access settings.

May this computer be safe from . . .

You have surely heard about viruses and hackers — that is, the programs and people that intentionally interfere with the normal operation of your computer. Whenever you connect one computer to another, you must be concerned about the possibility of an intruder.

The Java programming language is designed to work in a world of interconnected computers; therefore, the designers of Java built strong security features into the language. The following list outlines some of these features:

- **Run-time examination:** When your computer runs a Java program, the entire program is examined instruction by instruction to make sure that it contains only valid Java instructions that are prohibited from interfering with other programs or with the basic setup of your computer.

- **Restricted interactivity:** The Java language has built-in restrictions on establishing connections to other computers. Unless the user gives specific permission, a Java applet can only connect to the Internet location that the applet came from.

- **Restricted access rights:** The Java language has built-in restrictions on the ability of the program to read and write data. The program can access only the parts of your computer where it has received advance permission to be.

No security system is perfect

It's true that no security system is perfect. Security specialists have managed to find and fix flaws that make it theoretically possible to create a hostile Java applet. And they will no doubt find more such flaws.

Nevertheless, we have never met anyone who had a file destroyed or a system crashed by a Java applet. And we have had plenty of unpleasant encounters with viruses. So we feel pretty good about Java security as a practical matter.

Web page intelligence

The WWW is an easy and elegant way to provide access to information — technical references, product information, and marketing data. Java provides a way to add computer support in interacting with the data. For example:

- ✔ A Java applet on a page of product information can enable anyone who browses the page to calculate the cost of any given combination of products or options.
- ✔ A Java applet can enable an employee to calculate his pension benefits.
- ✔ A Java applet can administer a quiz on the contents of a technical reference.

An Open System

Many of the technical standards for computing hardware and software are *proprietary,* which means they are owned and well-protected by the companies who developed them. Individual companies have invested in perfecting a particular way of accomplishing a desired result. Understandably, they prefer not to share all the details with their competitors. So they use patents, copyrights, and secrecy to maintain a competitive advantage. Programmers often call these *closed* systems.

On the other hand, some information must be shared if systems developed by different teams are to work together.

Technical specifications for the Internet and the World Wide Web are developed and maintained by committees representing many interested parties. The specifications are published to the world at large. Any hardware or software product that matches the published specifications works with the Internet and the WWW. Such an arrangement is referred to as an *open system.*

With open systems, the published specifications establish a shared definition of how components of hardware and software from different sources must work together. You can assemble different components from different sources with the expectation that the combined system will work.

The Java language is an open system specification. Sun Microsystems, which developed the Java language, has published detailed specifications for Java. All products that adhere to the published specifications can work together. Many companies have developed Java software designed to interact freely with other companies' products.

As you read on, you, too, can join the community of Java developers.

New and Improved: Java 2

Like all things computer-related, the Java language evolves. The Java language we discuss in this book is Java 2, the second generation of the Java programming language. (The earlier generation of Java is represented by Java 1.0 and 1.1.) You are fortunate to begin discovering Java with Java 2 — you benefit from all the small questions and improvements by those who came before you. Java 2 incorporates a variety of small changes that make the language more consistent and logical than the earlier releases of Java. Java 2 also supports some important new capabilities you find in this book.

To a Java expert, the changes from Java 1.0 and Java 1.1 to Java 2 are important because these changes remove stumbling blocks and increase the power of the language. To you as a beginner, they represent relatively insignificant details. When you read code written in version 1.0 of Java, you may occasionally notice a line or two that seems slightly strange or out-of-date, but you understand. It's like listening to Golden Oldies. You see almost no difference between Java 1.1 and Java 2.

Because you may want to work with Version 1.0 code, we warn you about the differences as we come to them.

Chapter 2

Writing a Simple Program: Yet Another HelloWorld

*W*riting a program that prints Hello, World on the screen is the traditional way to start using every programming language. Why should we be different? As you may discover, laziness is also an honored tradition in programming. And so we, too, begin with yet another HelloWorld program.

If you already know a programming language such as Basic, Pascal, or C, you've probably encountered the HelloWorld tradition. If not, your initiation to the strange customs of programmers begins here.

Please give heed to these esteemed words to program by:

"We will encourage you to develop the three great virtues of a programmer: laziness, impatience, and hubris."

— Larry Wall, *Programming Perl,* 1991.

Some News about Java Programs

Before we plunge into the HelloWorld program, we have some news for you.

When you write a Java applet, you manipulate words, numbers, and pictures that appear on the screen of your computer. You expect your Java applet to have a *graphical user interface (GUI)*. That is, you expect your applet to display windows, buttons, and menus on your computer screen. You expect your users to point and click with a mouse or similar device to control the computer's actions. You expect information on the computer screen in a variety of colors, with different styles and sizes of type. The GUI enables you to do all these things to make your program easier for people to use.

The bad news

The bad news is that providing your program with a GUI is not easy. Deep down inside, what your computer does is staggeringly complicated. For example, just to maintain the display screen, your computer must keep track of the color and brightness of hundreds of thousands of points of light. A disk drive, mouse, and keyboard each brings with it a similar degree of complexity. The computer requires explicit instructions for what to do with each point of light on the screen, each keypress, each mouse motion, and so on.

The good news

The good news is that you're not the first to want the features offered by a GUI. Program code already exists to implement all the commonly used features and behaviors you want — standard graphical user interface features as well as many others. You can program almost anything you want without getting involved in the tacky details. You need only string together prewritten code to accomplish your goal.

However, the further news (good or bad, depending on how you choose to take it) is that you *do* need to find out how to select, assemble, and modify the prewritten code components. This book helps get you started.

A typical Java applet

A Java *applet* is a miniprogram written in Java and attached to a Web page. It enhances the Web page's presentation or enables the user to complete some specific task. A typical Java applet consists of a number of lines that identify the prewritten code components that you want to use, followed by some lines that modify them, if necessary, and fit them together. The thought process of a Java applet programmer is like that of a cabinet maker who lays out her tools and materials, cuts parts to size, and then assembles the finished product.

A GUI that doesn't stick to one platform only

One of the important benefits of Java is that it provides a graphical user interface (GUI, pronounced "gooey") that runs on a variety of computer hardware. The GUI makes computer screens more attractive and user friendly. But the GUI can prevent programs from moving easily from one platform to another. Most GUIs have been designed as proprietary software that works on one platform only. A program written for the Windows GUI requires considerable programming effort to make it run on a Macintosh or UNIX system, and vice versa.

The first GUI was developed by Xerox's PARC research center in the early '70s. This interface ran only on an $18,000 personal workstation called the *Star*. The Apple Macintosh operating system and, later, Microsoft Windows, made GUIs familiar to most personal computer users. Other software provides GUIs for UNIX-based systems.

But a program written for any one of these systems cannot run on the others without special adaptation. A program written in Java can run on any Java-enabled system with no adaptation whatsoever, permitting programs to be more widely distributed and more easily used.

As a result, Java code doesn't read like a bedtime story. Instead, the code reads like the assembly instructions for that bargain lawn furniture you bought at the discount warehouse. The first time you read the code of a Java applet, you may find it alarmingly inscrutable. Courage! With a little patience and persistence, you can figure out not only how to read Java, but even how to write it.

By the way, most of what we tell you about applets applies equally well to Java applications. A Java *application* is a stand-alone program that you can run without using a Web browser. For more about Java applications, see Chapter 18.

If you must program while you read

Some of our readers sit back, relax, and read the book first and then program later. Others sit down at the computer with this book and key in code as they read. If you belong to the *key as you read* group, now is a good time to install and test the materials on the CD or to download the JDK.

Be sure to go through the complete setup and test process before you try to use the code in the book.

HelloWorld with Attitude

With no further ado, we give you our version of the text of HelloWorld for Java:

```
import java.applet.*;
import java.awt.*;
/*
* HelloWorld
* @version 0.1
* @author dkoosis@isc.com
*/
public class HelloWorld extends Applet{
Label helloLabel = new Label ("Yo, you lookin' at me?");
public void init (){
    setBackground (Color.yellow);
    add (helloLabel);
    }
}
public class HelloWorld extends Applet
{
    Label helloLabel = new Label ("Yo, you lookin' at me?");
    public void init ()
    {
        setBackground (Color.yellow);
        add (helloLabel);
    }
}
public class HelloWorld extends Applet {
    Label helloLabel = new Label ("Yo, you lookin' at me?");
    public void init () {
        setBackground (Color.yellow);
        add (helloLabel);
    }
```

When you install this applet on a Web page and look at the page with a browser that's capable of receiving Java programs, a yellow square labeled with the greeting (Yo, you lookin' at me?) appears (see Figure 2-1).

Figure 2-1:
HelloWorld.

Applet Viewer: HelloWorld.class
Applet
Yo, you lookin' at me?
applet started

We are now going to walk you through everything that happens in the mind of the programmer on the way to making the little yellow square appear.

The standard prewritten code for an applet is in a group of files whose names begin with `java.applet`. I had better tell the computer where to find that code so that I'm not expected to write it all. Also, I know that I want to use at least some of the GUI features such as panels, labels, and buttons. Code for those features is in the *Abstract Windowing Toolkit* package — `java.awt`.

You are probably familiar with the use of the *wildcard* character *, which stands for any file. For example, in the following line of code, `java.applet.*` means "any file whose name begins with *java.applet.*"

```
import java.applet.*;
import java.awt.*;
```

It's good form to *document* my code with a title and version number so that my coworkers and I can easily identify a specific piece of code. Better start the documentation right away, so I won't forget later.

Information in a Java code file that is directed to human readers (the *documentation*), instead of to the computer, is set off as a *comment* by enclosing it between the characters `/*` and `*/`. In this book, we also put comments in italics.

```
/*
  * HelloWorld
  * @version 0.1
  * @author dkoosis@iscinc.com
*/
```

I am writing a Java applet. Fortunately, I can rely on prewritten code that defines the behavior of an applet. I'll just extend the standard applet code to add the special properties and behaviors that I want. The changes fall in-between the braces in the code.

Everything that falls between the first left brace { and the last right brace } is part of the definition of the HelloWorld applet.

```
public class HelloWorld extends Applet{
...
}
```

I'm going to want to stick some text onscreen. For that, I'll use prewritten code called a *Label*; I'll call my label `helloLabel`. And I know exactly what I want for the contents of the label, so I'll put that special property information between the parentheses.

Watch your capitalization — Java does!

Capitalization makes a difference. When you write Java code, you must pay close attention to how you capitalize words. As far as the computer is concerned, `HelloLabel` and `helloLabel` are two completely different names.

On the other hand, any amount of blank space is considered just "some white space." You can use indentation and extra space to make your code easier to read, or you can use just the bare minimum of space between words. The computer won't care.

For more about matters of code-writing style, see Chapter 22.

A label is one of those prewritten GUI features whose code is contained in the *Abstract Windowing Toolkit (AWT)*. To use a label here, the programmer gives the label a name and sets up its properties.

```
Label helloLabel = new Label("Yo, you lookin' at me?");
```

Now I'm finished identifying and setting up the parts. What do I want the applet to do? And when?

I want the applet to do its stuff right away — when the applet is down-loaded from the Web server. The *init method* is what defines the actions the applet takes when initialized, so I can include the actions in the applet's `init` method. I can set the background color of the applet to be yellow. Then I can add `helloLabel` to the applet's space on the screen.

You describe everything you want to happen when an application is *initialized* — downloaded from the Web server — in the `init` method.

```
public void init(){
setBackground(Color.yellow);
add(helloLabel);
}
```

From the Programmer's Mind to the Computer's Chips

As you probably know, the computer works in electronic ones and zeros. When you write code in a programming language, the code must be translated into the ones and zeros of true computer language before it can be used to run the computer. Fortunately, the computer, guided by other programs, can do this translation for you.

Several variations exist for how this translation process can be organized. Figure 2-2 shows how the process happens with Java.

Compiling

The programmer writes in Java, the programming language. Despite how the lines of code may appear to you at the moment, Java is a language intended to be understood by human beings. This human language form of the program is called *Java source code*. Java source code is saved on the developer's computer in files with the extension .java. For example, in the prior section, you read the contents of the file named HelloWorld.java.

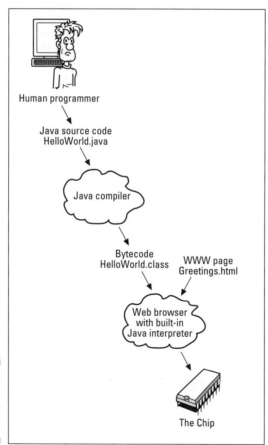

Human programmer

Java source code
HelloWorld.java

Java compiler

Bytecode
HelloWorld.class   WWW page
Greetings.html

Web browser
with built-in
Java interpreter

The Chip

When the Java source code is finished, the programmer turns it over to a computer program called the Java compiler. The compiler sorts and organizes the program into a form that can make efficient use of computer resources. The compiler also translates the program into a language of ones and zeros that is suited for computer use. This new version of the program is called *bytecode*. The bytecode for Java applets is saved in files with the extension `.class`. For example, `HelloWorld.class`.

Putting an applet on the page

A Java applet is designed to be incorporated as part of a World Wide Web document. In the same way that a Web page can contain a graphic image or a sound clip, the page can contain a Java applet.

HTML — the language of Web pages — stands for Hypertext Markup Language. HTML deserves the *markup* part of its name because it enables you to mark up text to indicate how you want the text to appear on a computer screen. HTML is a *hypertext* markup language because it also enables you to connect the onscreen text to text, images, and other objects (such as Java applets) that may reside anywhere on the Internet. If you don't already know about HTML, you find a very brief introduction to it in Chapter 3.

The following snippet of HTML code is the ⟨APPLET⟩ tag that gives the name of the file that contains the bytecode for the applet:

```
<APPLET CODE="HelloWorld.class" WIDTH=300 HEIGHT=50 >
</APPLET >
```

The best way to test your applet is to write a simple Web document with the appropriate ⟨APPLET⟩ tag in it. You can then view the HTML file with your Web browser and see the applet in action. For example, you might write the following HTML file as a test page for HelloWorld:

```
<HTML>
<HEAD>
<TITLE>Test page for HelloWorld</TITLE>
</HEAD>
<BODY>
<HR>
This line of text comes before the applet.<P>
<APPLET CODE = "HelloWorld.class" WIDTH=300 HEIGHT=50>
</APPLET>
<P>
This line of text comes after the applet.
</BODY>
</HTML>
```

You need to save this file with the extension `.html`. For example, use `HelloTest.html`.

To see the applet in action, make sure that `HelloTest.html` and `HelloWorld.class` are in the same directory. Use your Java-enabled Web browser to view `HelloTest.html`. You see something like Figure 2-3.

Where's the class code? If you don't tell it otherwise, your browser looks for Java class code in the same place as the HTML page that refers to the code. In Chapter 3, we show you how to tell the browser where else to look.

The virtual chip

When you view `HelloTest.html` with your Java-enabled Web browser, the browser

- ✔ Recognizes the Java `<APPLET>` tag
- ✔ Calls up the Java virtual machine program, which is built into the code of the Web browser or operating system

Every family of computer chips and every operating system uses its own unique code of ones and zeros for basic operations. A PC containing a Pentium chip uses different codes than a Macintosh containing a PowerPC chip, which uses different codes than a Sun workstation containing a Sun SPARC chip.

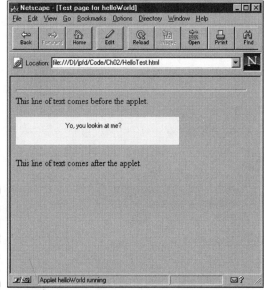

Figure 2-3:
HelloWorld
in its test
page,
HelloTest.

Doesn't the Java virtual machine really slow things down?

The Java virtual machine adds an extra translation step to every computer action. If the program were fully translated into the native codes of the computer chip before running, it would run faster.

For most Web applications, Java bytecodes run fast enough that performance isn't an issue. However, if squeezing the last drop of performance out of your Java applet is important, you can find tools called *just-in-time* compilers that enable you to do the final step of converting from bytecode to machine code in advance.

Still concerned about the effect of the Java virtual machine on performance? Sun Microsystems, Inc., manufactures a computer chip that uses Java bytecode as its internal machine code. A computer built with this chip (or provided with this chip on an add-in card) can run Java bytecode programs with no need for the Java virtual machine.

The Java bytecode in a `.class` file is the unique code understood by a special chip called the Java virtual machine. Unlike the Pentium or SPARC chip, if you open your computer, you don't actually see a chip for the Java virtual machine. The Java virtual machine is computer software that simulates a chip. At the time you run a Java applet, the bytecode runs on the Java virtual machine.

The advantage of a software-simulated chip is that it's portable. That is, Java programs can run on any kind of computer that uses the simulated chip. The disadvantage of a simulated chip is that it runs much slower than an actual computer chip, such as the Pentium or SPARC.

Remember:

- ✔ When you write a Java program, you write in Java source code.
- ✔ You then use the compiler program to create a file of Java bytecode.
- ✔ When you run a Java program, you instruct the computer to run your Java bytecode file.
- ✔ The computer uses the Java interpreter program to convert the Java bytecode into native machine code.

Inside the Computer's Chips

As you probably know, your computer stores information and programs in the form of millions of ones and zeros. These ones and zeros are recorded in memory chips by turning millions of electronic switches on and off inside the computer.

You don't need to know the details of how a statement such as

```
setBackground(Color.yellow);
```

is translated into ones and zeros, or how the ones and zeros result in making a part of the computer screen yellow. But a general picture of what goes on when you compile and run a Java applet is helpful.

When you run the HelloWorld applet, your computer works with the following chunks of memory that you have set up in your program:

- An applet scratch pad called `HelloWorld`
- A copy of the label blueprint
- A label scratch pad called `helloLabel`

Scratch pads

The computer sets aside an area of memory for each object you are working with — in the case of the HelloWorld program, the applet and the label. The computer keeps track of the properties and behavior of each object in the assigned area of memory for as long as the program uses the object. When the program finishes with an object, the computer releases the memory so that the memory is free for something else. You may think of this memory as a temporary *scratch pad*. It keeps track of an object while that object is in use and then gets discarded when the object is no longer in use.

For example, the `HelloWorld` scratch pad includes a note to the effect that background color is yellow. And the `helloLabel` scratch pad contains a note of the text that appears on the label. Of course, how much memory must be set aside and how that memory should be organized depends on the specific object. In the example, the scratch pad for `helloLabel` needs space to keep track of the words that are the content of the label.

Blueprints

In the case of the simple HelloWorld applet, you know in advance that you have only one panel and one label. But complete advance knowledge isn't always possible for more complex programs. For example, in a slightly more complex version of HelloWorld, the number of labels may depend on how the user responds to the program — the user input (see Figure 2-4).

To deal with this situation, the computer running Java applets maintains additional scratch pads that contain *blueprints* for setting up the kinds of objects you use in your program. (We talk about objects in Chapter 4.) In this way, if the computer needs to set up another label, the computer can refer to the label blueprint to find out.

- ✔ How much space to allow
- ✔ How to organize that space
- ✔ Standard information to include

Figure 2-4:
An applet
in which
the number
of labels
depends on
user input.

Write, compile, run, revise, compile, run, . . .

Unlike some programming languages (for example, some versions of BASIC), Java doesn't provide instant gratification. You must go through a series of steps to create and run the HelloWorld program.

Writing the code for your applet

You begin the process of writing the HelloWorld program by creating a file that contains the text of the program. Use a *text editor* to enter the text of HelloWorld, and save the text in a file with the same name as the applet — `HelloWorld.java`. The `HelloWorld.java` file is the program's *source code* file.

What is a text editor?

A *text editor* is a program that lets you type, edit, and save text without special format information, such as fonts. The simplest form of a text editor just lets you type text and save it. The Notepad accessory that comes with Microsoft Windows is an example of this kind of editor. We recommend that you write your first applet or two using a simple text editor like Notepad.

If you plan to do some serious programming, you will probably eventually want to invest in an *IDE* (Integrated Development Environment). An IDE includes a *programming editor* that makes the painful process of programming and debugging a bit easier. For example, programming editors recognize the key words of the programming language and highlight them

in a distinctive color. When you compile code and receive an error message, the programming editor automatically positions you to edit the line where the compiler detected an error.

Most IDEs also *automate* some of the common code-writing tasks you find out about in this book. But there's a catch. Before you can effectively use the automated tools, you need to understand what they do. So you still need to read this book.

The CD that accompanies this book includes a trial version of an excellent IDE, Inprise JBuilder. Sun's Java Workshop, Symantec Visual Café, and Microsoft Visual J++ are other examples of Java IDEs.

Compiling your applet

You must run the Java compiler. The input to the compiler is your Java source code file, `HelloWorld.java`, which you have written with your text or programming editor. The output of the compiler is a file named `HelloWorld.class`, which is the Java bytecode file.

If you use Inprise JBuilder or another IDE, a keystroke or click on a button tells the computer to compile the file you are writing.

You may get error messages when you run the compiler. To be honest, you *will* eventually get error messages when you run the compiler. People make mistakes. Sooner or later, you'll make some, too. We discuss error messages further in a later section of the chapter. If you are fortunate enough not to get error messages when you compile HelloWorld.java, that's only because HelloWorld is an extremely simple program.

Installing your applet in a Web page

Java applets are designed to live on a Web page. Therefore, to see the applet run, you must write it into a Web page. Use a text editor to enter the text of `HelloTest` (see the sample HelloTest Web page text in a previous section of this chapter) and save the file as `HelloTest.html`. Make sure that `HelloWorld.class` and `HelloTest.html` are in the same directory.

Testing your applet

Use your Web browser to view `HelloTest.html`. For example, if you are using Netscape, you can choose File⇨Open File and then use the dialog box to open `HelloTest.html`. If all goes well, you see the HelloWorld applet on its Web page, as shown in Figure 2-5.

If you get error messages

Error messages are displayed on the command-line screen and look something like this:

```
C:\JAVA\book>javac HelloWorld.java
HelloWorld.java:20: '}' expected.
}
 ^
```

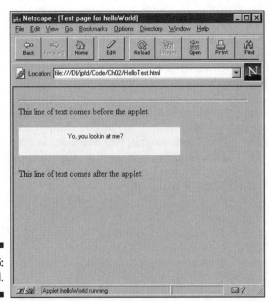

Figure 2-5:
Hello, World.

For a simple applet such as HelloWorld, the most likely source of error is a mistake in typing. Every left brace { must have a matching right brace } later in the code. Every left parenthesis (must have a matching right parenthesis). The semicolon (;) that appears at the end of most lines is vital. If the semicolon is missing, you receive an error message. Figure 2-6 shows the error message that you receive if you leave out a semicolon.

Another possible error source is carelessness in naming files. The source code filename must exactly match the name of the public class; the spelling and capitalization must be exactly the same.

As you can see from the sample error messages, the Java compiler is fairly helpful in pointing out obvious mistakes. Edit your Java source code file to correct the error and run the compiler again.

Creating HelloWorld: Just do it!

If you haven't already tried to enter and compile the HelloWorld program, we suggest that you stop reading and do some programming now.

Practice the physical steps of entering code, compiling, correcting, and testing so that the process becomes automatic. After you develop fluency in these steps, you won't even notice the mechanics of the process, and you can focus on the Java language and its capabilities.

Figure 2-6:
The Java compiler finds a missing semicolon.

You get used to this — honest

If this HelloWorld applet is your first exposure to programming, this process and jargon may seem hopelessly complicated. Please don't give up just yet.

The cycle of writing source code, compiling it into bytecode, and then running the bytecode from a Web page is the same for all applets. After a few repetitions, you may find the cycle natural and effortless.

Similarly, feeling a bit confused and frustrated by the strange appearance of Java source code is perfectly normal. You *will* get used to it quite quickly if you persevere.

Remember that you always have models to copy and modify. Professional programmers rarely start from scratch. Instead, professionals develop personal libraries of code snippets and examples. They refer to model programs and examples that are provided by software publishers. They save their own work, and they trade tips and tricks with other programmers through Internet discussion groups. See Chapter 20 for some Internet sources of sample code.

Chapter 3

Jumping to Java from HTML

- -

- -

*Y*ou must use HTML to create World Wide Web pages, and Java applets reside in Web pages. Therefore, to place your applet on a Web page and test it out, you need to know some HTML.

Similarly, you need to know at least a bit of HTML to read and use this book. On the other hand, this book isn't about HTML. (If you don't believe us, check the title page.) So if you're not already fluent in HTML, you may want to consult a very fine book, *HTML For Dummies,* 3rd Edition, authored by Ed Tittel and Steve James and published by IDG Books Worldwide, Inc., when you are ready to begin serious Web page design.

What you find in this chapter is just enough HTML overview and quick reference information to enable you to install and test Java applets.

HTML: The VAV (Very Abbreviated Version)

HTML stands for Hypertext Markup Language. It's called a *markup* language because it enables you to mark up text to indicate how you want the text to display on a computer screen. HTML is a *Hypertext* markup language because it also enables you to connect the onscreen text to text, images, and other objects (such as Java applets) that may reside anywhere on the Internet.

Text markup

The markup features of HTML enable you to indicate how Web browsers display your document onscreen. You mark up your text with special tags that control (turn on and turn off) format attributes and identify different parts of the document (see Figure 3-1).

Figure 3-1:
HTML tags
control
format
attributes.

For example, if you want a presentation like the one shown in Figure 3-1 on-screen, you must create the following HTML text:

```
<HTML>
<HEAD>
<TITLE>HTML Overview</TITLE>
</HEAD>
<BODY>
<HR>
<H1>This is a Heading 1</H1><P>
This is text that contains <I>italics</I>. And this is text that is <B>bold</B>.
</BODY>
</HTML>
```

The markup *tags* are the codes that appear inside angle brackets like <THIS>. Note that the tags themselves don't appear onscreen; that is, the Web browser doesn't display the tags. Instead, the tags control the appearance of the rest of the text (your actual *content*).

For each characteristic of the text, HTML has an *on* tag (<xxx>) and a corresponding *off* tag (</xxx>), which is indicated by /. For example, in this text

- <I> turns on italics and </I> turns off italics
- <B> turns on bold text and </B> turns off bold text
- <H1> turns on the attributes your browser has set for a level 1 heading and </H1> turns off the level 1 heading attributes

HTML has other tags for other attributes. With these tags and attributes, you can control not only the appearance of text, but also its placement. For example, you can use tags to center a block of text, to organize text into a numbered list, or to place text into the columns and rows of a table.

You may notice that the use of tags in HTML is very similar to the system of formatting codes used in many word processing programs. For example, if you are familiar with the *Reveal Codes* feature of WordPerfect, you notice that the idea behind HTML is very similar — tags that identify the formats being applied.

Because HTML is designed to work on a variety of systems with different graphic capabilities and different display resources, many display details are left up to the individual Web browser. For example, HTML provides for six levels of headings, with the ⟨H1⟩ tag being the most emphasized, and the ⟨H6⟩ tag being the least emphasized. But the exact style of type used to provide the emphasis depends on the browser.

Figure 3-2 is an example of the same HTML text as shown in Figure 3-1, but displayed on a different system with a different browser. As you can see, the browser tries to accomplish the level of emphasis that the HTML author wants with the resources available on the system that the reader is using.

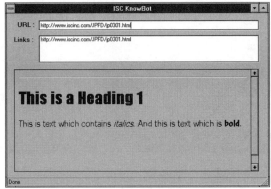

Figure 3-2:
An HTML document may look different on a different system, such as a Macintosh.

Functional markup

Besides directly controlling the appearance of text on the reader's screen, HTML tags may identify certain parts of the document by function. For example, in the HTML text of this example, the title is set off with ⟨TITLE⟩ and ⟨/TITLE⟩ tags:

```
<TITLE>HTML Overview</TITLE>
```

The title of the document appears in the title bar of the browser, rather than as part of the body of the document. The body of the document must be separately identified by `<BODY>` and `</BODY>` tags. Similar tags exist for other elements of information about the document (such as the document's author).

Links to other documents and files

What makes the World Wide Web exciting is the fact that documents and information from various sources can be linked together. One document may refer to another document that's maintained in a different location. And the user can jump from document to document by following the trail of references, with no need to deal with the mechanics of locating the host computer or establishing a connection and requesting the document.

For example, Figure 3-3 shows an HTML document with a hypertext link to the ISC home page (the authors' business — what a coincidence!).

Figure 3-3:
A hypertext
link.

A mouse-click on the highlighted words (in Figure 3-3, the words are underlined) causes your browser to locate the server for the ISC home page and display the page.

The HTML code that accomplishes this link is an *anchor* tag (`<A>` and `</A>`) that contains the WWW address of the ISC home page:

```
<HTML>
<HEAD>
<TITLE>HTML Links</TITLE>
</HEAD>
<BODY>
<HR>
<H1>Hypertext Links</H1>
<P>This is a link to the <A HREF="http://www.isc.com">
```

```
<B>ISC home page</B></A>.
</P>
</BODY>
</HTML>
```

This linking tag is a bit more complicated than text formatting tags, because you find two elements within the brackets of the initial tag. The first element is the name of the tag — `<A>`.

The second element in the tag is the *URL* (Uniform Resource Locator), or Web address, of the linked document identified by `HREF=`. In this case, `HREF="http://www.isc.com"` means that the linked document is at the Web address `http://www.isc.com`.

None of the information inside the brackets of the *begin anchor* tag (`<A>`) appears onscreen. However, the begin tag is followed by text that does appear onscreen, followed by the end anchor tag, `</A>`. Table 3-1 summarizes the HTML creation of the hyperlink.

Table 3-1	An HTML Hypertext Link	
Link Element	**The HTML Name**	**What It Does**
`<A HREF="http://www.isc.com">`	Begin Anchor Tag	Names the linked reference; note that the URL must be enclosed in quotation marks.
`<B>ISC home page</B>`	Anchor Text	Identifies the text that appears highlighted (in bold) on the browser screen.
`</A>`	End Anchor Tag	Closes the link.

Images in Your Web Pages

As we discuss earlier in this chapter, Internet pages are created as text. As a result, browsing the World Wide Web with a computer whose only input/output device is a teletype machine would be technically possible, although not much fun.

But most Internet users now have computers that can display high-quality graphic images, and many World Wide Web pages contain pictures. The graphic images are optional. They're maintained as separate files and incorporated into Web pages by means of an HTML tag in much the same way as a hypertext link to another HTML document.

Using the <IMG> *tag*

You can insert graphics into a World Wide Web page by using the HTML <IMG> tag. HTML enables a document to incorporate a graphic image that exists in a separate computer file or even a different part of the world.

Sorry for the jargon. *Graphic image* sounds so much more sophisticated than *picture.* And besides, the term *graphic image* makes the point that sometimes the image is an artist's rendering of text. For example, in Figure 3-4, the picture of the White House on this Web page is a graphic image, but the greeting *Good Afternoon,* rendered in fancy script, also happens to be a graphic image.

As we mentioned, the tag you use to incorporate pictures into a Web page is the <IMG> tag. For example, the picture of the White House in Figure 3-4 comes from the following HTML code:

```
<IMG SRC="/WH/images/bevel.jpg" BORDER=0  HSPACE=10
VSPACE=3 ALIGN=middle ALT="[White House image]">
```

Figure 3-4:
Web pages
can have
pictures as
well as
words.

In the case of the <IMG> tag, everything is packed into one tag; you don't need a separate end tag. Table 3-2 outlines the example <IMG> tag elements and their purposes.

URLs

Web pages are not the only type of resource on the Internet. In addition to Web pages, for example, you find Usenet newsgroups where users post information on a topic of shared interest and file archives where users may download material such as software upgrades and documentation.

A URL can point to any type of Internet resource. The first part of a URL is called the *protocol*, and it identifies the type of resource. HTTP, for example, specifies the *Hypertext Transfer Protocol*, the protocol for Web pages. A URL can point to some other type of resource such as an e-mail address, a file archive, a file on your local hard disk, or a

Usenet newsgroup. Depending on the protocol, your Web browser attempts to take some appropriate action. If the URL is an e-mail address, for example, Netscape Navigator pops up a window in which you can enter an e-mail message to be sent to the specified e-mail address.

Some valid protocols are

HTTP://	for a Web page
NEWS://	for a newsgroup
FTP://	for a file archive
MAILTO://	for an e-mail address

Table 3-2	The <IMG> Tag Elements
Tag Element	*What It Does*
SRC="/WH/images/bevel.jpg"	Gives the location of the file that contains the graphic image. (If the image isn't on the same server as the Web page, a complete URL is required.)
BORDER=0	Gives the style of border to put around the picture; 0 means no border.
HSPACE=10 VSPACE=3	Gives the amount of horizontal and vertical blank space to leave around the edges of the picture.
ALIGN=middle	Tells how to align the picture in relation to the text.
ALT="[White House image]"	Gives the text to display in case a particular browser can't handle graphics.

Whenever you use the <IMG> tag to insert a picture into your Web page, you must use the IMG keyword and the SRC= attribute to tell the browser where the picture is located. You can add a number of optional expressions to the tag to control how the picture is displayed (see Figure 3-5). Table 3-3 shows the optional expressions, called *attributes*, that you can use with the <IMG> tag.

Table 3-3   Optional Expressions (Attributes) for the <IMG> Tag

Optional Expression	What It Does
ALT="..."	The text between the quotation marks is what appears if the browser viewing the page isn't able to display graphics. This text is also displayed if the images are turned off in the browser (if the user turned them off to speed things up).
ALIGN= ...	Controls how the picture lines up with the text (see Figure 3-5)
HEIGHT= ...	Controls the vertical dimension of the picture
WIDTH= ...	Controls the horizontal dimension of the picture
BORDER= ...	Controls the appearance of a border around the picture
HSPACE= ...	Adds extra space to the right or left of the picture, between the picture and the adjoining text
VSPACE= ...	Adds extra space above and below the picture, between the picture and the adjoining text

Making a graphic link

You can use an image as a hypertext link. For example, clicking the "What's New" icon shown back in Figure 3-4 displays a new page of data. The HTML that accomplishes this link includes a begin anchor tag, followed by an image tag in place of text, and then the end anchor tag.

```
<A HREF="/wh/new/html/new.html">
<IMG BORDER=0 SRC="/wh/images/calendar.jpg" ALT="[What's
New icon]">
</A>
```

At Last: Including Applets in Your Web Pages

You can incorporate applets into Web pages in much the same way as you include graphic images. The HTML for incorporating an applet is very similar to the HTML for the <IMG> tag. Figure 3-6 shows several Hello applets on a Web page.

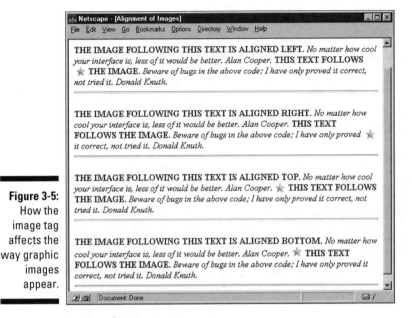

Figure 3-5:
How the
image tag
affects the
way graphic
images
appear.

Using the <APPLET> *tag*

The tag you use to incorporate applets into a Web page is the <APPLET> tag.
For example, the applets in Figure 3-6 are placed on the screen by the
following HTML tags:

```
<APPLET CODE="HelloAgainWorld.class"  WIDTH=100 HEIGHT=100
ALIGN=left>
<PARAM NAME=info VALUE="Hello.">
</APPLET>
```

```
<APPLET CODE=" HelloAgainWorld.class"  WIDTH=100 HEIGHT=100
ALIGN=right>
<PARAM NAME=info VALUE="Hi!">
</APPLET>
```

```
<APPLET CODE=" HelloAgainWorld.class"  WIDTH=100 HEIGHT=100
ALIGN=top>
<PARAM NAME=info value="How are ya?">
</APPLET>
```

```
<APPLET CODE=" HelloAgainWorld.class"  WIDTH=100 HEIGHT=100
ALIGN=bottom>
<PARAM NAME=info VALUE="Greetings!">
</APPLET>
```

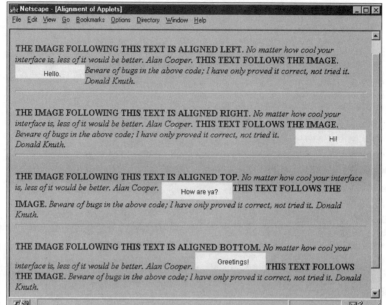

Figure 3-6:
Java
applets on a
Web page.

When you use the ⟨APPLET⟩ tag to insert an applet into your Web page, you use the keyword applet and the CODE= attribute to tell the browser where the Java bytecode for the applet is located. Then, you can add optional expressions to the tag to control how the applet is displayed — in the same way that you control how a picture is displayed. Table 3-4 describes the attributes that you can use with the ⟨APPLET⟩ tag.

Table 3-4	Attributes for the ⟨APPLET⟩ Tag
Attribute	*What It Does*
ALT="..."	The text between the quotation marks is what appears if the browser viewing the page isn't able to run Java applets.
ALIGN= ...	Controls how the applet lines up with the text. ALIGN works the same way as for graphic images. (Refer to Figure 3-5.)
HEIGHT= ...	Controls the vertical dimension of the applet's screen space.
WIDTH= ...	Controls the horizontal dimension of the applet's screen space.
BORDER= ...	Controls the appearance of a border around the applet.

(continued)

Attribute	What It Does
HSPACE= ...	Adds extra space to the right or left of the applet space, between the applet space and the adjoining text.
VSPACE= ...	Adds extra space above and below the applet space, between the applet space and the adjoining text.

The Web page can send information to the applet when it starts the applet. This information is sent by means of parameter tags (<PARAM>). A <PARAM> tag gives the name of the particular bit of information and its value. In the very next section, we show you how to write applets that use parameter input.

After any parameter tags, the final item required to run an applet is the applet end tag </APPLET>. Table 3-5 summarizes the <APPLET> tag elements and their purposes.

Table 3-5	The <APPLET> Tag Elements	
Tag Element	**The HTML Name**	**What It Does**
<APPLET CODE= "HelloW3. class" WIDTH=100 HEIGHT=100 ALIGN=top>	Begin Applet Tag	Identifies the linked applet; note that the URL of the applet code must be enclosed in quotation marks.
<PARAM NAME=info value="Hello">	Parameters	Optional inputs for sending information to the applet.
</APPLET>	End Applet Tag	Closes out the tag; it's required even when you have no parameters.

Passing parameters: A brief detour back to Java

When you want to use an HTML tag to give an applet some information, such as the contents of a label, you must also tell the applet how to find and use this information. *Passing* information to a Java applet involves three general steps (which we explain further with the example that follows):

1. **Set up a spot to keep track of the information, and then give the information a name.**

2. **Tell the applet to get the parameter and put the information in the spot you have prepared.**

3. **Use the passed information in place of something you would otherwise type in when you the write the applet.**

The following example and explanation illustrate the process of getting information to an applet:

```java
import java.applet.*;
import java.awt.*;
import java.lang.*;
/**
*                    HelloAgainWorld.class
*                    @version 0.1
*                    @author dkoosis@isc.com
*/

public class HelloAgainWorld extends Applet{

    Label helloLabel = new Label();
    String infoString = "unassigned";

    public void init() {
            infoString = getParameter("info");
            helloLabel.setText(infoString);
            add(helloLabel);
    }
}
```

This code is almost the same as the code for `HelloWorld` in Chapter 2. But instead of setting up a label with writing on it, we set up a blank label:

```java
Label helloLabel = new Label ();
```

The following line sets up a place in the computer's memory to keep the parameter. It also provides a name (`infoString`) so that you can refer to this information later, and it gives `infoString` a temporary value so we can trace the effects of the program.

```java
String infoString = "unassigned";
```

The `init` method defines what happens right after the applet is downloaded. The following line of code gets the parameter from the HTML page and puts the information into the place prepared for it (in the computer's memory).

```java
infoString = getParameter("info");
```

The following line of code uses the passed information. When we wrote this line of code, instead of typing the text that is to appear on the label, we typed the name given to this text — infoString.

```
helloLabel.setText(infoString);
```

A *string* is a series of characters that the computer treats as text. You can tell the computer that you want something to be treated as a string by enclosing the text in quotation marks:

"This is a string of number characters: 1, 2, 3, 4, 5."

We tell you more about Java strings in Chapter 10.

Movies and Talking Pages

A Web page can call up graphics stored in separate files by using a tag that gives the URL of the graphics file. Similarly, a Web page can include Java applets by giving the URL of the Java bytecode. In much the same way, other HTML tags enable you to call up motion, video, sound, and other types of data. Sometimes using these HTML features is a good alternative to writing Java applets if you don't really need the full power of Java. We recommend that you make yourself familiar with the features available. *HTML For Dummies,* 3rd Edition, which we mention at the beginning of the chapter, is a good resource.

Talking Back to the Internet

Using the HTML that we've shown you to this point enables users to read pages stored on a Web server. If they want to use an Internet *search engine,* sign someone's Internet *guest book,* or place a credit-card order, users must not only read data from the server, but also send data to the server.

Today, the standard way to send information to a Web server is by using HTML forms and *CGI* (the Common Gateway Interface). You make Web forms by using standard HTML tags that provide common data entry features: text entry fields, checkboxes, and selectable lists. When the users finish entering data, they can click a button that (depending on the page) typically says something like *Submit* or *Search* or *Place Order.* When users click the appropriate button, the data entered on the form is sent to a software program on the server. The program on the server can save the entered data to a database, run a search program and display results, or do anything else a programmer can dream up.

Programs that run on the end user's computer, like your Java applets, are called *client-side* programs. Programs that run on a centralized computer that works for many end users, like the programs that process CGI messages, are called *server-side* programs. By the way, server-side programs are often written in Java.

Communication with the server through CGI enables the users to request a database search or to place an order with a vendor. See Figure 3-7 for an example of a search request screen.

Java applets provide more powerful and flexible tools for creating user interfaces than are provided by CGI, but not all Web browsers are able to run Java applets at this time. You should be aware of the capabilities of CGI if you're concerned with receiving and responding to user input. In Chapters 15 and 16, we show you how to use Java-powered communications with the server.

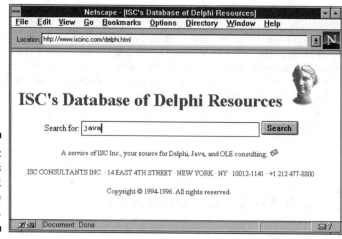

Figure 3-7:
CGI enables you to talk back to the Web host.

Chapter 4

The Object All Sublime: Object-Oriented Programming

• •

• •

*T*o begin writing more useful code and to understand the code you write, you must know a few technical terms and understand a few basic ideas about object-oriented programming.

A Primer on Object-Oriented Programming

If you have written some word-processing or spreadsheet macros or done a little programming in the BASIC programming language, you may already have noticed that Java code looks quite different from macros or BASIC. Many fundamentals that you know still apply, but the feel and thought processes of Java are very different from these *procedural* languages, in which the code is organized as a step-by-step description of what happens next.

In an object-oriented programming (OOP) language such as Java, the program code is organized in terms of *objects* that are members of *classes,* which are categories of objects that share features. These classes can, in turn, pass on features and create related classes through a process called *inheritance.* We discuss these concepts in more detail throughout this chapter. Object-oriented programming makes possible more flexible and more powerful code development.

A *class* is a description of some data and the procedures used to work with that data. All the standard *GUI* (graphical user interface) features — `Button`, `CheckboxGroup`, `Menu`, `Scrollbar`, and so on — are classes in Java. You also find classes for kinds of information that don't appear directly onscreen, such as `Date`, `String`, `AudioClip`, and `Image`. As we suggest in Chapter 2, we like to think of a class as a *blueprint*.

The developers of the Java language wrote many Java classes for you (including classes for the standard GUI features). And they made these classes available to you in the *Java Class Library* — *.Java/lib/classes.zip.* The `import` statements at the beginning of the HelloWorld applet (see Chapter 2) make this *library code* available to the applet.

In the HelloWorld applet, `Label` is an example of a class that's included in the Java Class Library. As we mention previously, you also find library classes for all the standard GUI features (such as `Button` and `CheckboxGroup`) and for other kinds of information that you may need to use (such as `Date` and `Image`).

One of the main things we show you in this book is how to use the Java Class Library. That is, we show you how to avoid writing code unless absolutely necessary — one of the primary skills of a good programmer!

An *object* is a specific set of data, based on the description in a class. The scratch pad pages we discuss in Chapter 2 are objects. In the HelloWorld applet, `helloLabel` is an object.

You can have more than one object based on a given class. For example, an applet can use many `Label`s. But every object must be based on a class — either a library class or one that the programmer has written herself. To write the applet that appears in Figure 4-1, you use the `Button` class definition to create two objects, `okButton` and `cancelButton`.

When you write a Java applet, you must always define one class yourself. That class is the applet. For example, the only class defined in the HelloWorld applet code is class `HelloWorld`.

Can you have more than one `HelloWorld` applet object? Figure 4-2 shows you the answer. Some objects contain families of other objects. Each of these `HelloWorld` applet objects includes a `helloLabel` object.

Writers and programmers aren't always consistent in their use of words to describe object-oriented programming features. In place of *class,* some people say *type* or *template.* In place of *object*, some say *instance.*

Figure 4-1:
How many
classes?
How many
button
objects?

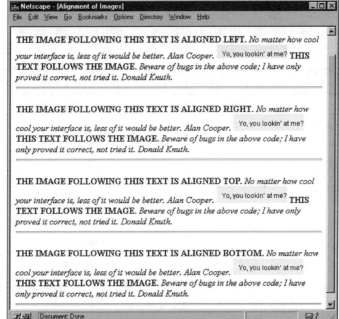

Figure 4-2:
More than
one
HelloWorld
applet
object.

A Closer Look at a Class and an Object

We want to begin with something that may seem pretty trivial — the label in the HelloWorld applet. The computer needs to keep track of at least a dozen distinct facts to establish and maintain the display of the label on the screen. If you don't believe us, think for a moment about what you would have to tell someone for him to re-create an accurate representation of the label on graph paper:

✔ Distance from left edge of screen (or graph paper)

✔ Distance from top of screen (or graph paper)

✔ Height of label

✔ Width of label

✔ Background color for the label

✔ Words to appear on the label

✔ Style of lettering

✔ Color of lettering

✔ And so on. . . .

If you want to put a second label on the screen, the computer needs to keep track of another set of label facts. You can imagine that the computer is maintaining a notebook of label information; Table 4-1 shows how this notebook may look:

Table 4-1	The Computer's Notebook of Label Facts	
Name	*HelloLabel*	*GoodbyeLabel*
Distance from left edge of screen	5	300
Distance from top of screen	5	300
Height	10	10
Width	100	100
Background color	yellow	blue
Content	"Yo, you lookin' at me?"	"So long."
Style of lettering	Times Roman	Times Roman
Color of lettering	black	white

In addition to this information about individual labels, the computer has a set of instructions on how to do various things with labels. For example, if you need to change the background color of a label, the *setBackground method* tells the computer how to look up the location and size of the label, locate and change the color of that area on the screen, and update the information in the notebook to indicate the label's new background color.

If an applet displays seven buttons, one for each day of the week, the computer must keep track of all the relevant details about each button — location, size, color, text, whether the button is released or pressed, and so on. However, the seven button objects share the same methods.

Similarly, when your computer displays a Web page with four copies of the *HelloWorld* applet, it must keep track of all the information about each applet object — including a different helloLabel object in each of the four applet objects. However, the methods for each HelloWorld applet object, and for each helloLabel object, are the same.

Managing your objects: Define, declare, instantiate

The computer's "notebook," with its list of information items and instructions, is the *class definition*.

Each time you create a new label, the computer must add another column of information about a specific label. If you want to do something to a specific label, you must identify which label you are interested in. The column of information with its identifying name is the object.

The important thing to notice is that you don't have to deal with all these details to create a label. After you define the Label class, the computer takes care of most of the work automatically.

You must do three key things to manage the life of objects:

✔ **Define a class.** Often you can use a class definition in the Java Class Library. Sometimes you may have to modify an existing class.

✔ **Assign a name for an object.** The technical term for this action is to *declare* an object. The code to declare an object consists of the name of the class followed by the name you are assigning to a particular object in that class. For example:

```
Label helloLabel;
```

✔ **Set up the actual data space for an object in computer memory.** The technical term for this action is to *instantiate* an object. The Java code you use to do this is called a *constructor*. The code to instantiate an object consists of the keyword new followed by the class name and often some additional information required for the setup of the object. For example:

```
new Label("Yo, you looking at me?");
```

You may often declare and instantiate an object at the same time:

```
Label helloLabel = new Label("Yo, you lookin' at me?");
```

Constructors and other methods

When you want to instantiate an object, you need to know the exact form of its constructor. The constructor code for each object is part of its class definition. You can look up the constructor code for library classes in the *Java Applications Programming Interface Reference* (the API reference), which is in the /docs subdirectory of JDK 1.1.1. The class definition of Label includes the following two constructors:

- ✔ Label(String label): Constructs a new label with the specified String of text. The notation (String label) tells you that what you put between the parentheses must be a String.

- ✔ Label(): Constructs an empty label. When you leave the parentheses empty, the label is empty.

In the following references, we show you both forms of the Label constructor in use. Notice that each code line ends with a semicolon.

In Chapter 2, Label(String label):

```
Label helloLabel = new Label("Yo, you lookin' at me?");
```

In Chapter 3, Label():

```
Label helloLabel = new Label();
```

Can you find the declarations in the following code? Can you find the constructor for HelloLabel?

```
import java.applet.*;
import java.awt.*;
import java.lang.*;

public class HelloAgainWorld extends Applet{

  Label helloLabel = new Label();
   String infoString = "null";

  public void init() {
     infoString = getParameter("info");
     helloLabel.setText(infoString);
     add(helloLabel);
  }
}
```

If you want to write a line in the code for another class that can enable objects of that class to change `helloLabel` in some way, use one of the `Label` methods. Like constructors, the methods for each library class are documented in the Java API Reference. For example, the specification for the `setText` method of `Label`:

```
setText(String)
```

sets the text for this label to the specified text.

The grammar of Java requires you to name the object that you're addressing, followed by a dot, followed by the name of the method, followed by a parenthesis. If any additional information is needed to complete the desired action, you include that information between the parentheses. And, of course, the whole statement ends with a semicolon. For example:

```
helloLabel.setText("This is my new text.");
```

Java's dot notation, as in the preceding example, is intended to be convenient and clear. It follows the model of "Hey, Joe. Please pass the salt." If you are used to another programming language with a different syntax, you may find it helpful to think of the *object* on the left side of the dot as a special parameter for the *method* on the right side of the dot.

TIP

Terse verse

In the example we use in this chapter, you go through several steps to send the `"info"` parameter string to the `helloLabel` object. `String` is a special case of ready-made object that does not require the use of a constructor. Also, you are not going to refer to the label string anywhere else, so you don't really need to give the label string a name by declaring it. You can just write `getParameter. . .` where you want the `"info"` parameter to appear:

```
public class HelloAgainWorld extends Applet{
Label helloLabel = new Label();
public void init(){
HelloLabel.setText(getParameter("info"));
add(HelloLabel);
}
}
```

Whether you use shortcuts like this is a matter of style and preference. Both versions of the code work equally well.

The Pix Applet Using Inheritance

Pix is an applet that illustrates the most important basic ideas and techniques of object-oriented programming in Java. This applet displays a variety of shapes on the screen. Each shape is accompanied by a label that states the name, perimeter, and area of the shape (see Figure 4-3).

As we show you in the Pix example, you can base one class definition on another and program only the differences using the inheritance process common to object-oriented programming. If you make changes in the original *parent* class (the "founder" of like classes), the changes are automatically *inherited* by the *child* class (the class derived from the parent and sharing features with it). Using this process saves an enormous amount of programming work. In Pix, we set up a generalized Pix class and then use *inheritance* to create specific shapes. (We talk more about inheritance later in this chapter.)

In the Pix example, we also show you that each object behaves like a *black box,* an important advantage of OOP. The class definition establishes what information the outside world provides to the object and what information the object provides to the outside world. You can use a class in your program without knowing the details of the object's private life. For example, the computation for the area of a circle is quite different from the computation for the area of a rectangle. To write a Circle class, you need to know how to calculate the area of a circle. But you don't need to know how to calculate the area of a circle to use the Circle class in the Pix applet.

Following is the code for the Pix applet. The code doesn't compile as it appears here; you need the other classes that we define in the following pages before the applet can run. We'll tell you when.

```
import java.applet.Applet;
import java.awt.*;
```

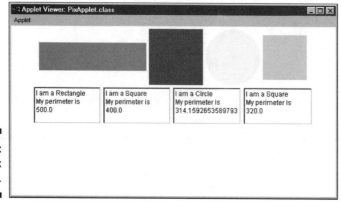

Figure 4-3:
The Pix applet.

```
/* Pix - an applet for exploring inheritance.
* author = dkoosis@isc.com
* version 0.1, 10 April 1996
*/

public class PixApplet extends Applet {

  public void init() {
      Rectgl r = new Rectgl(10,5,Color.red);
      Square s = new Square(10,Color.blue);
      Circle c = new Circle(20,Color.yellow);
      Square s2 = new Square(40,Color.green);
      add(r);
      add(s);
      add(c);
      add(s2);
      add(new PixLabel(r));
       add(new PixLabel(s));
      add(new PixLabel(c));
      add(new PixLabel(s2));
         }
}
```

Look for the classes and objects in the preceding code. You can pick out four obvious classes from the constructors: Rectgl, Circle, Square, and PixLabel. Rectgl and Circle are used to create only one object each, r and c. Square is used to create two objects, s and s2. PixLabel is used to create four objects, but the objects are not given names.

This applet also uses a Color class. You can tell that the color class is used by the references to it — Color.red, Color.green, and so on. Color.green refers to all the information and instructions needed to make a green color appear on the screen.

Rectgl, Square, Circle, and PixLabel are *not* library classes. To run the Pix applet, you must provide definitions of these classes.

Unfortunately, I can't spell out the name of the rectangular shape properly, because another library class uses the name *Rectangle* for a purpose that doesn't match my needs for this class. The correct solution to this dilemma would be to put my Pix classes in their own package, which would allow me to use any names I want for my shapes. But for this simple demonstration, I prefer to take the quick and dirty approach by selecting an unused name (Rectgl) for my class of rectangular shapes. By the way, I also chose to call the applet Pix because *Shape* is a name that's used in the Java class library.

Defining a `Rectgl` *Step-by-Step*

The following code is a definition of the class `Rectgl`. We explain the code step-by-step later in this section.

```
/* Rectgl */
class Rectgl extends Pix {
    /* Constructor */
    public Rectgl(int width, int height, Color c) {
        myDimension.width = width;
        myDimension.height = height;
        setColor(c);
    }
    /* Draw the shape */
    public void paint(Graphics g) {
g.fillRect(0,0,myDimension.width,myDimension.height);
    }
    /* Return this shape's area */
    public double getArea() {
        return myDimension.width * myDimension.height;
    }
    /* Return this shape's perimeter */
    public double getPerimeter() {
        return (myDimension.width + myDimension.height) * 2;
    }
    /*  Return a string describing the shape */
    public String getKind () {
        return "Rectangle";
    }
}
```

Now, we discuss the preceding code in a series of steps. We first show you the segments of code to discuss, and we then discuss the code segments in the paragraph that follows each segment. We proceed from the top down.

```
class Rectgl extends Pix {
```

The preceding code line is very similar to the line that begins the definition of your applet class. Just as the Hello examples extended the `Applet` class, we now extend the `Pix` class. *The brace { at the end of the line marks the start of the class definition contents.* The very end of the class definition has a matching close brace }. Everything between the braces is the contents of the class definition for `Rectgl`.

```
/* Constructor */
public Rectgl(int width, int height, Color c) {
        myDimension.width  = width;
        myDimension.height = height;
        setColor(c);
}
```

This preceding segment of code is a *constructor*. The text in parentheses on the first line tells what information you must provide to instantiate a Rectgl — in this case, two integers and a color. The information between the braces tells what the computer is to do when the code instantiates a Rectgl object. That is, the computer assigns the first number to be the width element of the shape's dimension and assigns the second number to be the height element. The setColor instruction tells the computer to use the given color for any graphics that are put on the screen. The code line in the Pix applet that instantiates Rectgl r matches this constructor:

```
Rectgl r = new Rectgl(10,5,Color.red);
```

If you try to put something other than two integers and a color between the parentheses of the constructor, the compiler gives you an error message and refuses to compile your code.

```
/* Draw the shape */
public void paint(Graphics g) {
        g.fillRect(0,0,myDimension.width,myDimension.height);
    }
```

The preceding and following lines of code are all *methods*. They represent things that a Rectgl object can do. The first method is the paint method. Everything that appears onscreen gets there via a paint method. The name g refers to the current graphics object — think of the graphics object as a paintbrush. Whenever the code of an applet or another object tells a Rectgl object "paint," the Rectgl tells the paintbrush to fill in a rectangular area myDimension.width wide and myDimension.height high.

Now we skip ahead in the code to the last method definition.

```
/* Return a string describing the shape */
    public String getKind () {
        return "Rectangle";
    }
```

The preceding method enables a Rectgl object to tell other objects (such as the applet and the PixLabel) what kind of shape it is. Whenever the code of an applet or another object tells a Rectgl object "getKind," the

Rectgl sends back the string "Rectangle". If your applet contains rectangle r and you want to make myLabel identify the kind of shape r is, you can use the getKind method.

```
myLabel.setText(r.getKind());
```

The getKind() method enables you to give an object a special public name that's different from the program code name of the object. Generally, however, if you need to find out the identity of an object, use the built-in methods toString(), getClass(), or getName(), or the operator instanceof.

Class and Method Definitions: Rules of Punctuation and Grammar

Here are some important specific rules about definitions:

- ✔ **Every method (except a constructor) either returns something or is void.** Notice that the first line of each method definition that we discuss in the previous section tells you what type of information the method returns — in the case of getKind, a string. Other methods of Rectgl return double, which is a number that may be a decimal fraction. And the paint method doesn't return anything, so the method is labeled void.

- ✔ **Every method definition tells you, between parentheses, what information the method requires to do its thing.** The Rectgl constructor requires two integers and a color. The paint method requires a graphic object — the *paintbrush*. The methods that do not require any information from the outside world have empty parentheses — ( ).

- ✔ **Every class definition begins and ends with a brace — { class definition }.**

- ✔ **Every method definition inside the class definition begins and ends with a brace — { method definition }.**

- ✔ **Every statement ends with a semicolon — ;.**

How to Work Less and Enjoy Programming More

You may have noticed that writing the code for a task as simple as putting a rectangle on the screen is a lot of work. And we still have yet to deal with a square and a circle.

Of course, you could probably copy much of the code you have written for Rectgl and then edit it. But you would run the risk of forgetting to make a necessary change or making a typo. Here's an elegant way to build on the work you have already done.

Using inheritance to build on your work

As the Pix applet demonstrated earlier in this chapter, Java has a feature called *inheritance* that allows you to base a new class definition on a class definition that already exists. In this way, you need to spell out only the differences, as we explain after you take a look at the class definition of Square:

```
class Square extends Rectgl {
/* constructor */
    public Square(int side, Color c){
    super(side, side, c);
}
/* Return a string describing the shape */
    public String getKind () {
        return "Square";
    }
}
```

We now discuss the preceding code in a series of steps. We show you the segments of code to discuss and then discuss them in the paragraph that follows each segment.

```
class Square extends Rectgl {
```

The preceding line of code tells you that a Square object is a special case of a Rectgl. When you construct a Square, you construct a Rectgl with some added or changed properties and methods specified in the class description.

```
/* constructor */
    public Square(int side, Color c){
    super(side, side, c);
```

The constructor for a square requires only one integer. The super (for superclass — another name for parent class) method refers to the class Square is based on — Rectgl. Instantiating a Square is the same thing as instantiating a Rectgl with both height and width equal to the Square's side integer.

```
/* Return a string describing the shape */
   public String getKind () {
       return "Square";
   }
```

Because `Square` is a different kind of shape, the method definition must return a different string to `getKind`. The computations for area and perimeter and the graphic operations to put a square on the screen are the same as for a `Rectgl`.

Planning ahead: Using abstract classes

If displaying these shapes is a one-shot deal, you may want to go ahead and write completely separate code for `Circle` and be done with the project. However, experience shows that more often than not, you should expect to expand or modify your applet later. What about adding a triangle?

When you have a family of related objects and want to manage them in an organized way, creating an object that bundles everything they have in common is useful. This *grandfather* object is likely not to exist in the real world, so we call it an *abstract* class.

For the Pix applet, the abstract class `Pix` is the starting point for all the individual shape classes. Notice that almost all the methods are empty. The one thing that the abstract `Shape` class actually does is to make sure that the shape's `preferredSize` and `minimumSize` are the same as the dimensions of the shape. This step is necessary to make any shape object display correctly on the screen.

```
abstract class Pix extends Canvas {
   Dimension myDimension = new Dimension();
   public void Pix() {
   }
   public Color getColor() {
       return getForeground();
   }
   public void setColor(Color c) {
       setForeground(c);
   }
   public void paint(Graphics g) {
   }
   public double getArea() {
       return 0;
```

```
    }
    public double getPerimeter() {
        return 0;
    }
    public String getKind() {
        return "unknown shape";
    }
    public Dimension preferredSize() {
        return myDimension;
    }
    public Dimension minimumSize() {
        return myDimension;
    }
}
```

Using this abstract class provides a framework to assure that all Pix have the same basic set of methods. All Pix can respond to paint, getKind, and so on. Making sure that the methods for the new shape are implemented in a meaningful way is up to the programmer who adds a new shape, but the abstract class provides the framework. And any other code that deals with Pix can handle the new shape without revision.

PixLabel

To see the benefits of the abstract class approach, look at the PixLabel class.

```
class PixLabel extends TextArea {
    public PixLabel(Pix s) {
        super( "I am a " + s.getKind()+ "\nMy perimeter is " +
            Double.toString(s.getPerimeter()) + "\nMy area is " +
            Double.toString(s.getArea()),3,15,SCROLLBARS_NONE);
        }
    }
```

PixLabel applies to any Pix object. The programmer who wrote the PixLabel class knows that every Pix has a getKind method that returns a string, a getPerimeter method that returns a double, and so on. Notice that PixLabel is based on a library class named TextArea. The constructor for TextArea calls for a string, the number of lines of text displayed, the number of columns wide, and a code telling whether to display scroll bars. In the same way that super in the code for Rectgl referred to the parent of Rectgl, here super refers to the parent class of PixLabel—TextArea.

A few tangled details about strings

In Java programming, text between quotation marks is always a string. Numbers used for computation are not strings and cannot be printed on the screen without first converting them to strings. So you must use a `.toString` method such as `Double.toString` before you can print a numerical result onscreen.

To indicate that you want to start a new line in a string of text, use `\n` — the newline code. For example, consider the following code:

```
"\nMy area is " +
Double.toString(s.getArea())
```

This code says:

1. Start a new line.

2. Begin with `My area is`.

3. Get the area of the object `s`, convert the numerical value to string form, and add the converted form to the string.

And lest we forget it, `Circle`

In case you want to try writing a `Circle` class definition on your own (before you look at our version), you need a few additional bits of information:

- Pix knows about height and width, but not about a radius. Your `Circle` class needs to declare a private integer variable to keep track of its own radius. At the beginning of the class definition, write a declaration like this:

```
private int myRadius;
```

- To obtain the value of Pi, use the method `Math.PI`.
- To fill in a circle, use the method `g.fillArc`:

```
fillArc(int x, int y, int width, int height,
int startAngle, int arcAngle)
```

where x and y are the location coordinates of the arc, width and height are the maximum dimensions of the circle, and `startAngle` and `arcAngle` give the angles of the two edges of a pie slice — for a circle, `startAngle` is 0 and `arcAngle` is 360.

Following is the code for our version of `Circle`.

```
class Circle extends Pix {
    private int myRadius;
    /* constructor */
    public Circle(int radius, Color c) {
        myRadius = radius;
      myDimension.width = myDimension.height = 2 * radius;
      setColor(c);
    }
    /* Display the shape */
    public void paint(Graphics g) {
        g.fillArc(0,0,(2*myRadius),(2*myRadius),0,360);
    }
    /** Return this shape's area */
    public double getArea() {
        return Math.PI * (myRadius * myRadius);
    }
    /* Return this shape's perimeter */
    public double getPerimeter() {
        return 2 * Math.PI * myRadius;
    }
    public String getKind() {
        return "Circle";
    }
}
```

Putting the applet all together

To compile and run the completed Pix applet, all the classes must be available to the computer at the same time. For purposes of learning Java, you can simply put the source code for all the class definitions in the same file with the applet class definition.

If you create related groups of classes that you use in more than one applet, you can save space and achieve more flexible access by creating a *package* or a *library*. Building packages and libraries is an advanced topic.

If you have some programming experience with other languages, you may wonder whether problems happen when different classes and objects use the same names to mean different things. For example, `getPerimeter` (that is, computing the measurement of the perimeter of the shape) involves a computation with Pi in the case of a `Circle` and an entirely different computation in the case of a `Rectgl`. One of the great advantages of programming in Java is that each object minds its own business. As long as your code makes clear which object is doing the work, each object keeps track of its own data and methods and faces no danger of confusion, regardless of what vocabulary you adopt. Programming gurus refer to this feature as *encapsulation*.

The Cartoon Version of "Hello, World!"

When we (David, Don, and others who talk about programming) talk about Java programs, we often speak as though program objects are people. For example, we talk about objects remembering data and methods, sending messages, and returning data.

Thinking this way makes programming more fun but also reflects an important idea behind the design of Java and other object-oriented languages. The developers of these languages believe that the structure of a program should reflect the structure of the problems that the program intends to solve. By designing classes that represent the real-world things you are working with, I can write programs with fewer errors and programs that are easier to maintain, modify, expand, and reuse.

Don't be concerned that you need an in-depth understanding of all the classes you come across. The Java Class Library contains hundreds of classes — all of them derived by inheritance from one class named `Object`.

Many classes deal with issues that don't concern you unless you are deeply involved in computer science. (Are your dreams haunted by *ThreadDeath* and *MalformedURLException?*) Other classes, such as colors and integers, deal with issues that you can hardly avoid.

If you use the objects that represent the things you need to deal with and ask these objects to do the things you need done, you find that (most of the time) you don't need to study the inner workings of these classes.

To encourage you to think like a professional programmer, we offer you the following dramatic interpretation of what happens when a Web page downloads the HelloWorld applet. Refer to the applet code as you read the script. Borrowing two hand puppets from a cooperative child (or at least putting an old sock on each hand) also helps. If you have neither children nor socks, look at the pictures in Figures 4-4 through 4-7.

```
public class HelloWorld extends Applet{
  Label helloLabel = new Label ("Yo, you lookin' at me?");
  public void init (){
    setBackground(Color.yellow);
    add(helloLabel);
  }
}
```

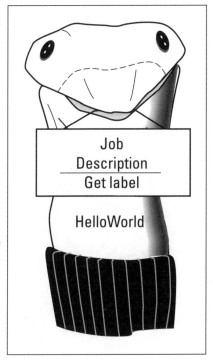

Figure 4-4:
Public
class
HelloWorld
extends
Applet(...

Web page: *(Offstage voice)* Hello, World!

HelloWorld: *(Pops up on stage. Takes scrap of paper labeled Job Description out of his pocket and looks at it.)* Hmm. I am going to need a Label. *(Refer to Figure 4-4.)*

HelloLabel: *(Pops up on stage.)* Yes?

HelloWorld: I'm going to call you HelloLabel, okay?

HelloLabel: Sure.

HelloWorld: And your text information is "Yo, you lookin' at me?"

HelloLabel: *(Pulls a T-shirt from his pocket and writes "Yo, you lookin' at me?" on the T-shirt with a marking pen. Puts on the T-shirt.) (See Figure 4-5.)*

Web page: *(Offstage voice)* Time to initialize!

HelloWorld: *(Looks again at scrap of paper from his pocket.)* Okay, first I have to turn my background yellow. *(Turns yellow; see Figure 4-6.)*

HelloWorld: *(Looks again at scrap of paper from his pocket.)* . . . And now I add HelloLabel! *(Reaches out and grabs HelloLabel to hold him up at the front of the stage; see Figure 4-7.)*

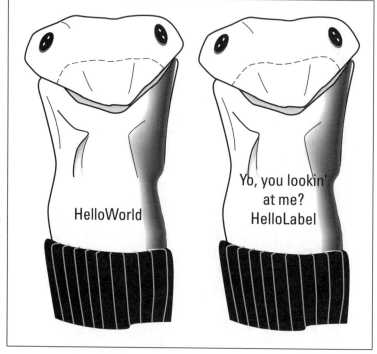

Figure 4-5:
`new`
`Label`
`("Yo,`
`you`
`lookin'`
`at me?")`

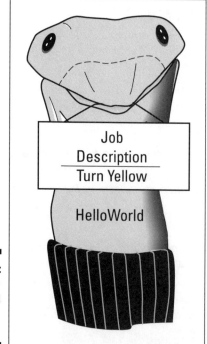

Figure 4-6:
`set-`
`Background`
`(Color:`
`yellow);`

Figure 4-7:
add
(HelloLabel);

Part II
Javanese

The 5th Wave   By Rich Tennant

"I think these JavaBots are just a bit too interactive!"

In this part . . .

To make the most of your leap into Java object-oriented
programming, we present the elements that let you
control what the Java applet users see and how they can
interact with the applet. We tell you some programmer's
tools and tricks and give you some useful coding and
testing advice.

Part II introduces the processes you use for making
choices with your code, repeating steps, understanding
the rules of program language grammar, and checking the
logic of your choices. Finally, we take a closer look at the
building blocks of the Java programming language. We
show you how to use code that already exists and how to
extend it (or build your own) to create the classes,
objects, and methods that you need.

Chapter 5

Where's the Action?

*W*hen you use Java, you can easily take for granted many of the things that the computer does for you. In fact, one of the great benefits of object-oriented programming is that you don't have to pay attention to all the tacky details in order to get a job done.

One of the tacky details that you have been able to take for granted so far is the arrangement of all your objects on the screen. You just write add, and an object appears on the screen. The object doesn't cover up what's already there or fall off the edge of the screen. At the risk of sounding like your mother, we say, "You should be grateful for this!"

Everything in Its Place

A family of objects called *Layouts* provides the service of organizing and arranging objects on the screen. When you say add, it's a layout that you're speaking to. The default Layout for applets — the one in charge if you haven't put another Layout in charge — is FlowLayout. So, when you write add(HelloLabel) in your code, with no other information about Layout, FlowLayout decides where the label appears.

Do you notice how easy it is to talk about objects as though they were personalities?

When you indicate nothing at all about how your visual components are to be displayed onscreen, the decisions about where to put things are made by FlowLayout. You can call on several other Layouts to arrange objects onscreen: BorderLayout, CardLayout, GridLayout, GridBagLayout. In this chapter, we show you two: FlowLayout and BorderLayout.

FlowLayout

FlowLayout arranges your objects on the screen in rows from left to right. When the current row has no more room for a new object, FlowLayout begins a new row. When the space that you allocated for your applet is full, nothing more appears until you make room for it by removing something else or resizing the applet (see Figure 5-1).

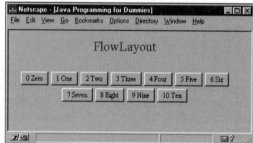

Figure 5-1:
Flow
Layout.

You use FlowLayout to arrange the shapes and labels of the Pix applet in Chapter 4, as well as the label of the HelloWorld applet. (See Figure 5-2.) You can tell FlowLayout how you want to align and space the rows of objects.

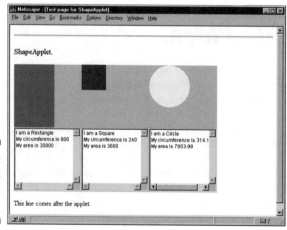

Figure 5-2:
Shape uses
Flow
Layout.

Class variables

The FlowLayout class includes its own special definitions of LEFT, RIGHT, and CENTER. Terms with special definitions are called variables. To clarify that you're referring to these definitions (variables), you must call on the class FlowLayout to handle this information.

You can't just say LEFT or CENTER, but instead must use the object-oriented notation and say FlowLayout.LEFT, FlowLayout.RIGHT, or FlowLayout.CENTER.

FlowLayout has three possible constructors that you can use. One lets FlowLayout just do its own thing; one tells it how to align the objects; and one tells it both alignment and spacing. Following are examples of each:

```
new FlowLayout(FlowLayout.RIGHT, 5, 10)
```

With the preceding constructor, you can create a FlowLayout that starts each row at the right edge and enables 5 units of horizontal space and 10 units of vertical space between each object.

```
new FlowLayout(FlowLayout.LEFT)
```

With the preceding constructor, you can create a FlowLayout that starts each row at the left edge and makes its own decision about spacing.

```
new FlowLayout()
```

This last constructor creates a FlowLayout that makes its own decision about both alignment and spacing (the default alignment is CENTER).

See Figures 5-3, 5-4, and 5-5 for the results of using different alignments.

Figure 5-3:
Flow
Layout
(Flow
Layout.Left)

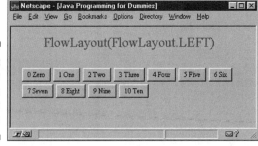

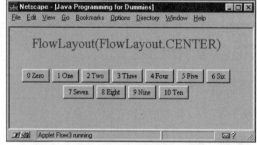

Figure 5-4:
`FlowLayout
(Flow
Layout.
CENTER.
5,10).`

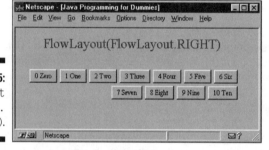

Figure 5-5:
`FlowLayout
(FlowLayout.
RIGHT,10,5).`

BorderLayout

BorderLayout, shown in Figure 5-6, is a class that gives you more control over where things go by setting up a five-part screen. The applet's screen real estate is divided into North, South, East, West, and Center.

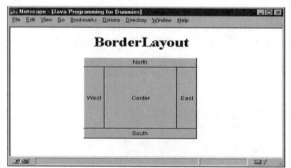

Figure 5-6:
BorderLayout.

To put an object onscreen with a BorderLayout, you need to tell the Layout where the object goes. For some arbitrary reason, when you refer to BorderLayout regions, you use strings. So, for example, to create the border, you write

```
new BorderLayout ():
```

and then you must say

```
myPanel.add( "North", MyLabel)
```

myPanel refers to the object whose Layout is managed by the BorderLayout.

Note the difference between the code to add an object to a BorderLayout and the code to instantiate a FlowLayout:

```
FlowLayout(FlowLayout.CENTER, 5,10)
```

but

```
myPanel.add( "Center", myLabel)
```

Building a screen layout

A typical way of organizing applet screen areas is to use a BorderLayout to set up some areas on the screen and then use a FlowLayout to fill each area with the objects that it needs. We use this approach in the example we work with in this chapter.

With BorderLayout, you can put more than one object in the same place. If you do this, the last object added covers up the previous objects.

When you use BorderLayout to put objects onscreen, BorderLayout gives the North, South, East, and West objects as much space as they require and then allocates what's left to Center.

If you think of the screen display for a typical personal computer program that uses a GUI, you get the idea of a BorderLayout. For example, a word processing program typically has a menu bar and some other user controls at the top ("North"). It has a status bar with other information at the bottom ("South"). Depending on the program, other controls often appear at the left ("West") and right ("East") edges of the screen. The space that remains in the center of the screen is the workspace where the user's typing appears ("Center").

A Panel is an object whose main purpose in life is to contain other objects. A Panel may contain buttons or other GUI controls, or it may contain other Panels in order to organize a display. In Java, you can use Panels to set up a screen display such as the one described in the preceding paragraph. You begin by using a BorderLayout of Panels. Then, you use a FlowLayout for each Panel, as follows:

```
setLayout(new BorderLayout());
Panel np = new Panel();
   add("North",np);
Panel sp = new Panel();
   add("South",sp);
Panel ep = new Panel();
   add("East",ep);
Panel wp = new Panel();
   add("West",wp);
Panel cp = new Panel();
   add("Center",cp);
np.setLayout(new FlowLayout(FlowLayout.CENTER, 10,5);
   np.add(new Label("Here I am."));
```

and so on. After `North`, `South`, `East`, and `West` have taken their shares of screen space, everything that's left belongs to `Center`.

So, What's the Big Event?

The user communicates with the applet by using a mouse or the keyboard. Whenever something happens to the mouse or keyboard while an applet is running, the applet is informed of this *event*. In fact, you can think one particular on-duty object as experiencing the event. For example, if you move the mouse pointer over a circle on the screen, the circle experiences the mouse event. The `Circle` object is responsible for informing the rest of the code that the mouse event has happened.

We say the `Circle` *posts* the event. (An event is a Java programming construct that enables a variety of objects to respond independently to the same bit of information. As you go deeper into Java programming, you find out about other types of events.)

Typically, one object posts events at any given moment. For mouse actions, the object responsible is the object located where the mouse pointer appears.

For keyboard events as well, one object is on duty at any given time. Depending on the platform, the object may be the one located where the mouse pointer appears or the last object where a mouse click occurred. We say that this object has the *keyboard focus* (see Figure 5-7). The object that has the focus posts keyboard events.

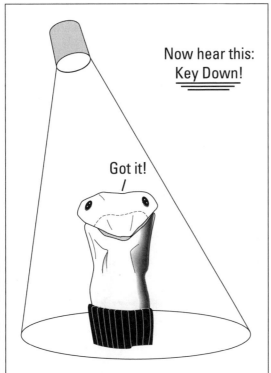

Figure 5-7:
The object
that has the
focus is
responsible
for keeping
track of
user input.

The other element in responding to user input is the code that says what to
do when the mouse is clicked or the key is pressed (see Figure 5-8). The
class that contains this code is called a *Listener*. The Listener must be
registered with the posting object in order to be informed of events. For
example, if you want some object to change color when the mouse pointer
enters the circle, you might write a Listener class called colorChanger. And
you would write code to add colorChanger to Circle's list of registered
Listeners. Then Circle will post a message to colorChanger every time it
experiences a mouse event.

A Listener registers for a given type of event; for example, mouse events or
keyboard events. A Listener can register with more than one posting object.
A Listener is required to have a method for handling each possible variation
of the type of event it's registered for. For example, a MouseListener is
required to have methods for each of the following mouse events:

Figure 5-8:
The object
that has the
focus posts
events to
registered
Listeners.

- mouseEntered
- mouseExited
- mousePressed
- mouseReleased
- mouseClicked

The methods in the Listener code give the response to the user input. For example, the mouseEntered method of colorChanger (a MouseListener) could send a message to other objects to change color.

When you write code to respond to user input, you need

- A target or posting object

  One or more Listeners must be registered with the target. (If no registered Listeners exist, the events that this object experiences go unnoticed and have no consequences.)

> ✔ A Listener object
>
> The Listener must specify methods to respond to all the variations of a given event type. (Of course, the response may be "do nothing.")

Monkeying with the mouse

The following is an example of the Java source code that you must write to deal with mouse events. If you include this method in the Pix applet, the square named s turns red when the mouse pointer moves over the object.

First, a colorChanger class (we explain the meaning of the Java keyword implements in Chapter 8):

```
class colorChanger implements MouseListener{
//Methods required to implement MouseListener interface
        public void mouseEntered(MouseEvent e) {
          s.setForeground(Color.red);
          s.repaint();
        }
        public void mouseExited(MouseEvent e) {
        }
        public void mousePressed(MouseEvent e){
        }
        public void mouseReleased(MouseEvent e){
        }
        public void mouseClicked(MouseEvent e){
        }
}
```

Then, you need to declare and instantiate a colorChanger object in the applet class:

```
        colorChanger Blush = new colorChanger();
```

Things have changed since 1.0

The way events are handled in Java 2 and 1.1 is different from the way they are handled in Version 1.0 of Java. We think the change is a big improvement. Just in case you don't believe us, we have included a section on the old Java 1.0 event model at the end of this chapter. A lot of Java 1.0 code is still in use, so the information may come in handy if some day you need to upgrade an old Java 1.0 applet, or if you simply want to read and understand a program written in Java 1.0.

And now the code to register the Listener with the target goes in the `init` method of the applet class:

```
public void init() {
        ...
        Square s = new Square(100,Color.blue);
        ...
        add(s);
        s.addMouseListener(Blush);
        ...
        }//end init
```

When the mouse moves into the screen area of the object, the object posts a `mouseEvent` message to the Listener. The Listener then changes the color of s. Note that the Listener doesn't necessarily have to change the color of the target. It may, instead, change the color of another object, play a sound clip of the national anthem, or whatever.

How about some code to change the color of the object to another color when the mouse leaves? This next code is a `mouseExited` method to turn an object cyan when the mouse leaves the target object. (Cyan is a bright greenish blue. You recognize it when you see it, even if the name isn't familiar.)

```
public void mouseExited(MouseEvent e) {
        s.setForeground(Color.cyan);
      s.repaint();
        }
```

Table 5-1 contains a list of mouse-related events and the methods that handle them.

Repaint is not advice from a decorator

When you write code that changes the intended appearance of an object, the code doesn't necessarily take effect immediately. If you want to be sure that the appearance of the object is updated to agree with its most current status, you need to use the `repaint()` method.

If an object doesn't seem to respond at all to a message that you send it, try repainting the object at the end of the method.

If you would rather have your object turn red and white, you have to write your own code.

Table 5-1	**What Can a Mouse Do?**
What Happened	*Method to Handle*
Responded to by `MouseListener`	
The user moved the mouse cursor into the screen area of the object.	`mouseEntered(Event e)`
The user moved the mouse cursor out of the screen area of the object.	`mouseExited(Event e)`
The user pressed the mouse button.	`mousePressed(Event e)`
The user released the mouse button.	`mouseReleased(Event e)`
The user clicked the mouse button.	`mouseClicked(Event e)`
Responded to by `MouseMotionListener`	
The user held down the mouse button and moved the mouse.	`mouseDragged(Event e)`
The user moved the mouse while the mouse button was released.	`mouseMoved(Event e)`

The mouse event e lets you find out some useful details about where the mouse cursor is: e.getComponent() refers to the component where the mouse cursor is located, and e.getX and e.getY give you the x- and y-coordinates of the mouse cursor at the moment the event happens.

The x- and y-coordinates are especially useful when you're writing a mouseDragged or mouseMoved method for a mouseMotionListener. The mouse events are constantly repeated as long as the mouse is moving. As a result, you get instant updates on the position of the mouse.

This next snippet of code draws a line wherever you drag the mouse:

```
public class Tracks extends Applet {
    mouseTracer Pencil = new mouseTracer(Color.black);
    public void init() {
        Rectgl r = new Rectgl(200,300,Color.red);
```

(continued)

(continued)

```
            add(r);
            r.addMouseMotionListener(Pencil);
        }//end init
}//end class
/*Use the Pix and Rectgl classes from Chapter 4
This mouseTracer keeps track of the X and Y coordinates
of the mouse and draws a line when the mouse
is dragged*/
class mouseTracer implements MouseMotionListener{
        private Color changeColor = new Color(0,0,0);
        private int startX = 0;
        private int startY = 0;
        //constructor
        mouseTracer(Color it){
            changeColor = it;
        }
        //Methods required to implement MouseListener interface
        public void mouseDragged(MouseEvent e) {
            Graphics g = e.getComponent().getGraphics();
            g.setColor(changeColor);
            g.drawLine(startX,startY,e.getX(),e.getY());
            startX=e.getX();
            startY=e.getY();
        }
        public void mouseMoved(MouseEvent e){
            startX=e.getX();
            startY=e.getY();
        }
}
```

Okay, so this code says

- `Graphics g=e.getComponent().getGraphics();` Check the identity of the object where the event is happening and take charge of the paintbrush for that object.

- `g.setColor(changeColor);` Dip it in the `changeColor` paint can. (In this example, black.)

- `g.drawLine(startX,startY,e.getX(),e.getY());` Draw a line from the location `startX`, `startY` to the `x,y` location where the mouse is now.

- Record the new location of the mouse as the new `startX`, `startY` location.

As long as the mouse drags, the event keeps repeating, and so the line follows the path of the mouse.

Keyboarding input

Usually, when you handle keyboard input, you use a `TextField`. The `TextField` has a built-in Listener, so you don't even have to write a Listener class. Instead, you can refer to the contents of a `TextField` by using the `getText()` method, and you can change the content of a `TextField` by using the `setText` method. Suppose you want to place the contents of the `myText` `TextField` into a Label named `myDisplay` and then erase `myText` so that you can type something new there. The following code will do the trick.

```
TextField myText = new TextField(infoString);
Label myDisplay = new Label("");
   ...
myDisplay.setText(myText.getText());
myText.setText("");
```

Occasionally, you may want to do something about keyboard input without using a `TextField`. If you do, you need to write a Listener.

For example, suppose you want to listen for any keys the user presses while the mouse is over `WestPanel` and display the typing on `EastPanel`. The target that posts the keying information is `WestPanel`, so you must add a `KeyListener` to `WestPanel`.

The code in the `KeyListener` class that you write must arrange to put a message in `EastPanel`. Here are some more code snippets. First the Listener class:

```
class kbListener implements KeyListener{
        private MousePanel it = new MousePanel(0,0,"");
        private String putString = new String("");
        //constructor
        kbListener(MousePanel target, String display){
        it = target;
        putString = display;
        }
        //Methods required to implement KeyListener interface
        public void keyPressed(KeyEvent e){
        }
        public void keyReleased(KeyEvent e){
        }
        public void keyTyped(KeyEvent e){
          putString = putString + e.getKeyChar();
          it.changeText(putString);
        }
}
```

What is this *public void* business?

Java needs to know two things about every method or variable in a class definition: scope and type. By keeping track of these two facts, Java protects you from writing the kind of code that may make your computer go out to lunch until you reboot.

Scope has to do with how widely information is shared between objects. If you want other objects to be able to use a method with code of the form `yourObject.method`, you must make the method `public`. Similarly, if you want other objects to use data from a class, as in `Event.HOME` or `FlowLayout.LEFT`, you must make the data item public.

Type has to do with the kind of data returned by a method. Some methods do not send out any result to the outside world. These methods are `void`. Other methods return a number of some type; for example, an integer — `int`.

There are also methods that send back a message of `true` or `false`. The technical name for true/false data is *Boolean* data (named after George Boole, one of the developers of mathematical logic).

Methods for event handling are usually `public` and `void`. We talk more about scope in Chapter 8, and more about type in Chapter 10.

Notice that the Listener is still pretty general. You haven't committed yourself to where the display appears yet. When you instantiate an object of the `kbListener` class, you tell the computer exactly where to display the message.

```
kbListener Tap = new kbListener(EastPanel, kbString);
...
```

Before any objects can make use of this Listener to respond to keying, you need to declare it and add it to `WestPanel`, where the keying will happen.

```
        WestPanel.addKeyListener(Tap);
```

Button, Button

A button is a typical GUI object. A button object reflects quite a bit of programming effort. Each platform and operating system has a built-in style of button that looks and behaves slightly differently from every other. Through some clever programming tricks that are too deep to explain in this book, Java enables you to use buttons in the native style of whatever system your applet happens to find itself in. If your applet is downloaded to a Web page on a UNIX workstation running Motif, the user sees a Motif-style button. On a Macintosh, the user sees a Macintosh-style button. On a PC running Windows, the user sees a Windows-style button.

As a Java programmer, you find that a ready-made button object in the Java Class Library saves you most of the work of creating buttons. The code to declare and instantiate a button is very similar to the code for a label.

```
Button okButton = new Button("OK");
```

To make something happen when the user clicks a button, you must provide guess what? A Listener!

```
class buttonListener implements ActionListener{
        private MousePanel it1;
        private MousePanel it2;
        private TextField from; private String words;
        //constructor
buttonListener(MousePanel target1, TextField source, MousePanel target2){
        it1  = target1;
        from = source;
        it2  = target2;
        }
        //Method required to implement ActionListener interface
        public void actionPerformed(ActionEvent e){
          words = from.getText();
          it1.changeText(words);
          from.setText("");
          it2.changeText("");
          }
        }//end buttonListener
```

Can't I just drag and drop?

Many IDEs (Integrated Development Environments — remember?) allow you to create a user interface by dragging and dropping GUI components onto an image of your user interface. For example, you can create an applet, and add a button by dragging the icon of a button onto the image of the applet. You can use the mouse to adjust the size and location of the button.

Behind the scenes, the IDE is writing Java code, similar to the code in this chapter, that you can view and edit. You can accomplish a great deal of design work very quickly by using the IDE. But when the time comes to fine-tune, revise, or troubleshoot, you still need to be able to read and write Java code.

The Programmer's Activity Box, Version 1.0

The following are specifications for a Java applet that pulls together all the various techniques we've covered so far for putting objects on the screen and making them respond to the user:

- ✔ The applet screen consists of five major panels: North, South, East, West, and Center.

- ✔ East and West are labeled with their names.

- ✔ On South, we put a button labeled South Button.

- ✔ On North, we put a blank text field 25 columns wide.

- ✔ All the panels are colored cyan. When the mouse enters any panel, the panel turns blue. When the mouse exits, the panel returns to cyan.

- ✔ You can type into the text field.

- ✔ When you click the South button, whatever you have typed into the text field is printed out on Center, and the text field is reset to blank.

See Figure 5-9 to understand the screen layout.

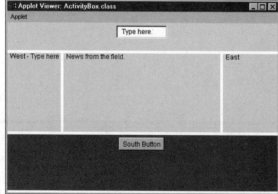

Figure 5-9:
The
Programmer's
Activity
Box.

To get this applet right takes a little advance planning. I need some ideas.

- The overall layout is a typical BorderLayout. To make it look good, I probably have to give the component panels a preferred size, the way I do for the Pix applet in Chapter 4.

- All the panels have the same behavior in response to the mouse. One MouseListener does the job. I have already seen how to do this.

- The button, the text field, and the label that displays text on the
  `Center` panel really belong to the applet as a whole, not to any
  individual panel. They interact with more than one of the objects
  onscreen.

Conducting a beta test

To check that a program does everything that the specifications call for
without problems, programmers create a version of the code for beta testing
(a *beta* is a test version of the program). The following code does everything
that the specifications call for. You may want to test this code on your
system.

(In the following code, we use an additional way to set off comments. A
double slash at the start of a line indicates that the line is a comment, for
documentation only.)

```
import java.awt.*;
import java.applet.*;
import java.awt.event.*;

/* ActivityBox Applet */
    public class ActivityBox extends Applet {
//Declarations
    String panelString = new String("News from the field.");
    String southString = new String("South Button");
    String infoString = new String("Type here.");
    String kbString = new String("East ");
    MousePanel cp = new MousePanel(100,100,panelString);
    MousePanel ep = new MousePanel(100,100,kbString);
    MousePanel np = new MousePanel(50,50);
    MousePanel sp = new MousePanel(100,100);
    MousePanel wp = new MousePanel(100,100,"West - Type here");
    TextField myText = new TextField(infoString);
    Button southButton = new Button(southString);
    colorChanger Blues = new colorChanger(Color.blue);
    buttonListener Zap = new buttonListener(cp, myText, ep);
    kbListener Tap = new kbListener(ep, kbString);
//init
    public void init() {
      setLayout(new BorderLayout(5,5));
          np.addMouseListener(Blues);
      add("North",np);
          np.add(myText);
```

(continued)

(continued)

```
        np.setBackground(Color.cyan);
            sp.addMouseListener(Blues);
            southButton.addActionListener(Zap);
        sp.add(southButton);
        add("South",sp);
        sp.setBackground(Color.cyan);
            ep.addMouseListener(Blues);
        add("East",ep);
        ep.setBackground(Color.cyan);
            wp.addMouseListener(Blues);
            wp.addKeyListener(Tap);
        add("West",wp);
        wp.setBackground(Color.cyan);
            cp.addMouseListener(Blues);
        add("Center",cp);
        cp.setBackground(Color.cyan);
    }
} //end applet
```

Notice that the code in the applet constructs a bunch of objects and sets
them up to interact.

```
/* MousePanel */
class MousePanel extends Panel {
    public String nameTag = "";
    Dimension myDimension = new Dimension(15,15);
//Constructor 1 - no name tag
    MousePanel(int h, int w) {
        myDimension.height = h;
        myDimension.width = w;
    }
//Constructor 2 - with name tag
    MousePanel(int h, int w, String nt) {
        myDimension.height = h;
        myDimension.width = w;
        nameTag = nt;
    }
//paint
    public void paint(Graphics g) {
        g.drawString(nameTag,5,10);
    }
//change text
    public void changeText(String s){
            nameTag = s;
            repaint();
    }
```

```
//getGetPreferredSize
    public Dimension getPreferredSize() {
        return myDimension;
    }
//getGetMinimumSize
    public Dimension getMinimumSize() {
        return myDimension;
    }
}
```

The Listeners do most of the interesting work. Notice that this `MouseListener` does something extra besides change the color of panels. It requests the focus whenever the mouse enters and it gives up the focus when the mouse leaves. This way, the `West` panel can take the keyboard focus in response to the location of the mouse.

```
class colorChanger implements MouseListener{
        private Color oldColor = new Color(0,0,0);
        private Color changeColor = new Color(0,0,0);
        //constructor
        colorChanger(Color it){
          changeColor = it;
        }
        //Methods required to implement MouseListener interface
        public void mouseEntered(MouseEvent e) {
          oldColor = e.getComponent().getBackground();
          e.getComponent().setBackground(changeColor);
          e.getComponent().requestFocus();
        }
        public void mouseExited(MouseEvent e) {
          e.getComponent().setBackground(oldColor);
          e.getComponent().transferFocus();
        }
        public void mousePressed(MouseEvent e){
        }
        public void mouseReleased(MouseEvent e){
        }
        public void mouseClicked(MouseEvent e){
        }
}

class buttonListener implements ActionListener{
        private MousePanel it1 = new MousePanel(0,0,"");
        private MousePanel it2 = new MousePanel(0,0,"");
        private TextField from = new TextField("");
```

(continued)

(continued)

```
        private String words = new String("");
        //constructor
        buttonListener(MousePanel target1, TextField source, MousePanel target2){
        it1  = target1;
        from = source;
        it2  = target2;
        }
        //Methods required to implement ActionListener interface
        public void actionPerformed(ActionEvent e){
          words = from.getText();
          it1.changeText(words);
          from.setText("");
          it2.changeText("");
          }
        }//end buttonListener

class kbListener implements KeyListener{
        private MousePanel it = new MousePanel(0,0,"");
        private String putString = new String("");
        //constructor
        kbListener(MousePanel target, String display){
        it = target;
        putString = display;
        }
        //Methods required to implement KeyListener interface
        public void keyPressed(KeyEvent e){
        }
        public void keyReleased(KeyEvent e){
        }
        public void keyTyped(KeyEvent e){
          putString = putString + e.getKeyChar();
          it.changeText(putString);
        }
}
```

The last brace marks the end of the keyListener class definition.

To test this applet, you have to put it into an HTML page. For example:

```
<HTML>
<HEAD>
<TITLE> A Programmer's Activity Box </TITLE>
</HEAD>
<BODY>
<H1>The Activity Box </H1>
<APPLET CODE="ActivityBox.class" WIDTH=500 HEIGHT=300>
```

```
</APPLET>
</BODY>
</HTML>
```

Try breaking the code

One of the dirty little secrets of programming is that bugs always occur. If
you have time and access to a computer right now, you can find that compiling this applet and playing with it for a while can be a useful exercise. You
can surely find features that you would like to tweak — behavior that is not
quite right.

When you find a problem, look back at the code and see whether you can
locate where you need to make changes.

To get started, explore what happens when you press a key that doesn't put
a character onscreen — for example, Esc or Backspace. Try making some
small changes in the code — one at a time — and see what happens. Chapter 6 provides some additional Java language features that give you better
control over your applets.

A class can listen to itself

So far, you have discovered an approach to handling events that reflect the
recommendations of many programming gurus. In this approach, you write
separate classes to do calculations, to display the user interface, and to
manage user input and other events. (This approach is called the *Model
View Controller,* or MVC paradigm.) Using this approach forces you to write
code that is relatively easy to use in more than one program. Personally, we
believe that this approach encourages you to think more clearly.

However, as you become more fluent in programming (trust us; you will),
you may become impatient writing a whole separate class just to respond to
one button. There is a faster way. A class may be its own Listener. As long as
it meets the requirement of providing a method for each method required by
the interface, any class may be a Listener. For example, an applet can also
be its own Listener:

```
class TicTacToe extends Applet
        implements MouseListener {

public void init() {
    ...
    addMouseListener(this);
```

(continued)

(continued)

```
    }
...
//Methods required to implement MouseListener interface
        public void mouseEntered(MouseEvent e) {
        }
        public void mouseExited(MouseEvent e) {
        }
        public void mousePressed(MouseEvent e){
        }
        public void mouseReleased(MouseEvent e){
        }
        public void mouseClicked(MouseEvent e){
          int x = e.getX();
          int y = e.getY();
          ...
/*find out where the mouse was clicked and respond
accordingly*/
        }
}
```

Handling Events in Java 1.0

Chances are good that you will see some Java 1.0 code and want to understand it. For this reason, here is a brief explanation of the way Java 1.0
handles events.

In Java 1.0, there are no Listeners. When an event occurs, all the active
objects hear about the event, and many objects may have methods to
respond. Typically, one object is responsible at any given moment. For
mouse actions, the object responsible is the object located where the mouse
pointer appears. For keyboard events as well, one object is on duty at any
given time. Depending on the platform, the object may be the one located
where the mouse pointer appears or the last object where a mouse click
occurred.

Several things can happen when an event is announced:

> ✔ The on-duty object may respond to the event and announce that the
> event has been taken care of. In this case, the other objects do not
> respond, even though they may also have methods for dealing with the
> event. The object announces that the event has been taken care of by
> returning `true` as a result of its event-handling method.

✔ The on-duty object may respond to the event but not announce that the event has been taken care of. In this case, other objects that have methods for dealing with the event may also respond. The object passes the event on to other objects by returning false as a result of its event-handling method.

✔ The on-duty object may have no method for handling the event. In this case, responsibility for handling the event passes on to the nearest object that does have a method to handle the event.

✔ Finally, the possibility exists for no object to have a method for handling the event. In this case, the event is ignored.

When you click a button with the mouse, the button generates an ACTION_EVENT, which you can handle with an action method:

```
public boolean action(Event evt, Object what) {
    String okString = new String ("OK");
    if (okString.equals(what)) {
        MyObject.repaint();
        return true;
    }
    return false;
}
```

When the object clicked is a GUI button, the information that the action method receives is ACTION_EVENT for the evt and the string that's the button's label for what. We go into the grammar of the if statement in Chapter 6. This if statement is a test to see whether the OK button is the button that was clicked. If the ACTION_EVENT was a click on the OK button, the button takes care of responding to the event and returns true to let other objects know that the event has been taken care of, or *consumed*. If the event was something else, the OK button doesn't know what to do, so it returns false so that other objects can decide whether they want to do something.

In a similar way, events are generated by mouse actions and key actions, and there are methods to handle them that generally correspond to the methods required by the Listener interfaces.

The important thing to remember about Java 1.0 code is that every object is its own Listener, and that events are passed on from object to object until they are "consumed" (that is, until a method returns true).

Deprecated code is outmoded code that is still temporarily supported by the programming tools in order to enable users time to rewrite it.

What happens to all that Java 1.0 code?

A lot of good code was written for Version 1.0 of Java. To give people time to adjust their code and their attitudes, the Java 2 tools still understand code written according to the old Java 1.0 rules. So you can compile and run an applet written in Java 1.0 — for now. The Java compiler warns you that you are using *deprecated* methods, but the code runs. Eventually, you may have to rewrite Java 1.0 code to keep up with changing times.

Chapter 6

Choices, Choices, Choices: if, else, and switch

● ●

In This Chapter

▶ Using selection statements in programs

▶ Writing grammatically correct `if` statements and `if...else` statements

▶ Writing grammatically correct `switch` statements

▶ Recognizing typical situations that call for using `if`, `else`, and `switch` statements

● ●

*Y*ou want to know Java because you want to add interactivity and dynamic behavior to your Web pages. The most basic Java language tools for making this happen are the `if` statement and the `switch` statement, which are called *selection* statements.

```
If(you already know how to use selection statements in a programming language){

  break; /* skip to the next section in this chapter */
  }
else{
  /* read this following section */
```

Selection statements are the brains of your Java applet. The `if` statement and its close relative the `switch` statement let your Java applets include methods that discriminate between situations and behave accordingly. All practical programs have decision points in them — and an `if` or a `switch` can be found in almost all of them. We already used a few unavoidable `if`s in the preceding chapters.

This chapter is about three basic kinds of decisions:

- ✔ Your applet must decide whether to carry out an action — use `if`.
- ✔ Your applet must choose between just two alternative actions — use `if...else`.
- ✔ Your applet must choose among a number of alternative actions — use `switch`.

Selection and Why You Need It

Before we get into the technical details of `if`, `else`, and `switch` statements, we offer a few examples of how we typically use them.

Listening to the user

Some programs do one thing and one thing only, with no need to respond to the outer world or changing circumstances. The HelloWorld applet in Chapter 2 and the Pix applet in Chapter 4 are examples of such programs. But you probably agree with us that programs that respond to the user in some way are more interesting and more useful.

Events enable your program to receive communications from the user (see Chapter 5). For example, a `KeyEvent` tells your applet that the user has pressed a key. And you can write a `keyPressed() keyDown()` method to respond to that fact.

But suppose that you want to do something different depending upon which key the user presses. To accomplish this, you must use a selection statement.

The `if` statement: When a simple "yes" will do

When you want your applet to perform one specific task after it receives one specific input, use an `if` statement.

Suppose that you want to modify HelloWorld so that it responds to user input. When you start the applet, you want the applet to display "Hello, world! Is anyone there?" Then if the user presses the letter *y* on the keyboard, the applet displays "Nice to meet you!"

The heart of the code to accomplish this is an `if` statement:

```
public void keyTyped(KeyEvent e){
        if ( e.getKeyChar() == 'y'){
        g.drawString ("Nice to meet you!", 10, 10);
    }
}
```

If the user presses the *y* key, the program displays "Nice to meet you!" on the screen. Otherwise, nothing new happens. This is a small but constructive step toward a more responsive program.

An `if` statement creates a side-trip from the main line of your program statements. See Figure 6-1.

Figure 6-1:
An `if`
statement
makes a
yes/no
decision.

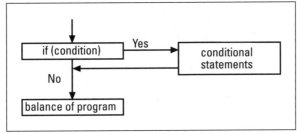

if...else: *When you want a choice*

You can make the program more intelligent by using an `if...else` construction. If the user presses the *y* key, the window displays Nice to meet you! But if the user presses any other key, the window displays Please press y for yes."

The code to accomplish this is an `if...else` statement:

```
public void keyTyped(KeyEvent e){
        if (e.getKeyChar() == 'y'){
            g.drawString ("Nice to meet you!", 10, 10);
        }
        else {
            g.drawString ("Please press y for yes.", 10, 10);
        }
}
```

The `if...else` statement creates two alternative paths in the main line of your program statements (see Figure 6-2).

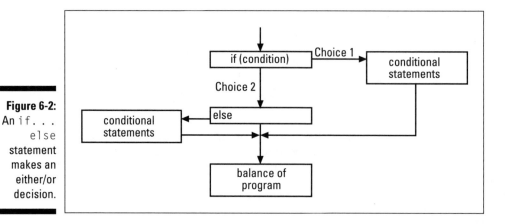

Figure 6-2:
An if...
else
statement
makes an
either/or
decision.

The switch *statement: When you have many choices*

The switch statement lets your program distinguish among a number of different alternatives. For example, the following code behaves differently according to which key is pressed. Inputs of *y, Y, n,* or *N* all call forth different displays. Any other key elicits the default response.

Look for the four special case responses and the default response in the code. Can you find them? (***Hint:*** Look for the keywords case and default.)

```
public void keyTyped(KeyEvent e){
    switch (e.getKeyChar()){
    case 'n':
        g.drawString("Can't fool me. I know you are there!",25, 25);
        break
    case 'y':
        g.drawString("Nice to meet you!",25, 25);
        break;
    case 'N':
        g.drawString("Can't fool me. I KNOW YOU ARE THERE!",25, 25);
        break;
    case 'Y':
        g.drawString("NICE to meet you!",25, 25);
        break;
    default:
        g.drawString("Please press y for 'yes' or n for 'no'.",25, 25);
    }
}
```

The switch statement creates a number of alternate parallel paths (see Figure 6-3).

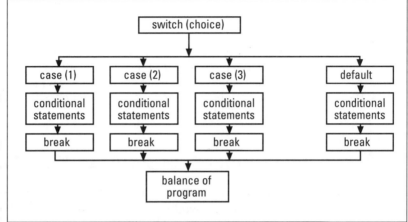

Figure 6-3:
A switch statement makes a multiple-choice decision.

More Reasons for Being Selective

Experienced programmers learn to recognize a variety of situations that automatically call for one of the three types of selection statements. As you begin to write Java programs, you develop your own catalog of selection situations that are typical of your subject matter and programming needs. We give you a few examples to get you started.

You don't have to do everything the user tells you

Even though you set up your program to respond to user requests, you don't have to accept everything that the user sends. Selection statements let you make sure that users provide valid input to the program. That way, you don't get information that you can't use or that can mess up your program.

For instance, suppose that you have an online auction application. The WWW page contains descriptions and images of the items up for sale. Users can send bids in directly from the Web page. (An example of this technique appears in Chapter 16.)

But you discover that some clowns think that sending in 29-cent bids on hundred-dollar merchandise is fun. Handling these nonsense bids slows down your system. You would rather let the end user's computer do the work of filtering out this kind of bid.

A Java applet can filter out all bids below a built-in minimum. This applet contains an `if` statement that compares the user's bid with the minimum bid:

```
if(userBid.value < minimumBid.value){
     g.drawString ("You must be kidding!");
}
```

With this code, when the value of `userBid` is less than the minimum value you have established, the bid is rejected before it's sent on to the server. Users who want to play games can still do so, but they won't make your server do extra work. Serious bidders get a faster response because the server needs to process only serious bids.

Know when you're up against the wall

Selection statements let you create Java applets that mimic the behavior of physical objects. For example, suppose that you want to create a handball game. When the ball hits the wall (the boundary of the onscreen panel containing your game), the ball bounces back in the opposite direction. An `if` statement can provide the desired bounce.

In the following code, `ball.xlocation` is the onscreen location coordinate of the graphic handball, and `court.xboundary` is the onscreen location coordinate of the panel boundary. The expression `(180 - ball.direction)` represents the direction that the ball bounces when it hits the wall.

Don't worry about the geometry of this. (Would we make this up?) Chapter 14 contains a complete example of a graphic simulation.

```
if (ball.xLocation >= court.xBoundary){
     ball.direction = (ball.direction-180)
}
```

Whenever the ball's location is the same as the wall's location (that is, whenever the ball hits the wall), the ball changes direction.

When you write your own video games, you can use selection statements to give life to the animated objects on the screen.

Follow the rules

Selection statements let you write programs that apply rules to a variety of situations. Consider the following problem:

You publish an online visual anatomy reference and you want to exercise some control over who gets to visit which pages. You decide on the following access rules for the "sensitive" pages.

- ✔ Everyone aged 18 or over may have access.
- ✔ Users 12 years and over may have access if they have registered parental permission.

Assuming that you can figure out a way to find out users' ages and to register parental permissions, building these rules into your Java applet using selection statements is easy:

```
if (user.age >= 18){
      grantAccess();
else{
      if (user.age >= 12){
        if (permission == true) {
            grantAccess();
        }
      }
}
```

```
} // this closes the "else" at the start of this chapter.
  // Read on to see why it is here.
```

Grammar Lessons

If you have experimented with writing and compiling Java code, you know that the Java compiler is very picky. A missing or misplaced semicolon, parenthesis, or brace is guaranteed to cause a bad result — usually an error message from the compiler; occasionally a misbehaving program. Each type of selection statement has very specific rules of form and punctuation.

The grammar of a simple Java if *statement*

Use the simple if statement described in this section when you want to deal with some special condition and keep on going. Figure 6-4 is a grammatical diagram of an if statement.

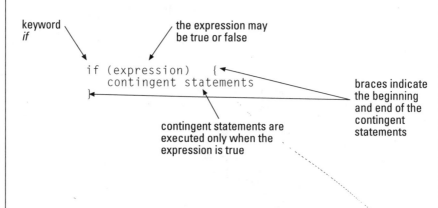

Figure 6-4:
Anatomy of
an if
statement.

Suppose that you want to convert all positive numbers to the equivalent negative value. For example, 1 is to be converted to –1 and 15 is to become –15. You use the following if statement:

```
if (value >0) {
        value = - value;
}
```

A few bracing words

In this book, we always enclose the conditional statements following an if or an else in braces. The rules of Java grammar enable you to omit the braces when there is only one statement, but we find that using the braces consistently makes the code easier to read and guards against those foolish little programming errors that are so hard to find and fix because they are so basic.

if . . . or else

Use an if...else statement when you want to create two alternative paths, and take one or the other depending on the condition you test with the if expression.

Figure 6-5 is a grammatical diagram of an if...else statement.

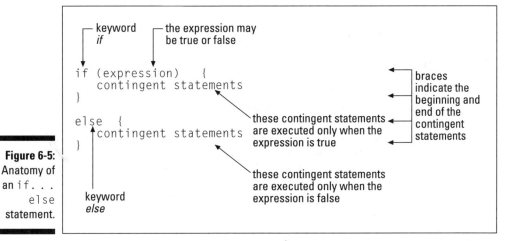

Figure 6-5: Anatomy of an if... else statement.

Suppose that you want to display all negative numbers in red and all other numbers in black. You may use the following if...else statement:

```
if (value <0) {
        text.color = Color.red;
}
else {
        text.color = Color.black;
}
```

For another example, suppose that

> ✔ Price is the price of the items ordered.
>
> ✔ Limit is the customer's credit limit.

When the price of the items ordered is greater than the online customer's credit limit, you want to use a method called requestDeposit. When the credit limit is greater than or equal to the price of the items ordered, instead use a method called holdAgainstLimit.

The code to accomplish this uses an `if...else` statement.

```
if (price>limit) {
        requestDeposit(price);
}
else {
        holdAgainstLimit(price);
}
```

Boxes within boxes, ifs within ifs

When you want your Java program to make more complex decisions, you are likely to use *nested* `if`s. That is, `if` statements appear among the conditional statements of other `if` statements. Consider the following variation on an example taken from the previous section.

Suppose that you want to display all negative numbers in red and all other numbers in black. In addition, you want to call special attention to numbers that fall outside established safety limits by causing the text to flash. Your program calculates a lower and an upper safety limit, either of which may be positive or negative. Values that are dangerously low flash slowly and values that are dangerously high flash rapidly. You may accomplish this with the following code:

```
if (value <0) {
/* The following happens when the value is negative */
      if (Number.value < lowlimit ){
        Number.showNum(slowFlash, Color.red);
      }
      else {
        if (Number.value > highlimit ){
            Number.showNum(fastFlash, Color.red);
        }
        else {
            Number.showNum(noFlash, Color.red);
        }
      }
}
/* The following happens when the value is positive */
else {
      if (Number.value < lowlimit ){
        Number.showNum(slowFlash, Color.black);
      }
```

```
    else {
      if (Number.value > highlimit ) {
          Number.showNum(fastFlash, Color.black);
      }
      else {
          Number.showNum(noFlash, Color.black);
      }
    }
}
```

A, B, C, D, or None of the Above

The if statement lets you deal with true/false situations. But often, you
want to write code that responds to multiple-choice situations. The switch
statement gives you this capability. Figure 6-6 shows you the anatomy of the
switch statement.

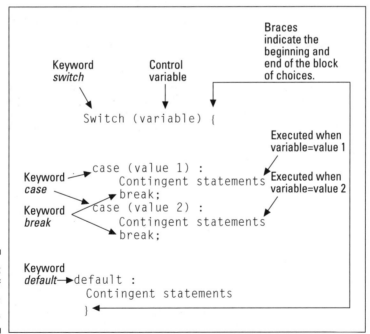

Figure 6-6: Anatomy of a case statement.

Matters of style

Don and David agree that using braces with a consistent style of indenting helps you to read the code. Put the closing brace for each `if` at the same level of indentation as the `if` closes. To do this, you have to leave each closing brace on a separate line.

You don't have to follow this advice. It is legal to omit the braces when there is only one statement, as in the following:

```
if (value <0) turnRed();
else turnBlack();
```

And indentation is never required. You can write the code that appears in the section "Boxes within boxes, `if`s within `if`s" such as this instead:

```
if(value <0){if(Number.value<lowlimit){Number.showNum(slowFlash,
    Color.red);}else{if(Number.value>highlimit){Number.showNum(fastFlash,
    Color.red);}else{Number.showNum(noFlash,Color.red);}}}
else{if (Number.value<lowlimit){Number.showNum(slowFlash,
    Color.black);}else{if(Number.value>highlimit){Number.showNum(fastFlash,
    Color.black);}else{Number.showNum(noFlash,Color.black);}}}
```

The style with no indentation or white space is pretty dreadful to read, but it saves space.

One common use of the `switch` statement is to evaluate and respond to user input from a GUI (graphical user interface). For example, when the user of your Java applet makes a menu selection or clicks a radio button, you can convert the result into a choice number that your applet may then evaluate with a `switch` statement to decide what to do next.

Here is an example. Suppose that you created a multilingual word processing applet with the following choices appearing on a Tools menu:

Word count

Spell check

Grammar check

Translate

If you make `itemNo` the reference number of the menu choice, the code that responds to this menu can look something like this:

```
switch(itemNo){
        case(1): //word count
          Doc.wordcount();
```

```
      break;
case(2): //spell check
    language=currentLanguage;
    Doc.spellcheck(currentLanguage) (currentDoc);
    break;
case(3): //grammar check
    language=currentLanguage;
    Doc.gramcheck(currentLanguage);
    break;
case(4): //translate
    fromLanguage=currentLanguage;
    showGetlanguageDialog(toLanguage);
    Doc.spellcheck(fromLanguage, toLanguage);
    break;
default
    showError();
}
```

In this code, the keywords are `switch`, `case`, `break`, and `default`:

- ✔ `switch()` sets up the variable that the program watches to decide where to go next.
- ✔ `case()` identifies the beginning of each branch.
- ✔ `break` identifies the end of each branch.
- ✔ `default` is the branch to follow if the `switch` variable does not match any of the cases.

The variable that you use for a `switch` must be one of the following:

- ✔ `char`
- ✔ `int`
- ✔ `short`
- ✔ `byte`

Specifically, you may not use a string or a floating-point number as a `switch`.

You find that many Java class variables are integers that have special names. This makes setting up a `switch` to handle them easy. For example, the `Color` class lets you refer to common colors by name, instead of by the numerical formula the monitor uses to display them. So, you can write a `switch` statement to take different actions depending on the color of an object.

If *and* switch*es together*

Couldn't I do the same thing with ifs?

Yes, anything that you can do with switch you can also do with if statements. One great advantage of switch is that it helps make your code easy
to read. Sometimes you may want to use ifs and switches together to make
for easier-reading code.

Sometimes you may want to use if statements to set the value of a switch
variable. For example:

```
if(value>1000){
      branch = 1;
}
```

Another example:

```
if (instring == "yes"){
      branch='y';
}
```

And another:

```
if (menuString.equals("Word Count")) {
      itemNo = 1;
}
```

Whose default is it, anyway?

default is the keyword for the conditional statements that are executed
when none of the case values match the switch variable.

```
switch (letter)
{
case'a':
      g.drawstring("You chose 'a'.", 25, 25);
      break;
case'b':
      g.drawstring("You chose 'b'.", 25, 25);
      break;
case'c':
      g.drawstring("You chose 'c'.", 25, 25);
```

```
        break;
case'd':
        g.drawstring("You chose 'd'.", 25, 25);
        break;
default
        g.drawstring("You chose none of the above.", 25, 25);
        break;
}
```

You don't have to take a break

The break that ends each branch of a switch sends you to the first statement that follows the complete switch. If you omit the break, the conditional code for the next case will also be executed. In a few special situations, you may want to make use of this feature.

For example, suppose that your applet contains the dialog box in Figure 6-7. The privileges that go with age are cumulative; any selection includes all the privileges of all selections lower down on the list.

Figure 6-7:
A dialog
box.

Between equals

Two different ways exist to express equality in an if statement, as follows:

If the things you are comparing are objects, you must use the equals method of the object. For example, menuString. equals("Word Count").

If the things you are comparing are numbers, characters, or Boolean values, use the double equal sign ==, which means *is equal to*.

Caution: Using a single equal sign = means *change so that it is equal to*. Do *not* use a single equal sign inside the parentheses of an if statement.

In this example, you may use code such as this:

```
switch (buttonNumber){
    case 1:
        drink=true;
    case 2:
        drive=true;
    case 3:
        pgfilms=true;
    case 4:
        gfilms=true;
        break;
    default:
        noteError();
        break;
}
```

In Java, the expression in an if statement is fully evaluated, including all side effects. If you are a hotshot C programmer, don't count on partial evaluation of expressions to speed your code or provide useful side effects.

Logic Chopping (Or Chopping for Logic)

Java, like most other programming languages, provides you with *logical operators,* the symbols that indicate the logical relationship between two quantities or concepts.

The following lists the logical operators.

Operation	*Symbol*
and	&&
inclusive or (a or b or both) See Figure 6-8.	||
exclusive or (either a or b, but not both) See Figure 6-9.	^
not	!
equal	==
less than	<
greater than	>

The impossible branch

When you are using a `switch` to evaluate the response to a menu or to some other user interface control, you may be very sure that your program can never reach the `default` branch of a `switch`. Nevertheless, it is a good idea to leave an explicit error branch in your code to make troubleshooting easier.

If you write completely error-free code, this practice is unnecessary. Send your résumé with supporting testimonials to the address on the authors' Web site.

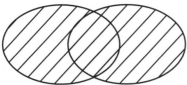

Figure 6-8:
`All B`
(inclusive
or).

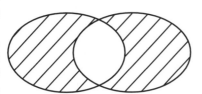

Figure 6-9:
`((All B)
&&
!(A&&B))B`
(exclusive
or).

For completeness, we've included a diagram of the other kind of `or` — the exclusive `or`. See Figure 6-9.

These operators enable you to write expressions such as the following:

Expression	What It Means
`if (a&&b)`	If both a and b are true
`if ((n<12)&&(b>5))`	If n is less than 12 and b is greater than 5
`if ((val1==21)||(val2<95))`	If val1 equals 21 or val2 is less than 95 or both are true (inclusive or)
`if ((val1==21)^(val2<95))`	If val1 equals 21 or val2 is less than 95 but not if both are true (exclusive or)
`if ((!fish)&&(!fowl))`	If not fish and not fowl

Often, a well-thought-out logical expression can take the place of a complicated series of nested if and else statements.

For example, consider once again the question of who may visit the "mature" areas of your Web site. To gain admission, a user must be 18 years of age or older, or 12 or older and have parental permission.

You can write all these restrictions as one logical expression (see Figure 6-10).

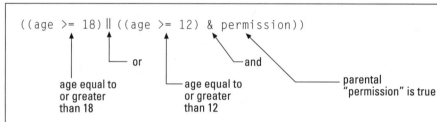

Figure 6-10:
Some logic.

Then you can put the logical expression in one simple if statement:

```
if((age>=18)||((age >=12)&& (permission==true))){
    ticket(true)
}
else {
    ticket(false)
}
```

When you find yourself writing complex if statements and copying the same selection statements to several different spots in your code, try writing your rules as one logical expression. You often find the resulting code more elegant.

Chapter 7

Round and Round: for and while

Computers are very fast and, as far as we know, they don't get bored very quickly. Because computers have these two great virtues, you can set them to doing repetitive tasks that you could never assign to a human being.

Iteration and Why You Need It

Iteration statements are the tools you use to put the computer to work on repetitive tasks. Java provides you with two kinds of iteration statements — `for` and `while`. Use iteration statements when you face these typical situations:

- ✔ A task must be repeated a specific number of times.
- ✔ A task must be repeated until a specific condition is met.

The `for` statement is the tool you use when a specific number of repetitions is needed. The `while` statement calls for repetition until a specific condition is met.

I'd like a dozen of those, please

Often you find situations where a set of steps must be repeated a specific number of times. For example, suppose you want to create a card-playing applet. To deal five cards, you can tell the applet to repeat the steps to select a card at random from the deck five times. The following code does exactly that. (We explain the detailed programming grammar shortly.)

```
for (int i =1; i <= 5; i++){
     dealCard();
}
```

A video game applet requires your applet to construct ten rocket bases onscreen. A for statement builds all ten without requiring you to repeat the code.

```
for (int i =1; i <= 10; i++){
     add(new rocketBase());
}
```

Whenever you see this kind of repetition, think of the for statement.

The for statement uses a counter to keep track of how many loops through the code are needed (see Figure 7-1).

Any object with a standard repeated structure is a candidate for the use of for loops. Spreadsheets and game boards are two examples of objects that have a standard repeated structure in two dimensions. The standard way to create these objects is by using a loop inside another loop. First, you write the code to create a row of squares, cells, or whatever. Then you write code to create a table by repeatedly creating rows.

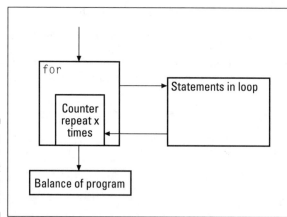

Figure 7-1:
The for statement uses a counter.

Loop-de-loop

Programmers talk about `for` and `while` *loops* because the program completes a series of steps and then starts over again at the top of the series, looping throughout the same code over and over again.

For example, a checkerboard is eight columns wide and eight rows deep. You can use a loop to create a row eight columns wide and then use another loop to create a board eight columns deep. The loop to create a row is nested inside the loop to create the board.

You can find an example of using a loop inside a loop to create a calendar in Chapter 11.

How many would you like?

You can get user input to control a `for` loop. As long as the object knows the number of times to go around the loop before it starts repeating, a `for` loop is fine. For example, if you write an applet to play cards with visitors to your Web page, you may need to deal the number of cards the user requests.

```
inputNum = getValidNum();
for (int i=1; i=<inputNum; i++){
    dealCard();
}
```

You'll know when it's done

In many cases, you don't know in advance how many times it will be necessary to go around the loop. The video game keeps firing rockets as long as the user has bases left to defend. Depending on the skill of the user, the program may go around the loop to fire a rocket many times or just a few.

Instead of using a counter, the `while` loop uses a logical test to know when to stop (see Figure 7-2).

If you have created an online shopping application in which users establish a line of credit and then place orders against their credit, you may use a `while` loop to accept orders as long as they have not used up the credit.

```
while( creditAmount >= purchaseTotal){
        getNextPurchase();
```

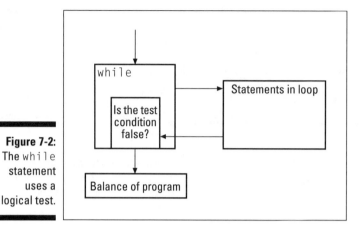

Figure 7-2:
The `while`
statement
uses a
logical test.

More Grammar Lessons

Just like selection statements, iteration statements must follow rules of form and punctuation closely. If you leave out a parenthesis, brace, or semicolon, the Java compiler complains. In addition, the counters and test conditions that tell when to exit from the loop must follow precise rules.

The grammar of a Java `for` statement

Use the `for` statement described in this section when you want to perform a series of steps a specific number of times. Figure 7-3 is a grammatical diagram of a `for` statement.

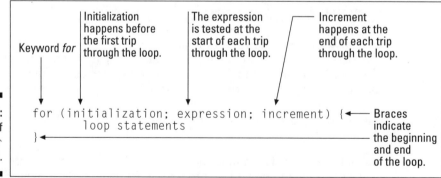

Figure 7-3:
Anatomy of
a for
statement.

The code that sets up the for loop appears within parentheses after the keyword for. It consists of the following:

- ✔ An initialization statement that sets the starting value of a counter
- ✔ A test expression that checks the value of the counter each time the loop completes
- ✔ An incrementing statement that changes the value of the counter each time the loop completes

Following this setup, the statements within braces (called the *body of the loop*) execute until the expression is no longer true.

An example of a for *loop*

Here is a detailed example to work through. The example puts the letter *X* into a string a variable number of times. The example may not represent something that you want to do every day, but you can type the code and experiment with it quickly. Before you try out this code, read it carefully. Begin by locating the for loop.

```
import java.applet.*;
import java.awt.*;
import java.lang.*;

import java.applet.*;
import java.awt.*;
import java.lang.*;

Applet{
        Label LoopLabel = new Label();
        String InfoString = null;
        int r = 0;
public void init() {
Applet{
        Label LoopLabel = new Label();
        String InfoString = null;
        int r = 0;
public void init() {

=

=

Integer.parseInt(getParameter("repetitions"));
```

(continued)

(continued)

```
   Integer.parseInt(getParameter("repetitions"));
  {
  {
        }
      }
    }
}
}
}
import java.applet.*;
import java.awt.*;
import java.lang.*;

public class Loop1 extends Applet{
   Label LoopLabel = new Label();
   String InfoString = null;
   int r = 0;
   public void init() {
      InfoString = getParameter("info");
      r =
Integer.parseInt(getParameter("repetitions"));
      for (int i=1; i <= r; i++) {
         InfoString = InfoString + "X";
      }
   }
   public void paint(Graphics g) {
      g.drawString(InfoString, 5, 10);
   }
}
```

To test this applet, you have to put it into an HTML page. For example:

```
<HTML>
<HEAD>
<TITLE> Loop Test </TITLE>
</HEAD>
<BODY>
<H1>Loop Test </H1>
<APPLET CODE="Loop1.class" WIDTH=500 HEIGHT=300>
<PARAM NAME=info VALUE="4">
<PARAM NAME=repetitions VALUE="4">
</APPLET>
</BODY>
</HTML>
```

Did you find the `for` loop? Let's go over the code of the `for` loop in detail.

The initialization statement is

```
int i=1;
```

This statement declares a variable named *i* and sets it equal to 1 at the beginning of the loop. This statement is executed only one time, when the loop begins.

```
i <= r;
```

The preceding is the test condition. As long as this test condition is true, the computer executes the statements in the body of the loop — the statements within the braces of the `for` statement. In this particular case, the loop is repeated as long as i is less than or equal to r. When i is found to be greater than r, the loop ends.

```
i++
```

This statement is read "increment i." It means increase i by 1. (You can also write i=i+1.) This statement executes each time that a pass through the loop completes.

Here is what happens if the value of r is 3:

1. **When the loop begins, i is set to 1. The test is performed — 1 is less than 3, so the test condition is true.**

   The body of the loop is executed, so that `infoString` becomes "3X." Then i is incremented. At the end of the first pass, i=2.

2. **The test is performed again — 2 is less than 3, so the test condition is true.**

   The body of the loop is executed, so that `infoString` becomes "3XX." Then i is incremented. At the end of the second pass, i=3.

3. **The test is performed again — 3 is equal to 3, so the test condition is true.**

   The body of the loop is executed, so that `infoString` becomes "3XXX." Then i is incremented. At the end of the third pass, i=4.

4. **The test is performed again — 4 is greater then 3, so the test condition is false.**

   The loop ends.

The road from parameter "repetitions" to int r

As noted in Chapter 3, parameters from the HTML page begin life as a series of typed characters, a string. If you want to do math with a parameter, you must convert it into an appropriate kind of number. Two lines of code in the example are devoted to transforming the parameter "repetitions" into an integer r that can be compared with the integer i.

```
int r = 0;
...
r = Integer.parseInt(getParameter("repetitions"));
```

- ✔ int r = 0 sets up an integer variable.

- ✔ getParameter("repetitions") brings in the string from the HTML page. The string may be "1", "3", or "25".

- ✔ r = Integer.parseInt(...) takes the string between parentheses and tries to convert it to an integer number. If successful, the statement stores the resulting number as r. (If the string is something like "B4U" or "please pass the salt", an error condition will result because these strings can't be converted to integers.) You can read more about Integer.parseInt. in Chapter 10.

TIP

Lazy fingers

The developers of the C programming language introduced a family of keying shortcuts that has been adopted in Java. Using these keying shortcuts is never required, but you certainly need to understand them when you look at code because these shortcuts have become standard among programmers.

```
i++ means i=i+1
i- means i=i-1
i+=2 means i=i+2
i-=3 means i=i-3
```

A nesting ground of fors

When you read Java code, one typical pattern that you notice is nested for loops — that is, one for loop inside another.

```
row...
row...
each
        column...
each
                ...
"+Integer.toString(row)+",
        Col:"+Integer.toString(col));
        }
"+Integer.toString(row)+",
        Col:"+Integer.toString(col));
        }
for (int row=1; row<=ROWS; row++) {
// for each row...
   for (column=1; column<=COLUMNS; column++) {
   // for each column...
     g.drawString
     ("Row: "+Integer.toString(row)
     +", Col: "+Integer.toString(col));
   }
}
```

In this code, you go through the column loop COLUMNS times for every time that you increment row. When row=1, the result looks like Figure 7-4.

Row: 1 Col: 1	Row: 1 Col: 2	Row: 1 Col: 3	Row: 1 Col: 4

Figure 7-4:
row = 1.

When `row=3`, the result looks like Figure 7-5.

Row: 1 Col: 1	Row: 1 Col: 2	Row: 1 Col: 3	Row: 1 Col: 4
Row: 2 Col: 1	Row: 2 Col: 2	Row: 2 Col: 3	Row: 2 Col: 4
Row: 3 Col: 1	Row: 3 Col: 2	Row: 3 Col: 3	Row: 3 Col: 4

Figure 7-5:
`row = 3`.

Counting by twos

It is perfectly legal, and sometimes useful, to change the counter in steps greater than one. For example, if you want to change the color of alternate columns in a table, your code might say (all on one line):

```
for (column=1; column<=COLUMNS; column+=2)
```

Similarly, you could start with a large counter number and work your way down with code like this:

```
for (column=MAX; column>=MIN; column--) {
```

We do not recommend that you change the value of your limits with code inside the loop. For example, do *not* write something like this:

```
for (column=MAX; column>=MIN; column--) {
    ...
   if (MIN>0){
        MIN=0;
   }
    ...
   }
```

Similarly, you should avoid changing the value of the counter inside the loop. Do *not* write something like this:

```
for (column=MAX; column>=MIN; column--) {
    ...
   column = column + adjustment;
    ...
   }
    ...
   }
```

The Grammar of while

Use the while statement described in this section when you want to perform a series of steps as long as a particular condition is true. Figure 7-6 is a grammatical diagram of a while statement.

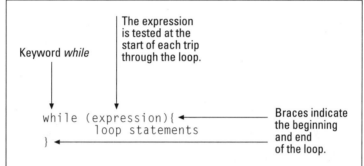

Figure 7-6: Anatomy of while.

The code that sets up the while loop appears within parentheses after the keyword while. The code consists of a test expression that checks the controlling condition before each pass of the statements that make up the loop.

Following this setup, the statements within braces (the body of the loop) execute until the test expression is no longer true.

Decoding a label

Suppose that you're writing an applet that helps the online customer order replacement parts for home appliances. The customer types in the model number of the appliance and then uses a visual interface to select the exact part that is needed. In order to display a graphic that closely matches the customer's real product, you want to know the color of the product.

Color information is coded into the model number. The first five to seven characters in the model number identify the product type and where it was assembled. Then the letter C is followed by a three-character code that indicates the color. For a human who knows the code, it is easy to scan until he or she finds the letter C and then pick out the three characters that follow. You can tell the Java applet to do the same thing using a while statement and the substring method of the String object.

The `substring()` method picks out a group of characters (a *substring*) from a string using the position numbers of the first character and the character that follows the end of the substring. By the way, the first position number in a string is 0. For example, if `modelNum` is `27318CRED6580`, the position number of the character 2 is 0. And `modelNum.substring(6,9)` is `RED`, because character number six in `modelNum` is `R` and character nine is `6` — the character following `D`. This is just a preview of `String` methods; for more information about `Strings` and their methods, see Chapter 10.

The following code does what a human reader does. It starts at the beginning of the line and reads until it comes to the letter `C`. Then the code picks out the next three characters.

Here is the sample code:

```
String letter = null;
String colorCode = null;
int n = 0;

while (letter.equals("C")==false) {
        letter = modelNum.substring(n,n+1);
        n++;
}
n++;
colorCode=modelNum.substring(n,n+3);
```

The applet checks the value of `letter`. `letter` is not equal to `"C"`, so the loop begins. Now the applet sets `letter` to be the first character in `modelNum` — the substring from position 0 to position 1 in `modelNum`. And the loop bumps up the value of `n` by 1.

The loop now checks the value of `letter` again. If `letter` is still not equal to `"C"`, you go through the loop again, setting `letter` equal to the next position in `modelNum`.

When `letter` equals `"C"`, the loop stops. The next three characters are the `colorCode`.

Give me a call

As you may have noticed, people like their phone numbers nicely broken up with a hyphen (`-`) and parentheses and so on. Computers do not. You can use a `while` statement to get rid of the hyphen in a phone number.

We use `substring()` again in this code. If we leave out the second position number when we use `substring()`, it returns a substring that ends at the end of the string. We also use another `String` method — `indexOf()`. The `indexOf()` method returns the position number of a given character or substring. If the target is not found, it returns -1. In this example, we use `indexOf("-")` to find the position of the first hyphen in the phone number.

```
String phoneNumber = "212-477-8800";
while (phoneNumber.indexOf("-") >= 0) {
       phoneNumber =
       phoneNumber.substring(0,phoneNumber.indexOf("-")) +
       phoneNumber.substring(phoneNumber.indexOf("-")+1);
}
// now phoneNumber == "2124778800"
```

Here is what happens in this `while` loop:

1. **When the loop begins, the first - is at position 3, which is greater than 0.**

   The computer takes the substring in positions 0-2 — `phoneNumber.substring(0,phoneNumber.indexOf("-"))` — and adds to the end of it the substring from position 4 to the end of the string — `phoneNumber.substring(phoneNumber.indexOf("-")+1)`. This becomes the new working version of `phoneNumber`. You have eliminated the first -, and you are ready to start the loop again.

2. **Now the first - is at position 6. The test expression is still true.**

   You repeat the substring trick to get rid of the next -, and you are ready to start the loop again.

3. **At the start of the third trip around the loop, you find no more - characters in** `phoneNumber`. `indexOf("-") returns -1`. **The test expression is false, and the loop ends.**

Keeping score

Your video game keeps score of how many Klingons you have exterminated and how many Tribbles survive on your side. As long as the number of Tribbles is at least 1/10 the number of Klingons, hope remains. If the number gets too small, a cloud of doom settles across the landscape.

The code is:

```
while ( (Tribble.count() / 10) >= Klingon.count() ) {
        playerThread.continue();
}
// no hope left...
cloudOfDoom.activate();
```

Locating the nearest exit

Loops are a vital tool for every programmer, but they must be handled with respect. You want to be sure that there is a way out of every loop. One of the most common programming mishaps is to lose track of the test in a `for` loop or a `while` loop in such a way that the loop just keeps going forever. For example, you could write:

```
for (i=n; i != 0; i--)
```

This works if `n` is a positive number. But what if `n` is negative? The test is never false, and the computer stays in the loop indefinitely. This condition is known as *infinite loop*.

The computer may simply hang there, unresponsive to the outside world. If you wait long enough, you may eventually get an interesting error message such as `out of memory`.

If you encounter these symptoms, try to reconstruct what the applet was doing, step by step, as it executes your code. Chances are high that you will find a point where there is an error or an overlooked situation in the test for a loop.

A personal confession

In the dark ages when all computer output was on paper, one of the authors (who will remain otherwise anonymous) wrote an elegant program to compute a table of mathematical functions for n from 1 to 1000. Being slightly dyslexic and thoroughly overconfident, he keyed > rather than < at a strategic point in the program. A 3-foot-high stack of computer printout decorated with five columns of zeros resulted, and he hasn't run out of scratch paper yet.

Chapter 8

Anatomy of a Class

. . . .

In This Chapter

▶ Defining the properties of a class

▶ Defining the methods of a class

▶ Public, protected, and private properties and methods

▶ Static properties and methods

▶ Defining an interface

▶ Creating a package

. . . .

*T*his chapter gives you a more formal overview of the parts that go together to make the code of a Java applet. Every applet consists of at least one class definition. Most useful applets use a number of other classes, some defined in the Java Class Library and others custom-built for the individual applet or for a family of applets.

When you read Java code, you can read more intelligently if you know what to expect. And as you begin to write Java code that uses a variety of classes, knowing how classes are organized is important.

Classes with Class

As discussed in Chapter 4, a class definition usually includes several main chunks of code in addition to the name of the class:

> ✔ **Declarations of class variables or properties:** The declarations give object variables — bits of information about the object — names so that the variables can be used or tracked. Usually the variables are instantiated and are given a starting value as well.

> ✔ **Constructors:** A class includes one or more constructors that tell what information must be provided from outside when an object of this type is instantiated and how that information is to be used in setting up the object.

> ✔ **Methods:** The methods are the object's job description. Each method is an action that the object understands, an instruction to which it can respond.

See Figure 8-1.

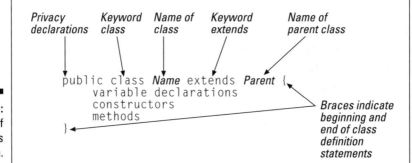

Figure 8-1:
Anatomy of
a class
definition.

No Trespassing

You have seen the keyword public a number of times in Java code by now. When a class, variable, or method is *public,* it's accessible to any other Java code that's running in the same machine at the same time. It's also possible for a class or some of its variables or methods to be *private.* When a class, variable, or method is *private,* it isn't accessible to any other code.

```
public class Rectangle extends Shape {
        public Rectangle(int width, int height, Color c) {
```

Any other code can make use of the Rectangle class created in this definition.

The following code, however, declares Circle public but makes radius_ private:

```
public class Circle extends Shape {
  private int radius_;
```

Any code can use the Circle class. For example, you can write another class called CircleFactory. CircleFactory can call on the Circle class to instantiate a circle and add it to the screen. And CircleFactory can determine in advance the size of the circle's radius by using the desired value in the constructor. But the new program cannot directly change the radius of the circle after it has been created. For example, you could *not* successfully write an applet that says

```
myCircle.radius_ = 27;
```

In Java, you can establish four different levels of privacy. (See Table 8-1.) For most purposes, you need to know only that anything labeled private simply doesn't exist outside the class in which it's declared. If you try to access private data or use a private method from an outside class, you receive an error message from the compiler.

If you want to be able to communicate with other objects to enable them to access data or otherwise send messages to an object, you must make the relevant methods or data public.

Table 8-1	Rules of Privacy
Declaration	*Visibility*
public	Visible to everyone
private	Visible to no one
(no declaration)	Visible to everyone in the same file or package
protected	Same as (no declaration) but visible for inheritance purposes only to everyone in the same file or package and to subclasses only in other files or packages

Variables

Variables that record some basic property of an object are usually declared at the top of the class definition. For each variable, you tell the computer what type of variable it is so that the computer can set aside the appropriate scratch pad space in memory to keep track of it. You can also assign a value right away, or you can leave the variable set to the default value for that type until you give it some new value later in the code.

A variable declaration includes

- ✔ A type or class name
- ✔ A name used to refer to the specific variable
- ✔ Optionally, a statement that assigns an initial value

> ## Minimizing errors
>
> In Java, making an error and changing the data of an object unintentionally would be difficult because you normally address each object by name. In other programming languages, being unclear about which bit of information belongs to which piece of code is much easier. In some cases, the same piece of information may be unintentionally changed in two different places. This can result in hard-to-find bugs that you remember fondly (or not) for many years.

Instance variables

Most of the variables that you use are *instance* variables. That is, every object based on the class template can have a different value for the variable, so the computer must set up scratch pad space for the variable each time that an instance of the class is created.

For example:

```
class ArcCanvas extends Canvas {
    int startAngle = 0;
    int endAngle = 45;
    boolean filled = false;
    Font font;
                        ...
```

Every `ArcCanvas` that you create has its own `startAngle`, `endAngle`, filled condition, and font.

Class variables

Sometimes a variable represents basic information that applies to a class as a whole. You have already seen a few typical examples:

- ✔ `PI`, which applies to all `Circles` (see Chapter 4)
- ✔ `LEFT`, `RIGHT`, `CENTER`, which apply to all `FlowLayouts` (see Chapter 5)

These variables are actually constants whose values you type into the code of the class definition. Traditionally, such constants are identified by entering their names as all capitals. red, blue, and yellow are variables of the class Color. The numbers that correspond to these standard colors may differ from system to system, but they do not vary from color object to color object. All color objects created on a given system have the same definition of red.

Class variables are identified by the keyword static in the declaration. For example:

```
public class Chart extends java.applet.Applet {
  static final int    VERTICAL = 0;
  static final int    HORIZONTAL = 1;
  static final int    SOLID = 0;
  static final int    STRIPED = 1;
```

Telling the world about variables

You may see classes in which all the variables are private. One standard approach to setting up communications between a Java object and the outside world is to give the object a set of public methods that respond to getValue requests for information about the object and that receive setValue instructions from the outside world. For example, myRadius is private data, but radius can be revealed to other objects by the method

```
public double getRadius()
```

Similarly, you may have a radius-setting method that sends in the desired new radius value by means of a message instead of directly changing the value of the variable.

```
public void setRadius(double r)
```

The advantage of this approach is that it enables you to deal with special situations only in the object that those situations affect. For example, you can write code to deal with negative values of r or other special situations as part of the Circle object. You may want to convert negative values to their positive equivalents, or to use a default value, or possibly to return an error message. The other objects that interact with Circle do not need to know about its inner workings.

In this way, if you discover some unanticipated circumstances after writing a class, you need only revise the code in one place.

Object Under Construction

Constructors contain instructions on how to create a new object of this class. A class may have more than one constructor.

A constructor consists of

- The name of the class
- The information required from outside to set up an object of this class
- Any necessary setup steps, such as putting initial values into the object's scratch pad variables

And, of course, constructors may be public, private, or protected.

Figure 8-2 shows the elements of a constructor.

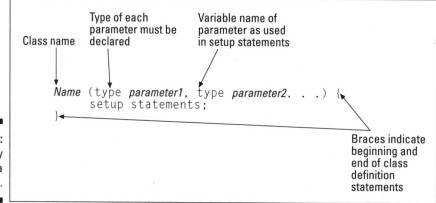

Figure 8-2:
Anatomy
of a
constructor.

For example:

```
MousePanel(int h, int w, String l) {
    dimension_.height = h;
    dimension_.width = w;
    label = l;
}
```

Any time that you list an item in the parentheses following the class name of a constructor, you must first identify its type and then give it a name. The name that you give the item is used in the statements in braces to put the value into the appropriate places in the new object.

The pattern of information that appears in parentheses is called the *signature* of the constructor. The signature of the preceding `MousePanel` constructor is `(int, int, String)`.

A second `MousePanel` constructor must have a different signature. For example, you may define a constructor that leaves the string set to some default value.

```
MousePanel(int h, int w) {
    dimension_.height = h;
    dimension_.width = w;
    label = defaultLabel;
    }
```

The signature of this constructor is `MousePanel(int, int)`.

How Do You Do That?

The third element in a class definition is *methods*. Methods are the job description of the class. An object responds to every message that refers to a method defined for its class (or the parent of its class). If you ask an object to do something that isn't included in its methods, your request is refused. (That is, you get a compiler error.)

The most common way for objects to communicate with each other is for one object to address another by its name and the required method.

```
Waiter.passThe(salt)
```

Like variables, methods can be public or private. Only methods that are not private may be used to communicate with the object. A private method is some computation that is a step in the object's internal work.

Just as you normally expect some response when you speak to a person, you expect some response when you send a message to an object. The method declaration tells what kind of response to expect.

Often, a method returns an item of data — a number or a string. Sometimes a method returns a yes/no response — Boolean `true` or `false`. And some methods return nothing at all — `void`.

A method definition consists of

- Privacy declarations, if any
- The expected return of the method
- The name of the class
- The information required from outside to complete the instructions
- The setup of any scratch pad space used only for this method
- The steps to complete the action

Figure 8-3 shows the elements of a method.

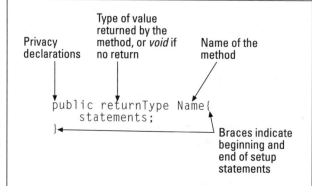

Figure 8-3:
Anatomy of
a method.

This next example is similar to one discussed in Chapter 5:

```
public void changeText(String s){
        nameTag = s;
        repaint();
}
```

This is a public class whose name is changeText. It happens to be a method of the class mousePanel. A mousePanel object, such as sp, may receive a message that says something like this:

```
sp.changeText("Glory be!");
```

When sp receives this message, it executes the steps in braces. That is, sp changes its nameTag to "Glory be!" and repaints itself so that the change becomes visible.

More than one way to circle the globe

Just as a class may have more than one constructor, it may have more than one method of the same name. When different ways exist to do the same thing, a class can have more than one method definition with the same name. The computer knows to apply the correct method by looking at the signature of the method. Of course, this means that you can't have two different methods with the same name and the same signature.

Many methods have a blank signature; that is, they take no information from the object that calls them. In this case, the method definition has an empty pair of parentheses. But the parentheses are still required so that the computer recognizes that it's dealing with a method definition. For example:

```
void init()
```

Table 8-2 shows examples of method calls and definitions.

Table 8-2	Some Method Calls and Definitions
Method call in displayPanel	***Method definition in*** myShape ***class***
myLabel="Generic Shape"; {Square.showName();}	void showName (){ add(myLabel); repaint(); }
Label says "Generic Shape"	
Square.showName("Irving");	void showName (String fullName) { myLabel = fullName; add(myLabel); repaint(); }
Label says "Irving"	

So's your old man: Laws of heredity

Classes inherit the methods of their parents. Inherited methods do not show up in the class definition of the child class, but they are available to call on as needed. Methods such as setBackground(), repaint(), and add() are inherited by many classes. Much of the time, you rely on a family of basic methods that are common to most of the classes with which you work.

A common programming trick is to override one of the inherited methods with a more specific method that serves a purpose of your applet.

The event-handling behaviors with which you work to attend to mouse and keyboard events are an example of overriding an inherited method with a custom method. These methods exist in the parent class `Component`, but you don't see them do anything visible until you override the inherited do-nothing method with a method that produces the result you want.

Managing a Large Family

As you begin to write more complex applets, you may find that you need to manage groups of related classes. Several techniques exist to help you keep large families of classes organized so that they don't become unruly.

Two techniques can help you make sure that, within a particular group, all classes (and their objects) speak the same language; that is, they have the same methods. These techniques are as follows:

- Creating an abstract class
- Creating an interface

A third technique makes sure that a group of classes are packaged together so that all are available at the same time: This third technique is creating a package.

Abstract classes and interfaces

We discuss an example of an abstract class in the Pix applet of Chapter 4. An *abstract class* is a class that has children but no instances of its own.

Pix is an abstract class. It sets up a structure of data and methods that its children can inherit and extend. You know that all the children of Pix — Circle, Rectangle, and Square — have methods to return a perimeter, an area, and a name, for example. And they all have the same `getColor` and `setColor` methods inherited from Pix.

But you still have to fill in specifics. For example, the Pix abstract class has an empty paint method — each specific shape must have its own paint method. And some of the other methods return a default value (such as "unknown shape") unless you provide more information.

```
abstract class Pix extends Canvas {
  Dimension myDimension = new Dimension();
  public void Pix() {
  }
  public Color getColor() {
    return getForeground();
  }
  public void setColor(Color c) {
    setForeground(c);
  }
  public void paint(Graphics g) {
  }
  public double getArea() {
    return 0;
  }
  public double getPerimeter() {
    return 0;
  }
  public String getKind() {
      return "unknown shape";
    }
  public Dimension getPreferredSize() {
    return myDimension;
  }
  public Dimension getMinimumSize() {
    return myDimension;
  }
}
```

Occasionally, you want to ensure that a number of classes have the same bundle of methods, even though they are not all children of the same parent class. One example discussed in Chapter 5 is the Listeners. Any class may be a Listener as long as it implements the appropriate Listener interface. That is, it must provide a specific set of methods for handling events of a given type. If a class implements the keyListener interface, you know that it has a keyTyped( ) method. When you're programming, you don't need to stop and make sure that the method is there.

Here is another example of a situation in which you might use an interface. Suppose you are creating classes for applets similar to the Pix applet but more complex. Your applets display a variety of geometric figures and text labels, and they compute areas, perimeters, volumes, and so on. See the family trees in Figure 8-4.

Pix				TextArea		Calculator		
Circle	Rectangle			PixLabel	Info Panel	Times		Sum
Hot Circle / Cool Circle	Hot Rectgl / Cool Rectgl	Rectangle		HotPix Label / CoolPix Label		Hot Times / Cool Times		Hot Sum / Cool Sum
		Hot Square	Cool Square					

= implements Emphatic

Figure 8-4: Some children in each family implement Emphatic.

You want to be able to draw attention to certain objects by means of an addEmphasis() method. For each type of object, the way you add emphasis is different. For geometric figures, the color changes. For text labels, the size of the type and the background color changes. For the results of computations, you add the words *is without doubt* in place of the equal sign. Of course, each type of object also requires a method to restore itself back to its original state — a restoreEmphasis() method.

You want to be sure that every object that may be asked to add emphasis has the necessary appropriate methods. So you declare an interface called Emphatic. When you define any class that requires Emphatic behavior, you declare that it implements interface Emphatic. This is a reminder to you and other programmers who may use your code that the Emphatic behaviors are implemented in this class. If you neglect to write one of the required methods, the Java compiler displays an error message when you try to compile the code.

When you use an *interface* declaration, you must still write specific procedures to implement all the behaviors in the interface for each class that implements the interface. The interface declaration puts the Java compiler to work only as a watchdog to make sure that you do the work. It doesn't do the work for you. An abstract base class can provide default behaviors that you change only where necessary, but an interface leaves all the work to you. Of course, like an interface, an abstract class needs a subclass that fills in the absent details before it's useful.

Packaging

So far, you have made sure that all the classes you need for your applet are available by putting them all in the same file. When you begin to build more complex programs and to use the same classes in more than one applet, this approach is inconvenient. You may find it easier to build a package instead.

A *package* is a group of classes that work together. When you write Java code, you can put a class into a package by declaring the package name in the first line in the file — package mypackage. After classes are written and packaged, you call on classes in a package by using an import statement. You are already familiar with some packages — java.applet, java.awt, and so on.

When you run the code as an applet, the browser or applet viewer needs to know where all the class files are located. The browser already knows where the class files for the Java library classes are located, but it looks for classes that belong to a package in a subdirectory with the same name as the package name.

The following steps show what you need to do when you want to create your own package:

1. **Declare the package.**

   Write the code for each class in the package. Add a package declaration as the first line of each code file. So every .java that goes into the package contains the same package declaration. For example:

   ```
   package mypackage;
   import java.awt.*;
   public class Droid extends Object {
   ...
   ```

2. **Put the compiled** .class **files in a directory named for the package.**

   Compile the code for each class in the package. For example, you may have a group of class files:

   ```
   droid.class
   bot.class
   actor.class
   ```

   Put all these files into a subdirectory named mypackage.

   While you develop your applet, the mypackage subdirectory can be a subdirectory of your current working directory. (For example, if your working directory is \projects\programming\, you can set up a subdirectory named `\projects\programming\mypackage\`) or you can add the package directory that you have created to the classpath declaration with a command such as `SET CLASSPATH Java.lib;` `\projects\programming\mypackage`.

Codebase

When you publish your applet on the Web, you may keep the applet code and package subdirectories in the same directory as the HTML file for the page that contains the applet. But you may want to organize your applet code in a directory separate from the HTML code. You can tell the HTML page where to look for Java code by adding a `CODEBASE=` statement to the HTML `<APPLET>` tag. For example:

```
<APPLET CODEBASE= http:\\www.isc.com\appletcode\
code="HelloAgainWorld.class" width=100 height=100 align=left>
<param name=info value="Hello.">
</APPLET>
```

In this case, when the Web browser reads the HTML page, it goes to the indicated URL to look for the applet code instead of looking in the same place where the HTML page is located. The browser looks for packages as subdirectories at the codebase URL.

A JAR full of classes

Unless otherwise instructed, your browser makes a separate call to the server for each Java class, image file, or sound file it needs to run an applet. The applet can start much faster if all the necessary materials are downloaded in one transaction. The way to accomplish this is to put the applet package in a JAR, along with any other necessary files.

But what, you ask, is a JAR? A JAR is a "Java Archive." That is, a single, compressed file that combines the contents of a number of files rearranged to take up the least possible file space.

If you are familiar with ZIP files, you will be pleased to hear that a JAR is a form of ZIP file, similar to the kind of file you get when you use PKWare's PKZip compression software to archive files.

To put your package in a JAR, you must use the JAR tool that is part of the JDK. The commands are similar to the commands you use to compile Java code or run the applet viewer.

Option Codes	JAR File	Input Files	Description
c f	myjarfile.jar	*.class	Puts all the .class files into myjarfile.jar.
c v f	bigjarfile.jar	*	"Verbose" puts all the files in the current directory into bigjarfile.jar and lists each file as it is compressed.

You can also display what is in a JAR file:

Option Codes	JAR File	Description
t f	myjarfile.jar	Lists onscreen all the files archived in myjarfile.jar.
t v f	bigjarfile.jar	"Verbose" lists onscreen all the files archived in bigjarfile.jar with file size and date and time information.

To use code that is in a JAR, you must ask for the JAR in the applet tag by adding the ARCHIVE = statement to the HTML <APPLET> tag. For example:

```
<APPLET CODEBASE= http:\\www.isc.com\appletcode\
code="HelloAgainWorld.class" ARCHIVE = "HelloStuff.jar"
width=100 height=100 align=left>
<param name=info value="Hello.">
</APPLET>
```

After you identify the archive, the browser takes care of locating and unzipping classes as needed.

Chapter 9

Recycle This Code

• •

• •

*T*he Java Class Library provides a number of prewritten classes that you can use directly to create useful applets. Among the most useful are the basic graphic user interface objects, such as buttons, checkboxes, and drop-down lists. This chapter gives you a guided tour through these GUI objects and through the Java Class Library documentation that you need as reference to use them.

Getting Started

To set up a graphical user interface for an applet, you must take care of two issues:

✔ Putting the GUI objects on the screen

✔ Responding to user input

Chapter 5 gives you an example of how to display and respond to a button. The Java Class Library documentation tells you everything that you need to know to do it again.

Looking it up

To use a class that someone else has written for you, you need to know its constructors, its public methods, and something about what the class does. For classes in the Java library, you can find all this necessary information in the Java API (applications programming interface) documentation. The Java API documentation is part of the Sun JDK (Java Developer's Kit) and is also provided as a component of other programming toolkits.

The documentation is organized by package. A class index exists for each package. The GUI classes are located in the `java.awt` package. So, to find out about the `Button` class, for example, look it up in the class index of the AWT (Abstract Windowing Toolkit) package. The event classes that you need to refer to in order to organize appropriate responses are in another package — `java.awt.event`.

The Java Class Library documentation is an HTML document. You move around in the documentation by clicking the hypertext links. This documentation was created by using a special program in the JDK called Javadoc to pull comments from the source code of the Java class libraries. (In Chapter 11, we show you how to use Javadoc to document your own code.)

If you follow the references for `Button`, you find the following:

- ✔ A family tree diagram
- ✔ A list of constructors, briefly explained
- ✔ A list of methods, briefly explained

The family tree diagram tells you the parent classes of `Button`. This is important information because `Button` inherits the methods of its parents. Although the methods you are most interested in are usually the methods defined in the class itself, sometimes you need to check what other methods are available. The family tree diagram enables you to check on the methods your class may inherit from parent classes.

Setup

To set up the button, you are primarily interested in its constructors. Keep following the hypertext links, and you can find the information you need to instantiate a button with a label.

`public Button (String label)`	Constructs a `Button` with the specified label. Parameters: `label` — the label of the button

The constructor code goes in the definition of the applet or object in which the GUI control appears. For example:

```
String southString = "South";
Button southButton = new Button(southString);
```

Response

When a GUI object exists, user interaction with the object causes events. Events are posted to registered Listeners. In order to respond to a button click or any other GUI event, you need to create and register a Listener object.

The methods of the GUI class tell you what kinds of Listeners may be registered with a particular class of GUI objects. Just look for add...Listener methods. For example, a button has only an addActionListener() method. A List, however, has both an addActionListener() method and an addItemListener() method.

The specifications for Listeners and the events they listen to are found in the documentation for the java.awt.event package. There, you learn that an ActionListener is required only to implement an actionPerformed() method. However, a mouseListener must have methods for mouseEntered(), mouseExited(), and three other possible conditions.

When you write an event Listener method, you may use methods of the given event type to get more information about what happened. For example, e.getX() and e.getY() tell you the exact location of a mouseEvent. Like the Listener interfaces, the various possible event types are documented in the java.awt.event package.

To write the following code, I had to look at two places in the java.awt.event documentation. First, I looked up the ItemListener interface to see what methods must be included in an ItemListener class. As it turns out, only an itemStateChanged() method is required.

Then, I looked up ItemEvent to see what methods of the event to use to get information about what is happening. I found that ItemEvent.getStateChange() returns SELECTED or DESELECTED to tell whether a click put a check mark in an empty box or removed the check mark from a box that had previously been selected. With this information, I was able to write an ItemListener that displays the results in a TextArea.

```
class boxListener implements ItemListener{
    private TextArea outTextArea = new TextArea(5,15);
    //constructor
    boxListener(TextArea outtext){
    outTextArea = outtext;
    }
    //Methods required to implement ItemListener interface
    public void itemStateChanged(ItemEvent e){
    if (e.getStateChange()==ItemEvent.SELECTED){
      outTextArea.append("Box checked!\n");
      }
  else {
      outTextArea.append("Box unchecked!\n");
      }
    }
}//end boxListener
```

Notice that the constructor tells any specific boxListener object what label to use for its messages. The code for the Listener must provide a way to keep track of the outTextArea by declaring and instantiating a TextArea with this code:

```
    private TextArea outTextArea = new TextArea(5,15);
    //constructor
    boxListener(TextArea outtext){
    outTextArea = outtext;
```

The examples used to explain event handling in this book show *pure* Listeners. That is, each Listener receives its event messages from a separate GUI object and sends result messages on to other GUI objects. However, it is possible for an object to be its own Listener or its own output target. For example, if you want a button to change color when clicked, you could extend Button to implement the appropriate Listener interface and change its own color. Or you could have a GUI display serve as Listener for a variety of controls.

Here is a list of the types of events you can work with:

ActionEvent	ItemEvent
AdjustmentEvent	KeyEvent
ComponentEvent	MouseEvent
ContainerEvent	PaintEvent
FocusEvent	TextEvent
InputEvent	WindowEvent

An Activity Box for More Mature Programmers

By referring to the AWT documentation, you can put together an applet that demonstrates each type of GUI user control. One block of code creates the controls and adds them to a panel. Another block of code contains the Listeners that respond to the events generated by the GUI controls. The finished product looks something like Figure 9-1.

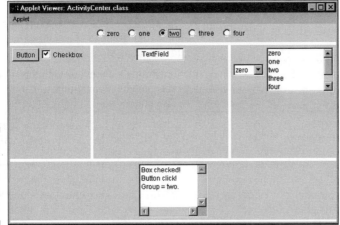

Figure 9-1:
Activity box
for more
mature
programmers.

Button

A button generates an event when the user clicks it with the mouse (see Figure 9-2). We've used examples of the code to instantiate a button and the code to respond to a user's click on a button in the "Setup" section of this chapter and in Chapter 5.

Figure 9-2:
A button.

Checkbox

A checkbox may be either checked or blank (see Figure 9-3). When the user clicks the checkbox, the state of the checkbox changes. If the checkbox is blank, it becomes checked; if the checkbox is checked, it becomes blank.

Figure 9-3:
A blank
checkbox.

An applet can refer to the checkbox variable that keeps track of the state of the checkbox. An applet can also respond to the event generated when a checkbox changes state.

Constructor	Result
Checkbox()	Constructs a checkbox with no label, no checkbox group, and initialized to a false (deselected) state.
Checkbox(String)	Constructs a checkbox with the specified label, no checkbox group, and initialized to a false state.
Checkbox(String, Boolean state)	Constructs a checkbox with the specified label, no checkbox group, and initialized to the given state.

When the user clicks on a checkbox, the checkbox changes state and generates an ItemEvent.

Because Java was created with the World Wide Web and Web browsers in mind, it enables your applet to talk to the browser. For example, you can watch for a checkbox event and display a message in the status bar of the browser with code such as the following. The showStatus() method displays a string in the status bar of the browser.

```
class boxListener implements ItemListener{
    //constructor
    boxListener(){
    }
    //Methods required to implement ItemListener interface
    public void itemStateChanged(ItemEvent e){
    if (e.getStateChange()==ItemEvent.SELECTED){
      showStatus("Box checked!");
      }
  else {
      showStatus("Box unchecked!");
      }
    }
}//end boxListener
```

The checkbox group, AKA radio buttons

The checkbox group GUI control is often referred to as *radio buttons* because the group behaves like the buttons on a car radio. Whenever one button in the group is selected, it turns off or deselects whatever other button in the group is currently selected. The checkbox group enforces a single choice among a group of options (see Figure 9-4).

Figure 9-4:
A checkbox group.

To use a checkbox group, you must instantiate a checkbox group as well as each of its checkboxes.

`CheckboxGroup()`	Creates a new checkbox group.
`Checkbox(String,CheckboxGroup, boolean)`	Constructs a checkbox with the specified label, specified checkbox group, and specified Boolean state.

The following code sets up a checkbox group:

```
CheckboxGroup myCheckboxGroup = new CheckboxGroup();
...
Checkbox[] checkList = new Checkbox[5];
...
  public void init() {
    add(checkList[0] = new
         Checkbox("zero",myCheckboxGroup,true));
    add(checkList[1] = new
         Checkbox("one",myCheckboxGroup,false));
    add(checkList[2] = new
         Checkbox("two",myCheckboxGroup,false));
    add(checkList[3] = new
         Checkbox("three",myCheckboxGroup,false));
    add(checkList[4] = new
         Checkbox("four",myCheckboxGroup,false));
    ...
  }
```

Thing [0] and Thing [1]

This title and the following code snippet for handling checkbox groups both use *array notation*. Arrays may be new to you if you have never done any programming.

The use of square brackets following a name in a variable declaration indicates that you are setting up a series of parallel items. Rather than give them separate names, you treat them as a group and refer to them by number — `checkList[0]`, `checkList[1]`, and so on.

In a variable declaration, [ ] indicates an array. A number inside the brackets indicates how many items are in the array. For example, `Checkbox[5]` means an array of five checkboxes. The meaning of the following code is "Instantiate an array of five checkboxes and name it `checkList`."

```
Checkbox[] checkList = new
       Checkbox[5];
```

You can refer to the individual checkboxes as `checkList[0]`, `checkList[1]`, and so on. You can even refer to `checkList[n]` and compute a value of n someplace to tell the computer which particular checkbox in the array interests you.

Oh, by the way, one of the charming little quirks that Java has inherited from its Bell Labs ancestors is that it begins counting at zero. So, the first item in an array is always item [0].

"Should array indices start at 0 or 1? My compromise of 0.5 was rejected without, I thought, proper consideration." - Stan Kelly-Bootle

You should be comfortable enough with Java to handle the following code for responding to a checkbox group event. This Listener is added to each of the individual checkboxes in the checkbox group. Read it carefully.

If you look up the documentation for `ItemEvent`, you discover two possible values that may be returned by `e.getStateChange()` — `SELECTED` and `DESELECTED`. The individual checkbox that is selected returns `SELECTED`. The checkbox that was previously selected and becomes `DESELECTED` also reports an `itemStateChanged` event. The `if` statement lets the code tell the difference between the box that was selected and the box that was deselected.

Notice that in this example, the result is printed in a text area. The characters \n mean start a new line. More about groups of characters with a special meaning in a moment.

```
class groupListener implements ItemListener{
      private TextArea outTextArea = new TextArea(5,15);
      //constructor
      groupListener(TextArea outtext){
      outTextArea = outtext;
      }
      //Methods required to implement ItemListener interface
      public void itemStateChanged(ItemEvent e){
      if (e.getStateChange()==ItemEvent.SELECTED){
```

```
        outTextArea.append("Group = " +
        e.getItem().toString()+".\n");
        }
    }
}//end groupListener
```

You have a choice

The `Choice` GUI object looks different from a checkbox group but has the same effect of forcing a single selection from a group of alternatives (see Figure 9-5).

Figure 9-5:
A choice.

To set up a choice, you declare and instantiate the `Choice` object; then you add items to it and add the object to the applet.

```
....
Choice myChoice = new Choice();
....
public void init() {
    ...myChoice.addItem("zero");
        myChoice.addItem("one");
        myChoice.addItem("two");
        myChoice.addItem("three");
        myChoice.addItem("four");
        myChoice.addItem("five");
        myChoice.addItem("six");
        myChoice.addItemListener(Choose);
        ep.add(myChoice);
```

Like the `CheckBoxGroup`, the `Choice` GUI object reports an `ItemEvent`. The code for a `ChoiceListener` is very similar to the code for a `CheckBoxGroupListener`.

```
class choiceListener implements ItemListener{
        private TextArea outTextArea = new TextArea(5,15);
        //constructor
        choiceListener(TextArea outtext){
```

(continued)

(continued)

```
    outTextArea = outtext;
    }
    //Methods required to implement ItemListener interface
    public void itemStateChanged(ItemEvent e){
      outTextArea.append("Choice = " +
      e.getItem().toString()+ " .\n");
      }
}//end choiceListener
```

You have more than one choice

List is another GUI control that resembles Choice, but its capabilities are quite different (see Figure 9-6).

Figure 9-6:
A list.

When you use a list, you can set up the list to permit the selection of more than one item. Also, using the List class provides you with a number of methods to manipulate the contents of the list after it has been instantiated. Just to give you an idea of what can be done, here is a selected list of methods (refer to the AWT documentation for the full list):

Method	*Action Performed*
add (String)	Adds the specified item to the end of scrolling list
remove(int)	Deletes an item from the list
getItem(int)	Gets the item associated with the specified index
getRows()	Returns the number of visible lines in this list
getSelectedIndex()	Gets the selected item on the list or –1 if no item is selected
getSelectedIndexes()	Returns the selected indexes on the list
getSelectedItem()	Returns the selected item on the list or null if no item is selected
getSelectedItems()	Returns the selected items on the list
isIndexSelected(int)	Returns true if the item at the specified index has been selected; false otherwise
makeVisible(int)	Forces the item at the specified index to be visible

Method	Action Performed
replaceItem(String,int)	Replaces the item at the given index
select(int)	Selects the item at the specified index
setMultipleMode	Sets whether this list should allow multiple (boolean) selections or not

User interaction with a List object generates three different kinds of events. When a user double-clicks a list item (as you may when selecting a file to run or open in a typical Windows application), the list generates an ACTION_EVENT. In addition, each time that the user clicks an item to select it or deselect it, the list generates a LIST_SELECT or LIST_DESELECT event with the index number of the selected item.

Put it in writing

Two Java GUI controls enable the user to input text: the text field and the text area. A text field accepts only one line of text. When the user presses the Enter key, the text field generates an ACTION_EVENT that reports the text string in the field.

The ACTION_EVENT and text string generated by a text field in which the user types **OK** is exactly the same as the ACTION_EVENT and text string generated when the user clicks a button labeled OK. If the same ActionListener is registered with both GUI objects, you need to check the event.target that is a property of the event to make sure that you are responding to a button, not a text field.

```
if (event.target == myButton) {
      showStatus("Button: OK");
}
```

Here is a simple Listener for a text field:

```
class textfieldListener implements ActionListener{
     //constructor
     textfieldListener(){
     }
     //Methods required to implement ActionListener interface
     public void actionPerformed(ActionEvent e){
     showStatus("TextField says:" + e.getActionCommand());
     }
}//end textfieldListener
```

A text area accepts multiline input. The area does not generate an action event when the user presses the Enter key. Instead, the user's text simply moves on to a new line in the text area, as shown in Figure 9-7.

Figure 9-7:
A text field
and a text
area.

The usual way for an applet to find out the contents of a text field or text area is to wait for a cue from some other control and then use the `getText()` method.

For example, the `buttonListener` may contain

```
public void actionPerformed(ActionEvent e){
  showStatus(textField.getText());
}
```

Go to the Library Often

Building on the examples in this chapter, you should be able to assemble a user interface that includes any of the standard GUI components. If you want to do something that is not included in our examples, look in the Java API documentation under the name of the class with which you want to work — `Button`, `Checkbox`, `TextArea`, and so on. Browse for a method that sounds like the one you want and read the description. Then do some experimenting.

Look out for the window

Our examples have been built on applets and panels. As you look at the class library, you see that `Window` and `Frame` are also available. These objects have the typical GUI close buttons, as well as the other features you would expect. For example, a `Frame` has a title bar and may have a menu. The procedures for adding GUI controls to a `Frame` are exactly the same ones already covered in this chapter. You can add a `MenuBar` with `Menus` consisting of `MenuItems` to a `Frame`. But we have a caution to add.

A `Frame` or a `Window` introduces an additional layer of complication in handling events and passing them on to other objects. Also, `Frames` and `Windows` expect you to be able to iconify or minimize the object and to close it. For applets that reside on a Web page, the added benefits often do not justify the added complexity. In any event, before you undertake working with windows and frames, make sure that you are fluent working with GUI controls on applets and panels.

More layouts

As you explore the contents of `java.awt`, you find three more `Layouts` — `GridLayout`, `GridBagLayout`, and `CardLayout`. `GridLayout` lets you set up a simple table of rows and columns. You can then place components in any given cell (see Figure 9-8).

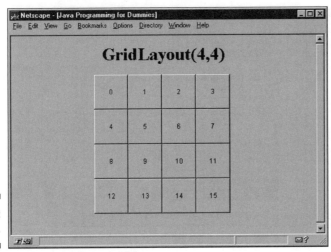

Figure 9-8:
GridLayout.

`GridBagLayout` lets you build a complex layout based on combinations of grid cells (see Figure 9-9). You find an extensive explanation of `GridBagLayout` in the Java API documentation.

`CardLayout` lets you fill a space with multiple layers, like a tabbed notebook (see Figure 9-10).

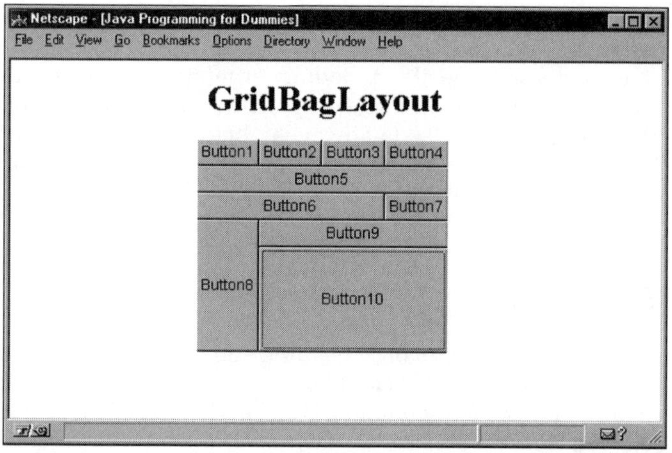

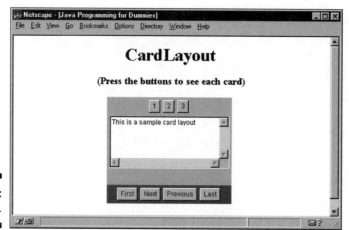

Figure 9-9:
GridBag
Layout.

Figure 9-9:
GridBag
Layout.

Figure 9-10:
CardLayout.

A Little Code for Dessert

Here is some sample code to get you started in using GUI objects. Experiment with the effects of giving your applet different dimensions on an HTML page. You may also want to try out some different layouts. And, test the resize() method that enables you to adjust the size of components so that the Layout doesn't exercise complete control of the size of components onscreen.

```
/** This is an activityCenter for more mature Java
 * programmers.
 */
import java.awt.*;
import java.applet.*;
```

```
import java.awt.event.*;
/* ActivityCenter Applet */
public class ActivityCenter extends Applet {
//Declarations
 Panel np = new Panel();
 Panel wp = new Panel();
 Panel ep = new Panel();
 Panel cp = new Panel();
 Panel sp = new Panel();
 Button myButton = new Button("Button");
 Checkbox myCheckbox = new Checkbox("Checkbox");
 Choice myChoice = new Choice();
 List myList = new List(5,true);
 TextArea myTextArea = new TextArea(5,15);
 TextField myTextField = new TextField("TextField");
 CheckboxGroup myCheckboxGroup = new CheckboxGroup();
 Checkbox[] checkList = new Checkbox[5];
 groupListener Click = new groupListener(myTextArea);
 buttonListener Zap = new buttonListener(myTextArea);
 boxListener Check = new boxListener(myTextArea);
 choiceListener Choose = new choiceListener(myTextArea);
 listListener Zip = new listListener(myTextArea);
 textfieldListener Taptap = new
 textfieldListener(myTextArea);
 dblclickListListener Zapzap = new
 dblclickListListener(myTextArea);
//init
        public void init() {
        setLayout(new BorderLayout(5,5));
        add("North",np);
        np.add(checkList[0] = new
        Checkbox("zero",myCheckboxGroup,true));
        np.add(checkList[1] = new
        Checkbox("one",myCheckboxGroup,false));
        np.add(checkList[2] = new
        Checkbox("two",myCheckboxGroup,false));
        np.add(checkList[3] = new
        Checkbox("three",myCheckboxGroup,false));
        np.add(checkList[4] = new
        Checkbox("four",myCheckboxGroup,false));
        checkList[0].addItemListener(Click);
        checkList[1].addItemListener(Click);
        checkList[2].addItemListener(Click);
        checkList[3].addItemListener(Click);
        checkList[4].addItemListener(Click);
```

(continued)

(continued)

```
np.setBackground(Color.cyan);
    checkList[0].setBackground(Color.cyan);
    checkList[1].setBackground(Color.cyan);
    checkList[2].setBackground(Color.cyan);
    checkList[3].setBackground(Color.cyan);
    checkList[4].setBackground(Color.cyan);
add("West",wp);
    myButton.addActionListener(Zap);
    wp.add(myButton);
    myCheckbox.addItemListener(Check);
    wp.add(myCheckbox);
wp.setBackground(Color.cyan);
myButton.setBackground(Color.cyan);
myCheckbox.setBackground(Color.cyan);
add("East",ep);
    myChoice.addItem("zero");
    myChoice.addItem("one");
    myChoice.addItem("two");
    myChoice.addItem("three");
    myChoice.addItem("four");
    myChoice.addItem("five");
    myChoice.addItem("six");
    myChoice.addItemListener(Choose);
    ep.add(myChoice);
    myList.add("zero");
    myList.add("one");
    myList.add("two");
    myList.add("three");
    myList.add("four");
    myList.add("five");
    myList.add("six");

    myList.addItemListener(Zip);
    myList.addActionListener(Zapzap);
    ep.add(myList);
    ep.setBackground(Color.cyan);
add("Center",cp);
    cp.add(myTextField);
    myTextField.addActionListener(Taptap);
cp.setBackground(Color.cyan);
add("South",sp);
    sp.add(myTextArea);
    myTextArea.setEditable(false);
```

```
                sp.setBackground(Color.cyan);
    }
} // end applet
class groupListener implements ItemListener{
        private TextArea outTextArea = new TextArea(5,15);
        //constructor
        groupListener(TextArea outtext){
        outTextArea = outtext;
        }
        //Methods required to implement ItemListener
        public void itemStateChanged(ItemEvent e){
        if (e.getStateChange()==ItemEvent.SELECTED){
          outTextArea.append("Group = " +
          e.getItem().toString()+".\n");
          }
        }
}//end groupListener
class buttonListener implements ActionListener{
        private TextArea outTextArea = new TextArea(5,15);
        //constructor
        buttonListener(TextArea outtext){
        outTextArea = outtext;
        }
        //Methods required to implement ActionListener interface
        public void actionPerformed(ActionEvent e){
        outTextArea.append("Button click!\n");
        }
}//end buttonListener
  class boxListener implements ItemListener{
        private TextArea outTextArea = new TextArea(5,15);
        //constructor
        boxListener(TextArea outtext){
        outTextArea = outtext;
        }
        //Methods required to implement ItemListener interface
        public void itemStateChanged(ItemEvent e){
        if (e.getStateChange()==ItemEvent.SELECTED){
          outTextArea.append("Box checked!\n");
          }
    else {
          outTextArea.append("Box unchecked!\n");
          }
        }
```

(continued)

(continued)

```
}//end boxListener
class choiceListener implements ItemListener{
      private TextArea outTextArea = new TextArea(5,15);
      //constructor
      choiceListener(TextArea outtext){
      outTextArea = outtext;
      }
      //Methods required to implement ItemListener interface
      public void itemStateChanged(ItemEvent e){
      outTextArea.append("Choice = " +
      e.getItem().toString()+ " .\n");
        }
}//end choiceListener
class listListener implements ItemListener{
private TextArea outTextArea = new TextArea(5,15);
      //constructor
      listListener(TextArea outtext){
      outTextArea = outtext;
      }
      //Methods required to implement ItemListener interface
      public void itemStateChanged(ItemEvent e){
        if (e.getStateChange()==ItemEvent.SELECTED){
        outTextArea.append(e.getItem().toString() + "
        selected in List.\n");
        }
      if (e.getStateChange()==ItemEvent.DESELECTED){
        outTextArea.append(e.getItem().toString() + "
        deselected in List.\n");
        }
      }
}//end listListener
class textfieldListener implements ActionListener{
      private TextArea outTextArea = new TextArea(5,15);
      //constructor
      textfieldListener(TextArea outtext){
      outTextArea = outtext;
      }
      //Methods required to implement ActionListener interface
      public void actionPerformed(ActionEvent e){
      outTextArea.append("TextField says:" +
      e.getActionCommand()+ ".\n");
      }
}//end textfieldListener
```

```
class dblclickListListener implements ActionListener{
     private TextArea outTextArea = new TextArea(5,15);
     //constructor
     dblclickListListener(TextArea outtext){
     outTextArea = outtext;
     }
     //Methods required to implement ActionListener interface
   public void actionPerformed(ActionEvent e){
   outTextArea.append("Double clicked:" + e.getActionCommand()+ ".\n");
     }
}//end dblclickListListener
```

If you don't want to grow your own, buy some JavaBeans

The classes in the Java AWT are not the only resource you have to create user interfaces for your applets. The developers of Java want to encourage commercial software developers to create and sell Java components that can be combined and used by end users to create their own custom applets. So they have created the JavaBeans standard.

The JavaBeans standard enables developers to publish classes that you can modify and customize without revealing the inner secrets of their code. As for an AWT class, you can look up the public methods and variables of a JavaBean object. And JavaBeans classes have methods designed to make them easy to customize. They are designed to fit easily into the visual editing tools of IDEs.

But you don't have to use an IDE to use JavaBeans. Except for small differences in how you declare and instantiate JavaBean objects, you can use JavaBeans in the same way you use AWT classes. You have to invest a little work to discover how to use a JavaBean, but much less work than would be required to create a complete spreadsheet or database viewer or whatever. Check the Web sites in Chapter 21 for sources of JavaBeans.

Why should VB programmers have all the fun?

By the time you read this, you will be able to recycle most Java code without typing a single line. Instead, you will simply drag a picture of a JavaBean and drop it onto a picture of your Java program. This is the way that programmers recycle code in Visual Basic and Delphi, for example, and it's a very powerful technique, indeed.

The magic is in the JavaBean. Recycling Java classes can be a chore if you need to look up the Javadoc or read the source code to figure out a class's properties and methods. A JavaBean is a chunk of code — a component — that follows an agreed-upon standard for telling visual programming environments and other tools about its methods and properties. Visual programming tools like JBuilder or Symantec Café can inspect a JavaBean, learn its methods and properties, and use that information to make life easier for you, the programmer. Instead of searching the source code for the right variable to change the background color to red, you simply select from a menu of valid colors that your visual programming environment presents to you.

A smart programming tool can go even further. It can use the information a JavaBean provides to let you connect several beans together to create a complex user interface or perform a complex task. Think of it as the software equivalent of Lego.

The JavaBeans standard also provides the capability to save and restore data — referred to as *persistence*.

The Java Foundation Classes

The Java Foundation Classes (JFC) include a set of GUI components — the Swing component set — that extends and replaces the AWT. These components are completely written in Java; they don't rely on platform-specific libraries as does the AWT. JFC provides JavaBeans-compliant Swing components that implement complex user interface widgets such as toolbars, tree views, and tables, to name a few. These components can have the same look and feel across all platforms, or they can be made to take on the look and feel of the native platform. With the JFC, you have the choice of writing an applet that has an identical look and feel on UNIX workstations and on Windows PCs, or writing one that changes its look and feel to match the platform it is running on.

For some time, the JFCs may not be widely available. For example, today you need to use a special plug-in and a special HTML tag in order to run JFC on Microsoft browsers. So the AWT seems like the best place for beginners to start. But we strongly recommend that you take a look at the JFCs for added GUI features after you master the basics of using the AWT.

Chapter 10

Finding Your Type

● ●

In This Chapter

▶ Describing data types for numbers and letters

▶ Using `integers`, `longs`, `floats`, and `doubles`

▶ Converting numbers among the number data types

▶ Using math library functions

▶ Using class wrappers

▶ Dividing letters into characters and strings

▶ Identifying characters and special codes

▶ Editing, comparing, and analyzing strings

● ●

*A*n important fact of human communication (and miscommunication) is that the meaning of a statement depends on what type of object the statement is about. When you say "Don't mix apples and oranges," essentially, you are talking about *data types*. In their famous vaudevillian routine "Who's on First . . ." Abbott and Costello were experiencing a data-typing problem. (The expression *Who* referred to an object of data type *name of baseball player*, instead of an object of data type *interrogative pronoun*.)

Java insists on knowing the type of every item of data at all times. For example, Java requires you to name the data type for every variable at the time you set up the variable. This feature makes Java what programming gurus call a *strongly typed* language.

In other sections of the book, we touch on several of the standard Java data types in passing. In this chapter, we review all the basic types.

About Data Types

As you know, the computer represents all data as patterns of ones and zeros. But sometimes the ones and zeros are interpreted as a number, sometimes as a letter, and so on. If you or the computer lose track of how a particular pattern of ones and zeros is to be interpreted, the resulting interpretation may be amusing or catastrophic, but it's rarely what you intended.

The following sections tell you all about describing your data types. We divide our discussion into two primary categories of data, numbers and letters. Within these primary categories, we talk about specific data types and the methods that you can use to work with them. And we hope the discussion helps you get the data interpretation results that you intend!

Categorizing Your Numbers

Most computers are built around the idea of using a standard amount of memory space for each number. This design enables computers to do mathematical computations very quickly, but it also imposes some limitations on how large or how accurate a number may be. You find two basic types of numbers to work with in Java, as in most computer languages:

- **Whole numbers:** When working with whole numbers, we never round things off. Instead, we always use exact numbers. The financial industry likes to use whole numbers because the results are then accurate to the last penny (if you are counting in pennies). The disadvantage of working with whole numbers is that you may run out of space to represent numbers and some fractions and other numbers can't be represented with reasonable accuracy using only whole numbers.

- **Fractional numbers:** With fractional numbers, we represent numbers as a whole number plus a decimal fraction. The fractional number type enables you to handle much larger and smaller numbers, but only to a certain number of decimal places of accuracy.

Java has four different basic types of whole numbers and two types of fractional numbers. The data types differ in whether they are whole numbers or fractional numbers and in how much memory space is allocated to each number. (Advanced programmers can use two do-it-yourself types that let you set up your own rules for special situations. They are called BigInteger and BigDecimal.)

Describing whole numbers

Java uses the following data types for whole numbers:

- ✔ byte: An 8-bit whole number; a byte can only be a whole number between –128 and +127.

- ✔ short: A 16-bit whole number; a short number can be a whole number between –32768 and +32767 only.

- ✔ int: A 32-bit whole number; an int number can be a whole number between –2147483648 and +2147483647 only.

- ✔ long: A 64-bit whole number; a long number can be a whole number between –9223372036854775808 and +9223372036854775807 only.

To give you a sense of scale, you can't quite compute the national debt accurate to the penny as an int, but you can comfortably do so by using a long. The data types byte and short are rarely used. For most purposes, you can use int even when you could get away with using a byte or short.

Describing fractional numbers

Java uses the following data types for fractional numbers:

- ✔ float: A 32-bit floating point number as large as + or –3.40282347 times 10 to the 38th power. A float number can be as close to zero as + or – 1.40239846 times 10 to the –45 power.

- ✔ double: A 64-bit floating point number as large as + or – 1.79769313486231570 times 10 to the 308th power. A double number can be as close to zero as + or –4.94065645841246544 times 10 to the –324 power.

Unless you are doing scientific calculations that require an unusually high degree of precision or exceptionally large numbers, you are not likely to use doubles. And unless you make other arrangements, when a number has more than six digits, the computer displays floats and doubles in a special notation, as follows:

1.239874E5 means 1.239874 times 10 to the fifth power. That is, 1.239874 ×100,000 = 123,987.4

2.431502E-2 means 2.431502 times 10 to the –2 power. That is, 2.431502 × 0.01 = 0.02431502.

5.632714E9 means 5.632714 × 1,000,000,000 = 5,632,714,000.

1.354321E-4 means 1.354321 × 0.0001 = 0.0001354321.

(If you want to work with large numbers and still avoid this *scientific notation*, see the rules for a BigDecimal.)

What you can do with numbers

You can perform all the basic arithmetic operations with any of the six number types described in the previous sections. That is, you can add, subtract, multiply, and divide; you indicate these operations in the code by using the operators +, -, *, and /, respectively. You cannot mix different number data types in the same computation.

A warning about division. When you divide fractional numbers — float and double — the result is carried out to as many decimal places as are available and then rounded off. When you divide whole numbers — byte, short, int, long — the result is not rounded off. Instead, any remainder after division is simply dropped.

For example, 5/2==2. Programmers call this action *truncation*. If you want to find the remainder, you can use a special operator called the *remainder operator* (%) that calculates the remainder only, for example, 5%2==1. That is, when you divide 5 by 2, the remainder is 1. Also, 13/4==3, and 13%4==1.

Table 10-1 gives a short summary of the operations that you can perform with numbers.

Table 10-1   A Summary of Mathematical Operations in Java

Operator	Code Line	What It Means
+	intx = inta+intb; floatx = floata+floatb;	Set x equal to a + b.
-	intx = inta-intb; floatx = floata-floatb;	Set x equal to a - b.
*	intx = inta*intb; floatx = floata*floatb;	Set x equal to a*b.
/	intx = inta/intb; floatx = floata/floatb;	Set x equal to a / b. For int, short, and long, the result is truncated.

Operator	Code Line	What It Means
%	`intx = inta%intb;`	Set x equal to the remainder of a / b. Applies only to `int`, `short`, and `long`.
+=	`intx += inta; floatx += floata;`	Add a to the old value of x and save the result as x.
-=	`intx -= inta; floatx -= floata;`	Subtract a from the old value of x and save the result as x.
*=	`intx *= inta; x floatx *= floata;`	Multiply a by the old value of x and save the result as x.
/=	`intx /= inta; floatx /= floata;`	Divide the old value of x by a and save the result as x.

Remember, the grouping of mathematical operations makes a difference. Consider the following example:

```
(4 x 5) + 3 = 23
```

but

```
4 x (5 + 3) = 32
```

You should always use parentheses to group mathematical operations to clarify what is going on in your mind and to make sure that the calculations are executed in the correct order.

Numbers in an object wrapper

You can mix the data types for numbers together in computations, but you need to be very careful to keep track of the results. (Combining an integer with a double results in a double; combining an integer with a float results in a float, and so on.) It's usually safer to convert from one type of number to another. You can specifically convert all numbers in a computation to the same type before you perform the computation; for example, adding up a column of numbers.

The Java Class Library includes a group of number classes in the `java.lang` package. The parent class for all these classes is called `Number`. Each of the classes that extends `Number` has a similar set of methods that take care of a variety of useful conversions. If you expect to need any of these number conversions, you declare and instantiate an object *wrapper* instead of relying on the basic *unwrapped* number type.

If your number is instantiated in an object wrapper, that is, if you declare an instance of the appropriate number class, you can use these forms of conversion:

Object Method	*What It Does*
`myNumber.doubleValue()`	Returns a number in the `double` data type
`myNumber.intValue()`	Returns a number in the `int` data type
`myNumber.floatValue()`	Returns a number in the `float` data type
`myNumber.longValue()`	Returns a number in the `long` data type
`myNumber.toString()`	Returns a `string` representing the printed value of the number

If you have not instantiated an object wrapper, you can use the class methods to make conversions. For example:

Class Method	*What It Does*
`Integer.doubleValue(myNumber)`	Converts `myNumber`, which happens to be an `Integer`, to its `double` value
`Long.doubleValue(myNumber)`	Converts `myNumber`, which happens to be a `Long`, to its `double` value
`Double.intValue(myNumber)`	Converts `myNumber`, which happens to be a `Double`, to its `int` value

When a number is represented as a string — for example, when used as an applet parameter — you can convert the string back to a number:

Class Method	What It Does
`Integer.parseInt(myString)`	Translates `myString` to its integer form
`Long.parseLong(myString)`	Translates `myString` to its long form

If you want to maintain very precise control over the behavior of your numbers, (for example, to set up special rules about rounding, and so on) look at the `BigDecimal` and `BigInteger` classes in the `java.math` package.

Using Special Mathematical Functions

If you are in need of special mathematical functions or values, study the Java API (Application Programming Interface) documentation for `java.lang.Math`. This class has a number of class methods that make standard mathematical functions and constants available to you. The next listing shows you a few samples:

Math Class Function	What It Does
`Math.E`	Enables you to use the constant **e**
`Math.PI`	Enables you to use the constant pi
`Math.abs(myNumber)`	Returns the absolute value of `myNumber`
`Math.max (myNumber, yourNumber)`	Returns the greater of two numbers
`Math.pow(myNumber, exponent)`	Raises a number to a power, for example, `pow(4,2)`= 42=16
`Math.random()`	Generates a pseudorandom number between 0.0 and 1.0
`Math.sqrt(myNumber)`	Returns the square root of `myNumber`

You also find a full set of trigonometric functions, and so on. Check out the `java.lang.math` documentation!

Categorizing Your Letters

When dealing with letters and words, you need some different data types. Java has two basic data types that enable you to work with letters and words, rather than numbers.

Describing characters

The data type char is for a single character. Java uses the *Unicode* standard to represent characters. That is, Java enables 16 bits to represent each character. Unicode represents not only the Latin alphabet, but also a wide variety of other scripts and character sets. In this book, we work only with the ASCII - Latin alphabet subset of Unicode, because most hardware systems offer only minimal support for other alphabets as yet. In theory, you could write your Java applet to handle strings in Armenian or Thai or Han ideographs.

To represent a char value, type the character within single quotation marks — 'a'. A few special char values represent special codes that you cannot type directly — backspace, tab, and so on. You can represent each special code by using an *escape sequence* that consists of the \ character followed by another character. See Table 10-2 for these special characters, their associated escape sequences, and ASCII character numbers.

Table 10-2	Representing Special char Values in Java	
Special Function	*Escape Sequence*	*ASCII Number*
backspace	\b	8
horizontal tab	\t	9
newline	\n	10
formfeed	\f	12
carriage return	\r	13
double quote	\"	34
single quote	\'	39
backslash	\\	92

Suppose that you want to test whether myChar is a backspace character; you can write the testing code in this way:

```
if (myChar=='\b') {
   do something;
}
```

Also, an object wrapper for `char`, named `Character`, offers some useful class methods:

Method	What It Does
Character.isDigit(myCharacter)	Returns true if myCharacter is a digit — 0123456789
Character.isUpperCase(myCharacter)	Returns true if myCharacter is an uppercase letter
Character.isLowerCase(myCharacter)	Returns true if myCharacter is a lowercase letter
Character.isSpace(myCharacter)	Returns true if myCharacter is white space (space, tab, or so on)

The following sample code snippet uses some `Character` methods. Suppose that you want to evaluate a keyboard response to a multiple-choice question. The user's response is saved as

```
char userInput
If (Character.isUpperCase(userInput)) {
   switch (userInput) {
     case 'A': statements; break;
     case 'B': statements; break;
     ...
     default; statements; break;
   }
      }
If (Character.isLowerCase(userInput)) {
   switch (userInput) {
     case 'a': statements; break;
     case 'b': statements; break;
     ...
     default; statements; break;
   }
      }
```

Working with strings in Java

The second data type for letters, String, works with letters as a series of characters — from one letter to many words. Strings have a special status in Java; they are allowed to break the rules of object-oriented style. Strings can be manipulated with the + operator and do not require formal instantiation. These departures from the normal Java style for handling objects are a concession to the millions of programmers who are used to handling strings in a certain way and who must work with strings every day.

String is a class that instantiates itself whenever needed. The formal way to declare and instantiate a string is perfectly acceptable:

```
String myString = new String ("Foo!");
```

However, simply saying the following is equally acceptable:

```
String myString = "Foo!";
```

Also, you can combine two strings by using the + operator. For example, if AString equals "ice" and Bstring equals "cream," you can combine them with this next statement:

```
CString = AString + Bstring;
```

The resulting string is "icecream."

The technical term for combining two strings is *concatenate*. When used with strings, the + sign is the *concatenation* operator.

By the way, if you want to be an object-oriented purist, you can use a method called concat that does exactly the same thing as the operator + for strings. For example, you can say either of the following:

```
CString = AString.concat (BString);
```

or

```
CString = AString + BString;
```

The String methods

A number of methods enable you to do interesting things with strings. You can find descriptions of all these methods in the Java API documentation, but the following overview can help orient you to the kind of methods available:

✔ **Edit:** One family of methods enables you to make changes to strings. You can convert a string to all uppercase or all lowercase. And you can substitute one character for another everywhere that character appears in the string.

✔ **Compare:** Another family of methods lets you make comparisons between strings. You can test whether two strings have the same contents, whether they start or end with the same characters, and so on.

✔ **Analyze:** A last family of methods lets you identify and pull out the letters from particular positions in a string. For example, you can pull out the first letter, or the third letter, or the second through tenth letters of a string. And you can find where in a string a particular character appears.

Editing methods

You can use edit methods to change or format a string. For example, you may often like to make sure that user input is consistently received in all uppercase or all lowercase letters. That way, you can make consistent comparisons and enforce consistent appearance of text. To convert a string to all uppercase or all lowercase, use the appropriate method:

```
newString=myString.toLowerCase;
newString=myString.toUpperCase;
```

You can also replace a given character with another one. For example if you want to replace all appearances of the letter A with the number 1, you can write this line of code:

```
newString=myString.replace('A', '1');
```

If you want to get rid of white space at the beginning or end of a string, you can use the trim method:

```
newString=myString.trim()
```

Comparison methods

Comparison methods return a true or false answer and can be used in selection and iteration statements.

You must use the equals method to compare strings. Java enables you to make a comparison of strings by using the == operator, but the result may be misleading. To Java, == means that both strings have the same location in computer memory, which may be true for some strings that are identical, but is not true for all strings.

The following are `equals` methods that you may use; they're pretty self-explanatory, but remember that they each return a logical value (that is, true or false).

```
(myString.equals(AString))
(myString.equalsIgnoreCase(AString))
(myString.endsWith("ed"))
(myString.startsWith("http//"))
```

Analyzing methods

You can pick a string apart character by character with the analyze methods. For example, suppose that you are analyzing a URL, an Internet address. You want to find the first dot and then pick out the character immediately following it. The following code finds the *index* (the position number in the string) of the first dot and then finds the character at that-position-plus-one.

```
key = tempAddress.charAt(1+inString.indexOf('.'))
```

Other methods let you find *substrings* (that is, part of a string), the last index of a particular character or substring (if that element appears more than once), and so on. Another handy method tells you the length of a string.

```
n=myString.length()
```

You can find a preview of working with these methods in Chapter 7.

Other Data Types

As you become a more sophisticated programmer, you will develop a library of classes of your own that impose rules about what operations are permitted and how to convert between one class and another. Keep in mind the model of how the basic Java types behave. For example, you may develop a class called `Prospect` that organizes name and address information about people, and you may also develop a class called `Customer`. You probably want to write a `Prospect.toCustomer` method that enables you to make the conversion in a planned way.

Keep the data type model in mind as one way to reach a deeper understanding of the classes designed by the applet programmers.

Part III
Caffeinated Pages

In this part . . .

Part III shows you how Java programming can be really fun and useful, too! In this part, we present a bevy of applets that help you practice your programming skills. This part gives you great, simple applets that can stimulate your own creativity in the process.

The applets in Part III include a calendar that you can use in a variety of ways, scrolling ticker tapes and bouncing animations, framed input forms and lists of choices, fractals, and online shopping carts. Along with each specific example, we give you ideas for other ways to apply that applet's elements, techniques, and structures. By the way, these applets have all been tested in Java 1.1.

Chapter 11
A Calendar Class

*N*ow that we've covered some fundamentals, we want to take a look at a more sophisticated Java applet. If you ever use a computer program to track your personal finances, manage a project, or tally up your billable hours, you probably have to input dates — the date you write a check, the date you expect a project to be completed, the date you start your vacation.

Can We Meet Next Friday?

Some programs require you to input a date directly. To select November 7, 2000, you may type 11/7/2000, for example. Typing dates this way is fairly convenient for the computer but often inconvenient for people. Knowing what day a particular date falls on is helpful. You may remember that you wrote a check on Monday or that your best client prefers not to meet on Fridays. November 7 in the year 2000 may not mean much to you, but if we point out that it's the first Tuesday in November, you may recognize the date as another presidential election day in the United States.

To accommodate our human foibles and to reduce data-entry errors, current computer programs that require date input usually provide calendar-like interfaces — such as the one pictured in Figure 11-1 — for selecting dates.

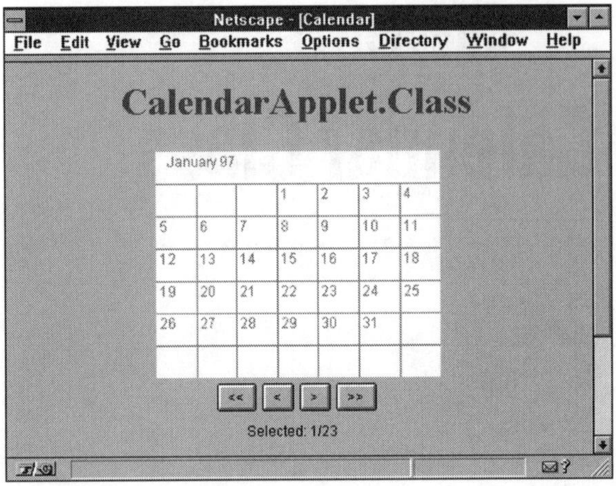

Figure 11-1:
A calendar-
style date
selector.

In the next few pages, we show you how to implement a calendar class that you can use to select dates using the familiar calendar-style interface. It's not a finished product, but it is a beginning upon which you can build to create an applet that you can use in your own Web sites.

The class that we envision has the following job description:

✔ It must display dates in a calendar format, one month at a time.

✔ It must enable the user to move backward and forward in steps of a month or a year by clicking buttons.

✔ It must enable the user to select a date by clicking it with the mouse.

With these modest ambitions, we move ahead.

Strategy

Spending a little time thinking about the big picture is a good idea before you get too involved in writing detailed applet code. Issues that are wise to consider include the following:

✔ What existing classes provide the behaviors that you want in your applet?

✔ What new classes do you need to create and where can you use existing classes unchanged?

> ✔ How will the user interact with the applet?
>
> ✔ How will the applet interact with the Web page?
>
> ✔ What kinds of revisions can you anticipate and how can you make them easy?

Choosing your ancestors wisely

As the designer of a new Java class, you can choose the parents. What's more, you can have the class inherit whichever of your parents' capabilities and qualities that you want. To a large extent, your ability to get things done with Java, at least at first, is a measure of your ability to choose your ancestors wisely; that is, to find an existing Java class that meets — or nearly meets — your needs.

The basic Java Class Library includes hundreds of classes that provide the nuts and bolts of any Java applet. With time, you may buy or borrow additional Java classes that do the particular things your programs need to do. Sometimes you may need to build your own classes, as we do in these chapters.

As you may expect, related classes are usually grouped together in a *package*. You can't learn the entire Java Class Library at once, nor do you need to. Instead, you can work with one related group of classes at a time.

Where does your calendar fit in the family tree? Already, you know a lot. The calendar appears onscreen and responds to user input. In this regard, your calendar behaves a lot like some other objects you may have seen in earlier chapters: Button, TextField, and Choice come to mind. See the branches of the family tree in Figure 11-2.

Figure 11-2: Calendar and its immediate family.

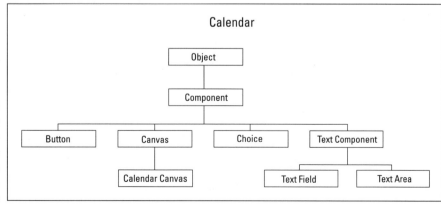

If you study the Java Class Library, you discover that all the objects that appear onscreen and respond to user input are derived from the `Component` class. It would seem reasonable, then, to derive your calendar from `Component`. If you look further, however, you see that the `Canvas` class, derived from `Component`, is the one intended for use in constructing special-purpose GUI controls. You can derive your Calendar class from `Canvas`.

Don't write code if you don't have to

The buttons and labels in the standard Java AWT are sufficient for your purposes in this applet. The standard graphics methods are also plenty to create a calendar. All you need is to draw some straight lines and possibly fill in the color of some areas.

On the other hand, the buttons are intended to step forward and back a month and a year. The built-in Java date object doesn't have these capabilities. In this case, you need to extend the class by adding methods that enable you to step forward and backward in units of a month or a year.

Making yourself (or your applet) at home on a page

An applet is a funny sort of computer program, really, because it lives as a guest within a Web page. Like any guest, your applet is more welcome if it is considerate of its host. In particular, giving the host Web page control over the appearance of your applet onscreen is a good idea. In this chapter, we show you how to let users specify your applet's size and color. This technique gives a Web page designer (perhaps you) an easy way to use your applet in a variety of pages, with different colors and different layouts, without having to modify Java source code to accommodate each change.

You can provide additional parameters to control background and foreground color. You can make the calendar large or small, red, blue, yellow, or green, according to the needs of the particular Web page you are creating, just by using different parameters in the `<APPLET>` tag.

Code Me Some Code

The complete code for the Calendar applet appears in the "The Complete and Unexpurgated Code" section later in this chapter. Before you look at the complete applet code, review these highlights.

Listening to the Web page

The way that applet users communicate their preferences to an applet is with parameters embedded in the HTML <APPLET> tag. As you may recall, the <APPLET> tag requires at least a height and width attribute as part of the basic tag. You can grab the values of the applet height and width as parameters, the same way you would grab any other applet parameters:

```
int height = Integer.parseInt(getParameter("height"));
int width = Integer.parseInt(getParameter("width"));
```

To work with the height and width values as numbers, you have to convert the string, returned by getParameter(), to an integer. The Integer class provides a static method, parseInt(), that does exactly that.

Remember that static methods, which are indicated by the keyword static in the method declaration, are special. They work even when you have not instantiated an object of their class. In other words, saying Integer height = new Integer is not necessary.

In the Calendar example, we just parse the "height" and "width" applet parameters. You see how to set background color and foreground color with parameters in the "Finishing Touches" section later in this chapter, but we leave the job of writing the final code to you.

Painting a pretty face

A large part of the calendar code is taken up with painting the calendar on the screen. Whenever you present a new month onscreen, you display the month's name and you lay out the dates so that each date appears in the proper day column. Following are the graphics functions that you use:

- drawLine(x1, y1, x2, y2) — Use this function to draw lines that divide the canvas into a grid of seven rows and seven columns.

- drawString(string, x, y) — Use this function to write out the month name and to display each date number in the appropriate column and row.

The applet uses two `for` loops to draw the lines on the calendar:

```
public void paint(Graphics g) {
    // paint the row dividers
  for (int i=rowHeight; i<r.height; i+=rowHeight) {
      g.drawLine(0, i, r.width, i);
    }
    // paint the column dividers
    for (int i=columnWidth; i<r.width; i+=columnWidth) {
      g.drawLine(i, rowHeight, i, r.height);
    }
```

Handling current events

The applet has four buttons and a label for communicating with the user of the Web page. To handle button presses and mouse clicks, you need an `ActionListener` and a `MouseListener`. The applet class implements both of these interfaces. If you copy the `monthCanvas` class and install it in another applet, you need to put similar event-handling code in the new applet. For example, if you create an ExpenseAccount applet, you must add the code you see below to the `ExpenseAccount` class, along with any other code for handling other action events. See Chapter 5 and Chapter 9 for models of how to handle events with various combinations of Listener interfaces.

```
/** CalendarApplet handles two kinds of events:
 *    1) button clicks which increment or decrement
 *    the current month
 *    2) mouse clicks on a given screen location
 */
public void actionPerformed(
    java.awt.event.ActionEvent event) {

    if (event.getSource() == prevYear) {
      monthCanvas.decrementYear();
    }
    else if (event.getSource() == prevMonth) {
      monthCanvas.decrementMonth();
    }
    else if (event.getSource() == nextMonth) {
```

```
        monthCanvas.incrementMonth();
    }
    else if (event.getSource() == nextYear) {
        monthCanvas.incrementYear();
    }
    else if (event.getSource() == monthCanvas) {
    }
}


// MouseListener interface:
public void mouseClicked(java.awt.event.MouseEvent me) {
    Calendar d =
    monthCanvas.positionToDate(me.getX(), me.getY());
    selectLabel.setText("Selected: " +
    DateFormat.getDateInstance().format(d.getTime()));
}


public void mousePressed(java.awt.event.MouseEvent me) {
}


public void mouseReleased(java.awt.event.MouseEvent me) {
}


public void mouseEntered(java.awt.event.MouseEvent me) {
}


public void mouseExited(java.awt.event.MouseEvent me) {
}

}
```

Do you have a calendar?

The basic work of the CalendarApplet requires calculations with dates.
You need to calculate on which day of the week a particular date falls and to
determine whether the year is a leap year. Or you need to get someone else
to do it for you.

Fortunately, the Java utility package for Java 2 includes a Date class and a
GregorianCalendar class, and the java.text package contains a
SimpleDateFormat class. These tools do most of what you want. The Date
class keeps track of a moment in time, measured in milliseconds.

Beware Java dates

The Java `Date` class counts milliseconds since 12 a.m. January 1, 1970. A date in this form is very precise, but it is a very big number. Rumor has it that some folks at Bell Labs know why 1970 was selected as the beginning of computer time. We don't.

The basic Java `Date` class is fine for many purposes, but for many others, you need to use a Calendar class to translate Java dates into something human computer users understand. In Java 1.0, the tools for handling dates are much more limited than in Java 1.1 and Java 2. Keep this in mind as you read Java 1.0 code. You are likely to see home-brew solutions that are no longer necessary.

The `Date` class provides the following methods:

- ✔ `getTime(long)` — This function provides the current value of a date.
- ✔ `setTime(long)` — This function sets the current value of a date.

`GregorianCalendar` class translates time (remember, it's in milliseconds) into more useful everyday units of measure, such as months and days. For example:

```
curDate.get(Calendar.MONTH);
curDate.get(Calendar.DATE);
curDate.get(Calendar.DAY_OF_WEEK));
```

Finally, `SimpleDateFormat` handles putting dates into text strings that you can write onscreen.

```
SimpleDateFormat formatter = new SimpleDateFormat
("MMMMyyyy");
String dateString = formatter.format(curDate.getTime());
```

Labeling the dates

To label the dates:

1. Record the current time and the name of the current month:

```
tmpDate.setTime(curDate.getTime());
int curMonth = curDate.get(Calendar.MONTH);
```

2. Find the first day of the week.

The applet needs to know which column is the right place to begin putting in dates. That is, the applet needs to know what day of the week is the first of the month. This code locates the first day in the month and then backs up the date counter to whatever date is the Sunday before the first of the month.

```
curDate.add(Calendar.DATE,-(curDate.get(Calendar.DATE)));
curDate.add(Calendar.DATE, -(curDate.get(Calendar.DAY_OF_WEEK))+1);
```

3. Paint the date for each day.

Nested for loops go through the cells of the calendar, painting the dates as they go. Note that dates outside the current month are skipped:

```
//paint the dates
//for each row...
    for (int row=1; row<ROWS; row++) {
//for each column...
    for (int column=0; column<COLUMNS; column++) {
      if (curDate.get(Calendar.MONTH) == curMonth) {
/* Write the date.  Convert the integer date to a string by concatenating it
   with "" */
        g.drawString(   ("" + curDate.get(Calendar.DATE)),
          (column * columnWidth) + 3,
          (row * rowHeight) + (rowHeight / 2) );
        }
        curDate.add(Calendar.DATE, 1); //?
      }
    }
```

The Complete and Unexpurgated Code

In this section, we give you the complete code for the applet class and each of the other classes it uses that are not part of the standard Java Class Library.

Calendar applet

```
/**     CalendarApplet - an applet to demonstrate
 * the MonthCanvas component.
 * MonthCanvas displays a calendar-style interface to dates.
 * @version  0.3, 13 Apr 1997
```

(continued)

(continued)

```java
* &copy; 1996 by <a href="http://www.isc.com/">
* ISC Consultants Inc.</a>, all rights reserved.
*/
import java.applet.Applet;
import java.awt.*;
import java.awt.event.ActionListener;
import java.awt.event.MouseListener;
import java.util.*;
import java.lang.*;
import java.text.*;

/** A simple applet that demonstrates the Calendar class */
public class CalendarApplet extends Applet
      implements ActionListener, MouseListener {

    private MonthCanvas monthCanvas = null;
    private Button prevYear = null;
    private Button prevMonth = null;
    private Button nextMonth = null;
    private Button nextYear = null;
    private Label selectLabel =
                          new Label("No Date Selected");

    public void init() {
      int height = Integer.parseInt(getParameter("height"));
      int width = Integer.parseInt(getParameter("width"));
      monthCanvas = new MonthCanvas(width,height-60);
      monthCanvas.addMouseListener(this);
      add(monthCanvas);

      prevYear = new Button(" << ");
      prevYear.addActionListener(this);
      add(prevYear);

      prevMonth = new Button(" < ");
      add(prevMonth);
      prevMonth.addActionListener(this);

      nextMonth = new Button(" > ");
      add(nextMonth);
      nextMonth.addActionListener(this);

        nextYear = new Button(" >> ");
      add(nextYear);
```

```
        nextYear.addActionListener(this);

      add(selectLabel);
   }


   /** CalendarApplet handles two kinds of events:
    *   1) button clicks which increment or decrement
    *       the current month
    *   2) mouse clicks on a given screen location
    */
   public void actionPerformed(
           java.awt.event.ActionEvent event) {

      if (event.getSource() == prevYear) {
         monthCanvas.decrementYear();
      }
      else if (event.getSource() == prevMonth) {
         monthCanvas.decrementMonth();
      }
      else if (event.getSource() == nextMonth) {
         monthCanvas.incrementMonth();
      }
      else if (event.getSource() == nextYear) {
         monthCanvas.incrementYear();
      }
      else if (event.getSource() == monthCanvas) {
      }
   }


// MouseListener interface:
public void mouseClicked(java.awt.event.MouseEvent me) {
   Calendar d =
      monthCanvas.positionToDate(me.getX(), me.getY());
   selectLabel.setText("Selected: " +
      DateFormat.getDateInstance().format(d.getTime()));
}


public void mousePressed(java.awt.event.MouseEvent me) {
}


public void mouseReleased(java.awt.event.MouseEvent me) {
}
```

(continued)

(continued)

```
public void mouseEntered(java.awt.event.MouseEvent me) {
}

public void mouseExited(java.awt.event.MouseEvent me) {
}

}
```

MonthCanvas *class*

```
/** MonthCanvas is a component to display dates with
*    a calendar-style interface.
*/
class MonthCanvas extends Canvas {

    final static byte ROWS = 7; // rows in calendar
    final static byte COLUMNS = 7; // columns in calendar

    private Calendar curDate = new GregorianCalendar();
    private Calendar tmpDate = new GregorianCalendar();

    // date of the first Sunday (possibly from the
    // preceding month) in this calendar view
    private Calendar firstDayInCalendarView =
                                new GregorianCalendar();
    private int rowHeight;
    private int columnWidth;
    private Rectangle r;
    private Dimension dimension = new Dimension(150,150);

    public MonthCanvas() {
        initialize();
    }

    public MonthCanvas(int width, int height) {
        setBounds(0,0,width,height);
        initialize();
    }
```

```
/** all constructors call this initialization routine */
private void initialize() {
    setBackground(Color.white);
    setForeground(Color.gray);
    r = getBounds();
    columnWidth = r.width / COLUMNS;
    rowHeight = r.height / ROWS;

    // resize so that columns and rows fit evenly
    setBounds( 0, 0, (columnWidth * COLUMNS),
                     (rowHeight * ROWS));
    r = getBounds();

    // save the height and width as a Dimension for
    // use by getPreferredSize() and getMinimumSize()
    dimension.width = r.width;
    dimension.height = r.height;

}

public void incrementMonth() {
    curDate.add(Calendar.MONTH,1);
    repaint();
}

public void decrementMonth() {
    curDate.add(Calendar.MONTH,-1);
    repaint();
}

public void incrementYear() {
    curDate.add(Calendar.YEAR,1);
    repaint();
}

public void decrementYear() {
    curDate.add(Calendar.YEAR,-1);
    repaint();
}

public void paint(Graphics g) {
```

(continued)

(continued)

```
        // paint the row dividers
        for (int i=rowHeight; i<r.height; i+=rowHeight) {
            g.drawLine(0, i, r.width, i);
        }

        // paint the column dividers
        for (int i=columnWidth; i<r.width; i+=columnWidth){
            g.drawLine(i, rowHeight, i, r.height);
        }

        // paint the month name
        SimpleDateFormat formatter =
                    new SimpleDateFormat ("MMMM yyyy");
        String dateString =
                    formatter.format(curDate.getTime());
        g.drawString(dateString, 10, (rowHeight/2));

        // find the 1st (Sun)day in this calendar view
        tmpDate.setTime(curDate.getTime());
        int curMonth = curDate.get(Calendar.MONTH);
        curDate.add(Calendar.DATE,
                -(curDate.get(Calendar.DATE)));
        curDate.add(Calendar.DATE,
                -(curDate.get(Calendar.DAY_OF_WEEK))+1);
        firstDayInCalendarView.setTime(curDate.getTime());

        // paint the dates
        // for each row...
        for (int row=1; row<ROWS; row++) {
          // for each column...
          for (int column=0; column<COLUMNS; column++) {
            if (curDate.get(Calendar.MONTH) == curMonth) {
                g.drawString(
                    ("" + curDate.get(Calendar.DATE)),
                        (column * columnWidth) + 3,
                    (row * rowHeight) + (rowHeight / 2));
            }
            curDate.add(Calendar.DATE, 1);
          }
        }

        // restore the date
```

```
            curDate.setTime(tmpDate.getTime());
    }


    /** returns the date corresponding to a
     *   position (x and y coordinate) in the
     *   current calendar view
     */
    public Calendar positionToDate(int x, int y) {
       int column = x / columnWidth;
       int row = (y / rowHeight) - 1;
       Calendar returnDate = new GregorianCalendar();
       returnDate.setTime(firstDayInCalendarView.getTime());
       returnDate.add(Calendar.DATE,
                          (row * COLUMNS) + column);
       return returnDate;
    }


    /** Return the calendar's preferred size */
    public Dimension getPreferredSize() {
        return dimension;
    }


    /** Return the calendar's minimum size */
    public Dimension getMinimumSize() {
        return dimension;
    }
}
```

Finishing Touches

Two methods that you ought to implement before you set your applet loose
on the world are the following:

> ✔ String[][] getParameterInfo() — This method documents
> your classes' parameters. The [][] that you see tells you that
> getParameterInfo() returns a two-dimensional array of strings.
> We tell you more about arrays, Thing [0] and Thing [1], in Chapter 9.
> Put simply, getParameterInfo() returns the name, type, and descrip-
> tion of each HTML page parameter that your applet understands. Look
> at this sample implementation:

```
    String[][] getParameterInfo() {
 String parameterInfo[][] = {
 // name    type   description
         "volume",    "1-100",  "how many fish",
         "speed", "1-10",  "swimming speed",
         "hunger", "boolean",  "are the fish hungry?"
                      };
 return parameterInfo;
 }
```

✔ `String getAppletInfo( )` — This method is intended to provide information about the author, version, and copyright of the applet. Another sample implementation:

```
String getAppletInfo() {
String appletInfo = "FishTank, v2.0, by Robert Ahab";
return appletInfo;
 }
```

You can invoke `getAppletInfo( )` and `getParameterInfo( )` from the applet viewer menu.

Controlling the color

Now that plain gray Web pages are giving way to a variety of colors, Web designers appreciate having control over an applet's color. This control is a nice touch that's easy to implement using an applet parameter.

The HTML document that references your applet may look like this:

```
<HTML>
<HEAD><TITLE>Testing Color Settings</TITLE></HEAD>
<BODY bgcolor=#0000FF >
<APPLET class=FishTank.class height=100 width=100 >
<PARAM name=bgcolor value=#0000FF >
</APPLET>
</BODY>
</HTML>
```

The `<BODY>` tag uses the (not yet standard) `bgcolor` parameter to set the Web page background to the color blue. The value #0000FF is the hexadecimal number representing blue. Keeping with convention, you provide the FishTank applet with a `bgcolor` parameter as well. As you can see, the Web designer wants to set the applet background to match the Web page background.

This next snippet of code illustrates how to fetch the applet parameter and set the background color:

```
int bgcolor = Integer.valueOf(getParameter("bgcolor"));
setBackground(new Color(bgcolor));
```

Commenting about comments

If Java is your first programming language, now is a great time to develop some good programming habits. Get in the habit of writing programs for people, not for computers. Strive to write code that's easy to read and understand.

Making your programs easy to understand is so important that Java provides three ways to denote comments in your code, as illustrated here:

/* */	This comment style, which is familiar to C programmers, can span multiple lines.
//	This style, as in C++, runs until the end of the line.
/** */	Use this style for text that you want to appear in automatically generated documentation.

No performance penalty occurs for using comments in Java. The compiler strips comments from your code when it generates the class file.

You can't nest /* */ comments in Java. In other words, you can't place one /* */ comment inside another. The only time that you're likely to be annoyed by this is when you want to temporarily disable, or *comment out,* a block of code that contains comments.

That third style of comment (/**), as we mention previously, deserves further discussion. The Java Developer's Kit (JDK) includes a simple documentation tool, called Javadoc, that can help you document your classes. Javadoc parses declarations and specially marked comments from your Java code files and generates reference documents in HTML format. Consider the following snippet of code from the Button class:

```
/** A class that produces a labeled button component.
@version  1.16 08/17/95
@author   Sami Shaio
*/
public class Button extends Component {
```

Figure 11-3 shows a portion of the corresponding HTML page generated by Javadoc.

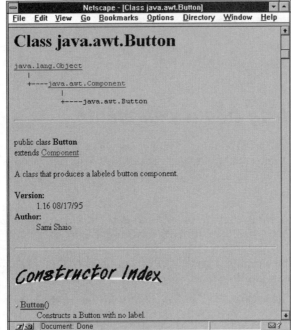

Besides showing an inheritance diagram, Javadoc displays a class's public and protected methods along with any documentation comments that appear in the code. The special tags @version and @author, when used in a documentation comment, are displayed as you see in the figure.

Chapter 12

A Ticker Tape Class

● ●

In This Chapter

▶ Making a minimal ticker tape

▶ Getting files from a remote server

▶ Dealing with exceptional occurrences

▶ Working with threads

● ●

*I*n this chapter, you build an applet that fetches the contents of a text file and displays it in a scrolling ticker tape. The contents of the text file can be the bargain special of the hour, today's cafeteria menu, the local weather report, or anything else you'd like.

To build this applet, you need to know how to open and read a file and how to paint scrolling text onscreen. As with the `Calendar` component in Chapter 11, we *subclass* (that is, we derive characteristics of) the `TickerTape` class from the `Canvas` class.

I/O, I/O, into the Streams We Go

I/O is shorthand for Input/Output, which is programmer-speak for getting data in and out of programs. We've already shown you some very important kinds of input: key presses and mouse clicks. And we told you how to work with output to the screen in the form of the Java `paint()` method. (See Chapters 5 and 8.)

Some common places to which you can send data (output) or from which you can fetch data (input) include

✔ A file on your DOS PC disk

✔ A tape drive on your UNIX machine

✔ A Web server on the Internet

We're sure that you can think of many other examples. (We're also sure that, in a few years, you'll find storage devices and network server programs of which you haven't even dreamt.) From the application programmer's point of view, data sources and data links are all the same. You either want to write data or read data, and you'd rather not be bothered with the differences between files, network connections, tape drives, keyboards, and so on. In other words, you don't care how many cylinders the car has, you simply want it to start when you turn the ignition key.

Streams provide the abstraction you seek. That is, the `Streams` classes provide a common way of accessing various I/O devices, whether these devices are files, network connections, keyboards, or something else. To open and read a file, our code uses several of the `Streams` classes: `InputStream`, `DataInputStream`, and `BufferedInputStream`.

Fetching a File from the Server

The data source for the ticker tape applet is a plain text file residing in the same directory as the applet. The message in this plain text file is the message displayed on the ticker tape. The text file could be on your local directory, on a company Web server — or anywhere you can get to with your Web browser. Fetching a file is surprisingly easy. Include the code fragment that follows in your applet to fetch a file; we go over the code in detail in the next section.

```
private final static char URLSeparator = '/';
private String messageFile = "message.txt";

/** fetch the message file into a string */
private String fetchMessageString() {

    String messageString = new String();

    // construct the URL of the message file
    String urlString = getDocumentBase().toString();
    urlString =urlString.substring(0,urlString.
    lastIndexOf(URLSeparator))
        + URLSeparator + messageFile;

    // fetch the message file
    try {
        URL url = new URL(urlString);
        InputStream inStream = url.openStream();
        BufferedReader dataStream =
```

```
            new BufferedReader(new InputStreamReader(inStream));
            // stuff the message into messageString
            String inLine = null;
            while ((inLine = dataStream.readLine()) != null) {
                messageString += inLine;
            }
        }
    catch(MalformedURLException e) { // catch bad URLs
        showStatus("Invalid URL: " + urlString);
    }
    catch(IOException e) { // catch IO errors
        showStatus("Error " + e);
    }
    return messageString;
}
```

Examining the parts

Now we want to look at the various parts of the code. Near the beginning of the code you just looked at, you find a useful method worth remembering — `Applet.getDocumentBase()`.

This method returns the URL of the HTML file that includes your applet. We use `getDocumentBase()` to construct the URL of a file called *message.txt*, which is in the same directory as the HTML file (your Document Base).

If you want to ensure that an applet can be run only from a particular Web page, you can put a test in your code that looks something like this:

```
final String myURLString = "http://www.mycompany.com/ mypage.html";
        if (getDocumentBase().toString().equals
            (myURLString) == false) {
    showStatus("Please run this applet from " +
        myURLString);
}
else {
    runMyApplet();
}
```

The `getDocumentBase()` method has a close cousin with which you should also become familiar — `Applet.getCodeBase()`.

This method returns the URL of your applet's class file (your Code Base).

Opening the input text file

If you return to the example code, you notice some blocks of code labeled try and catch. We explain try and catch in a moment, but first, you need to open the input text file:

```
URL url = new URL(urlString);
InputStream inStream = url.openStream();
BufferedReader dataStream = new BufferedReader(new
InputStreamReader(inStream));
// stuff the message into messageString
String inLine = null;
while ((inLine = dataStream.readLine()) != null) {
    messageString += inLine;
}
```

These few preceding lines of code open a network connection, fetch the text file over the Internet (or from the local file system), and put the file contents in the String variable messageString. That's a lot of work for such a small amount of code.

The URL class provides an object wrapper for a valid Internet URL. The methods getProtocol( ), getFile( ), getHost( ), and getPort( ) return the different parts of the URL. The method openStream( ), which you use in the code, opens a network connection to the URL. openStream( ) returns an InputStream, which in itself is not very useful. With an InputStream, however, we can create an InputStreamReader and then a BufferedReader. And a BufferedReader lets you read the contents of the URL. Here's how you do it:

✔ First, use InputStream to instantiate an InputStreamReader.

✔ Then, use the InputStreamReader to instantiate a BufferedReader.

The BufferedReader has two important advantages over a plain old InputStreamReader. Instead of reading from the file at each read request, which can be relatively slow, the BufferedInputStream reads big chunks of text into memory and services subsequent read requests from this memory image. Also, BufferedInputStream provides you with the handy method readLine( ), which reads an entire line of text at once.

Because the Ticker Tape applet is most likely used to display short messages, using BufferedReader is not really necessary. In more typical situations, however, you may be reading larger files and may want to follow the example we provide.

If you've ever had the pleasure of writing network programs in the past, you'll be impressed by the simplicity and power of Java's networking classes. Java includes — in the package `java.net` — a group of powerful, yet easy-to-use, networking classes that makes building Internet applications easier than ever before.

Handling Exceptional Occurrences

Next we want to discuss exceptional occurrences; that is, we want to talk about `try` and `catch`. (We said we'd get back to them!) These constructs of the Java language are intended to help you deal cleanly with those errors that commonly occur while your program is running. Perhaps your program fails to establish a network connection, or a user enters an invalid filename. Java's approach to dealing with errors — which is the same as in C++ and Delphi — is called *exception handling*. Exception handling enables you to expect the best and prepare for the worst. You may read example code such as this:

```
try
    to construct a valid URL from the variable named
        urlString
    to open a buffered input stream to the URL
    to read the contents of the URL into the variable named
        messageString
catch the exceptional condition when the URL is invalid
catch the exceptional condition when we cannot open and
read the file
```

Exception handling is a robust and fairly easy-to-use idiom for dealing with errors. The implementation of exception handling can also be confusing. For now, we explain just what you need as a beginning Java programmer.

Some of the more useful Java classes handle error conditions by *throwing an exception*. When you use a method that throws an exception, you're required to provide a way to *catch* that exception. Even as a beginner, you need to know enough about exception handling so that you can make good use of classes — such as `URL`, `InputStream`, and `Thread` — that throw exceptions.

The constructor declaration for the `URL` class looks like this:

```
public URL(String spec) throws MalformedURLException
```

Notice that this method *throws* a particular exception named
MalformedURLException. As you may guess from the name, the exceptional circumstance that MalformedURLException refers to happens when
you try to construct a URL with a string that can't possibly be a valid URL. In
order to use this method, we have to provide a catch for the
MalformedURLException. The following code shows how:

```
try    {
        URL url = new URL(urlString);
}
catch(MalformedURLException e) {
        showStatus("Invalid URL: " + urlString);
}
```

If the urlString parameter contains a valid URL, such as http://
www.idgbooks.com/, then showStatus() isn't called. If, on the other hand,
urlString contains some nonsense, such as *hohoho,* showStatus()
displays the message Invalid URL: hohoho.

Exception handling is an advanced topic. For now, just be careful to follow
the examples we give you and include try and catch code blocks when we
use them with certain Java classes.

Running Your Tasks by a Thread

As you type away at your computer, perhaps a clock program discreetly
displays the current time in a corner of your screen. With every passing
second, the clock program redraws itself, or at least, redisplays the time in
the corner of your screen. A clock program is a handy utility. But if this
utility prevents you from doing other work, it would be pretty useless. After
all, if you just wanted to tell time, you would buy a clock instead of a computer.

Fortunately, your computer system can handle multiple tasks at once. You
can crunch numbers in your spreadsheet, listen to music on your
computer's CD player, and download your e-mail from the Internet all at the
same time.

Just as we like our computers to run more than one program at a time, we
often like our programs to handle more than one task at a time. For example,
a word processor should prepare output for the printer without interrupting
your typing. Your Web browser should display text and accept mouse clicks
even while it's still busy downloading that 100K picture of your company's CEO.

In Java, we can run separate tasks in separate threads of execution, or simply, *threads*. The next code is an example of a thread:

```
     class MyExample extends Canvas implements Runnable {
  private Thread thread;
  private boolean isRunning = false;
// constructor
  public MyExample() {
     thread = null;
  }
// methods
  public void start() {
     if (thread == null) {
        thread = new Thread(this);
     }
     isRunning = true;
     thread.start();
  }


  public void run() {
     while (isRunning) {
           doTheWork();
           try { Thread.sleep(sleepTime); }
           catch(InterruptedException e) {
                 /* don't do anything */ }
     }
  }


  public void stop() {
     if((thread != null) & thread.isAlive()) {
        thread.stop();
        isRunning = false;
        thread = null;
     }
  }
}
```

The class in the preceding code implements the Runnable interface (see Chapter 8 for more about interfaces), which provides the basic plumbing we use to run some code in its own thread.

All the preceding code is a framework around the method doTheWork() — just a made-up name for this example. This framework sets up doTheWork() to run as a separate thread. When run as a thread, this specific method can share computer resources with other tasks in a way that may be managed by the applet programmer, the browser, and the operating system. For example, the applet programmer can tell the thread to sleep for some milliseconds every iteration of the code, or the programmer can assign the thread a priority relative to other activities of the computer.

The heart of the setup for a thread is one method, run(), which is invoked by the run-time system whenever the computer yields time for this thread to perform its work. Besides the actual doTheWork() activity, the run() method must include try and catch blocks such as the ones we show you in the sample code.

If the run-time system yields time to some other thread, our thread catches an InterruptedException. We don't take any action when our thread is interrupted in the preceding code, and action isn't generally needed. But we are required to provide code to catch the exception, even when we don't do anything with it.

The start() and stop() methods are housekeeping activities used to make sure that a thread doesn't become duplicated in computer memory and take up computing resources unnecessarily. The start() method checks to make sure that the thread isn't already running. The stop() method eliminates all references to the thread that we instantiated by setting the thread to null, thus enabling the run-time system to reclaim the resource.

The Complete and Unexpurgated Code

The following is the complete code for the applet class and the TickerTape class that it uses. To use this applet as it is written, you must have a file (named *message.txt*) that contains the desired message and is located in the same directory as the applet class file. Figure 12-1 shows what the Ticker Tape applet looks like on a Web page. Remember, in real life, the message scrolls across the screen.

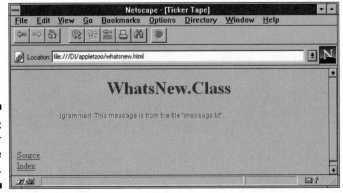

Figure 12-1:
The Ticker
Tape
applet.

```
/**
* @version  0.3, 13 Apr 1997
* &copy; 1996 by <a href="http://www.isc.com/">
* ISC Consultants Inc.</a>, all rights reserved.
*/

import java.awt.*;
import java.applet.Applet;
import java.net.*;
import java.io.*;

/** TickerApplet */
public class TickerApplet extends Applet {

  private final static char URLSeparator = '/';
  private String messageFile = "message.txt";
  private TickerTape tickerTape = new TickerTape();

  /** fetch Message String */
  private String fetchMessageString() {
    String messageString = new String();
    // construct the URL of the message file
    String urlString = getCodeBase().toString();
    urlString = urlString.substring( 0,
                  urlString.lastIndexOf( URLSeparator))
                + URLSeparator + messageFile;
    // fetch the message file
    try {
      URL url = new URL(urlString);
      InputStream inStream = url.openStream();
      BufferedReader dataStream =
        new BufferedReader(new InputStreamReader(inStream));
      // stuff the message into messageString
      String inLine = null;
      while ((inLine = dataStream.readLine()) != null){
        messageString += inLine;
      }
    }
    catch(MalformedURLException e) { // catch bad URLs
      showStatus("Invalid URL: " + urlString);
    }
    catch(IOException e) { // catch IO errors
      showStatus("Error " + e);
```

(continued)

(continued)

```
    }
    return messageString;
  }

  /** init */
  public void init() {
    add(tickerTape);
    tickerTape.setText( fetchMessageString());
  }

  /** start */
  public void start() {
    tickerTape.start();
  }

  /** stop */
  public void stop() {
    tickerTape.stop();
  }
}


/* TickerTape class */
class TickerTape extends Canvas implements Runnable {

    private Dimension preferredDimension =
                                  new Dimension(400,10);
    private int messageWidth;
    private int messageX;
    private int messageY;
    private int currentX;
    private int sleepyTime = 50;
    private int scrollStep = 2;
    private final static int INSET = 2;
    private String messageString = "Default Message";
    private Thread thread;
    private boolean isRunning = false;

    /** constructor */
    public TickerTape() {
        thread = null;
        setBackground(Color.blue);
```

```
        setForeground(Color.white);
        setFont(new Font("TimesRoman", Font.BOLD, 14));
    }

    /** run */
    public void run() {
        while (isRunning) {
            scroll();
            try {
                Thread.sleep(sleepyTime);
            }
            catch(InterruptedException e) {
                // caught an exception
            }
        }
        thread = null;
    }

    /** stop */
    public void stop() {
        if((thread != null) & thread.isAlive())
            isRunning = false;
    }

    /** start */
    public void start() {
        setSize(preferredDimension);
        messageX = getBounds().width;
if (thread == null) {
            thread = new Thread(this);
            thread.setPriority(Thread.MIN_PRIORITY);
        }
        isRunning = true;
        thread.start();
    }

    /**scroll*/
    private void scroll() {
        // if the message has scrolled off the edge
        // of the canvas, wrap it around
        if(messageX < (-messageWidth)) {
            messageX = getBounds().width ;
        }
```

(continued)

(continued)

```
        else {
            messageX = messageX - scrollStep;
        }
        repaint();
    }


    /**setext*/
    public void setText(String s) {
        messageString = new String(s);
        FontMetrics fontMetrics =
                    getGraphics().getFontMetrics();
        messageWidth =
                    fontMetrics.stringWidth(messageString);
        messageY = fontMetrics.getHeight() -
                    fontMetrics.getDescent() + INSET;
        preferredDimension.height = fontMetrics.getHeight()
                                    + (INSET * 2);
    }


    /** Return the Ticker's preferred size */
    public Dimension getPreferredSize() {
        return preferredDimension;
    }


    /** Return the Ticker's minimum size */
    public Dimension getMinimumSize() {
        return preferredDimension;
    }


    /**paint*/
    public final void paint(Graphics g) {
        g.drawString(messageString,messageX,messageY);
    }
}
```

Chapter 13

Sprites: Faster Than a Speeding Rabbit

In This Chapter

▶ Programming strategy for making a simple sprite

▶ Working with arrays

▶ Using double buffering

▶ Getting faster code with final methods

*S*prite is a generic term for an image that you can move around the screen independently of the other elements on the screen. Sprites are typically an important element of graphical computer games or animations. A sprite object is an elegant example of how object-oriented programming enables you to reuse code.

When you run the applet represented by this chapter's code sample, you see bouncing squares and someone else bouncing around, also. See Figure 13-1 for a look at our sprites. Each sprite object has the following properties:

✔ A direction or *heading*

✔ A speed

✔ An image

In this chapter, we show you how to create a Sprite class. Then we show you how to use sprite objects in a simple applet that you can easily modify to try different techniques. In Chapter 15, we use the same sprite objects to create a more complicated simulation game.

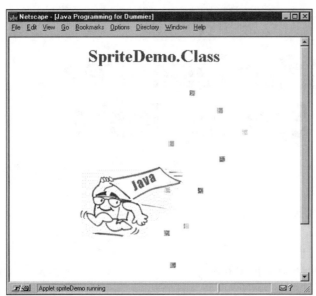

Figure 13-1:
Sprites.

The Strategy for Displaying Moving Graphics

You can see how to make words move onscreen in Chapter 12. But a picture is worth a thousand words, they say. So here is the word on how to make pictures move.

Avoiding screen flicker

When you build an applet that involves displaying a moving component onscreen, such as the Ticker Tape applet in Chapter 12, you need to consider the issue of screen flicker. Depending on your computer system, the ticker tape may blink unpleasantly as the message moves across the screen. You can do something about this flicker. The flicker exists because the `update()` method of onscreen display sets the entire component region to the current background color before calling `paint()` to draw the component from scratch. If this process takes enough time, you see the component blink with each call to `paint()`, resulting in a flickering effect.

The component's default `update()` method looks like this:

```
public void update(Graphics g) {
//fill the onscreen graphics region with the current
//background color
    g.setColor(getBackground());
    g.fillRect(0, 0, width, height);
//call paint to render the component from scratch
    g.setColor(getForeground());
    paint(g);
}
```

Using the preceding algorithm can result in pretty obnoxious screen flickering, especially if your applet paints itself frequently. For the Ticker Tape applet, we left in the flicker to avoid complicating the code.

But for a sprite, whose purpose is to provide smooth animations, we have to do a better job of eliminating screen flicker. The best way to reduce flickering is through a technique called *double buffering*. See what you think of this idea: Instead of clearing and painting the onscreen image, you do all your dirty work offscreen on a scratch pad. Then in one efficient step, you copy the completed offscreen scratch pad to your visible onscreen workspace.

Following is a code snippet for the double-buffering process:

```
//create a scratch pad the same size as our onscreen
//image
    Image scratchPad = createImage(this.size().width, this.size().height);
//get a Graphics object for our scratch pad
    Graphics scratchPadGraphics = scratchPad.getGraphics();
    public final void update(Graphics g) {
//paint to our off-screen scratch pad - the messy stuff
//happens here
        paint(scratchPadGraphics);
//copy our scratch pad to the screen
        g.drawImage(scratchPad,0,0,null);
}
```

Instead of drawing directly to the screen, the double-buffering version of `update()` passes the scratch pad to `paint()`. When the `paint()` method completes its work, `update()` copies the finished image from the scratch pad to the screen.

As a final touch, you declare your `update()` method to be *final*. And because final methods can't be inherited, Java doesn't have to figure out which `update()` method to call at runtime. The compiler can take advantage of this preknowledge to generate code that runs slightly faster (or as the programmers simply say, *faster code*).

If you intend for a method not to be inherited, declare it *final* by including the word `final` after `public` in the declaration statement. Making this declaration enforces your intentions and provides the bonus of slightly faster code.

Displaying graphics files

Displaying graphics files is very simple in Java. The next code segment shows how your applet loads the picture `joe.gif`, residing in the same directory as the applet class file:

```
img = getImage(getCodeBase(), "joe.gif");
```

Then you can draw the image by placing the following line in the `paint()` method:

```
g.drawImage(img, x, y, null);
```

In the preceding code, the `img` parameter is an image object and `x` and `y` are the coordinates where the image is to appear onscreen. (The fourth parameter, which is null in this case, enables you to declare something called an `ImageObserver` object that collects data about the downloading of images. We won't go into the advanced topic of `ImageObservers` here.) So the code boils down to specifying what image and where.

That's really all there is to it!

Bouncing the image around

How do you make the drawn images bounce around onscreen? You need to test for where the sprite is onscreen and then change the sprite's direction if it's at an edge of the applet's onscreen space. The following code shows the method for testing the sprite's location:

```
// check for boundary bounce conditions
            if (contains ((int)demoSprites[i].positionX,
                    (int)demoSprites[i].positionY)) {
            if (((demoSprites[i].positionX -
                demoSprites[i].width/2) <= 0) ||
                ((demoSprites[i].positionX +
                demoSprites[i].width/2) >= getSize().width))
            demoSprites[i].bounceVertical();
            if (((demoSprites[i].positionY -
                demoSprites[i].height/2) <= 0) ||
```

```
                    ((demoSprites[i].positionY +
                      demoSprites[i].height/2) >= getSize().height))
                    demoSprites[i].bounceHorizontal();
              }
       }
```

And this next code shows how to change the sprite's direction; that is, the `bounce` methods:

```
       }
public void bounceVertical() {
       direction = (0 - direction) % 360;
    }
}
```

If you want the sprites in your application to do something other than bounce (explode, come in the opposite side of the applet window, or whatever) you can modify this code.

The Complete and Unexpurgated Code

You find two components to this code — a `Sprite` class and an applet that uses `Sprite` objects. The following is the complete code for the `Sprite` class. Please don't miss the comments and explanations that we include in the midst of this code!

```
/** Sprite class allows you to create moving objects on the screen */
class Sprite extends Panel {
    //constants that can be used outside the class
    final static int NORTH = 180;
    final static int SOUTH = 0;
    final static int WEST = 270;
    final static int EAST = 90;
    final static int MAXSPEED = 12;

    //constants accessible only to children of the class
    protected final static int DELTA = 4;
    protected final static int DEFAULTSIZE = 10;

    //some geometrical information
    float positionX = DEFAULTSIZE;
    float positionY = DEFAULTSIZE;
```

(continued)

(continued)

```
    float width = 0;
    float height = 0;
    protected double speed = 0;
    protected float radius = 0;
    protected int direction = SOUTH; //in degrees from SOUTH

    //everything else
    protected boolean isMoving = false;
    protected Image myImage = null;

    /**
     * protected constructor is only accessible to derived classes
     * derived class is expected to set myImage and dimensions
     */
    protected Sprite() {}

    /** this constructor creates a default graphical representation */
    Sprite (Component c) {
        myImage = c.createImage(DEFAULTSIZE, DEFAULTSIZE);
        Graphics gr;
        gr = myImage.getGraphics();
        gr.setColor(Color.red);
        gr.fillRect(0, 0, DEFAULTSIZE, DEFAULTSIZE);
        setDimensions();
    }
*/

  protected Image myImage = null;
  /**
   * protected constructor is only accessible to derived     * classes
   * derived class is expected to set myImage and
       * dimensions
   */
  protected Sprite() {}
  /** this constructor creates a default graphical     * representation
   */
  Sprite (Component c) {
     myImage = c.createImage(DEFAULTSIZE, DEFAULTSIZE);
     Graphics gr;
     gr = myImage.getGraphics();
     gr.setColor(Color.red);
     gr.fillRect(0, 0, DEFAULTSIZE, DEFAULTSIZE);
     setDimensions();
  }
```

As you can see, the default appearance of a sprite is a red square 10 x 10 pixels. (DEFAULTSIZE has a value of 10.) Not very interesting. Also, you see that myImage is the offscreen scratch pad used to implement double buffering. The heading (the sprite's direction) can be specified in degrees or, as a convenience, using the NORTH, SOUTH, EAST, and WEST constants.

Apply these direction constants (NORTH, SOUTH, EAST, and WEST) as if you're looking at the computer screen as a road map. That is, NORTH is toward the top of the screen, SOUTH is toward the bottom of the screen, and so on.

```
/** this constructor accepts an image to be used for drawing Sprite on screen */
    Sprite (Image img) {
        myImage = img;
        setDimensions();
    }


    /**
     * this constructor accepts an image to be used for drawing Sprite on screen
     * and its coordinates
     */
    Sprite (Image img, int posX, int posY) {
        myImage = img;
        positionX = posX;
        positionY = posY;
        setDimensions();
    }
```

The following code makes the sprite move.

```
/** sets the direction of Sprite */
    public void heading (int dir) {
        direction = dir;
    }


    /** sets the speed between 1 and MAXSPEED */
    public void setSpeed (double sp) {
        if ((sp >= 1) && (sp <= MAXSPEED)) {
            speed = sp;
        }
    }


    /** causes the Sprite to move */
    public void startMovement () {
        isMoving = true;
    }
```

(continued)

(continued)

```java
/** causes the Sprite to stop moving */
public void stopMovement () {
    isMoving = false;
}


/** tick method is called by parent on every time tick.
 * it moves the Sprite along its direction if necessary
 */
public void tick () {
    if ((isMoving) && (speed > 0)){
        positionX += ((float)speed / MAXSPEED) * DELTA *
                    Math.sin((2 * Math.PI * direction) / 360);
        positionY += ((float)speed / MAXSPEED) * DELTA *
                    Math.cos((2 * Math.PI * direction) / 360);
    }
}


/** causes the Sprite to bounce off the vertical wall */
public void bounceVertical() {
    direction = (0 - direction) % 360;
}


/** causes the Sprite to bounce off the horizontal wall */
public void bounceHorizontal() {
    direction = (180 - direction) % 360;
}


public void paint(Graphics g) {
    g.drawImage(myImage, (int)(positionX - width/2),
                (int)(positionY - height/2), null);
}


protected void setDimensions() {
    // wait until image is loaded
    while (myImage.getHeight(this) == -1) {
    }
    width = myImage.getWidth(this);
    height = myImage.getHeight(this);
    radius = (float) (Math.sqrt(Math.pow(height, 2) + Math.pow(width, 2)) / 2);
}
}
```

What's going on here? Java's image-handling classes are smart enough that they don't keep you waiting while they download a potentially large image from a potentially slow data source. Instead, when you request an image, the Java classes start loading the image in a separate thread (see the Chapter 12 discussion about threads) and let you continue with your work.

```
(float)speed / MAXSPEED) * DELTA *
            Math.cos((2 * Math.PI * direction) / 360);
    }
  }
  /** causes the Sprite to bounce off the vertical wall */
  public void bounceVertical() {
    direction = (0 - direction) % 360;
  }
  /** causes the Sprite to bounce off the horizontal wall */
  public void bounceHorizontal() {
    direction = (180 - direction) % 360;
  }
/** causes the Sprite to bounce off the horizontal wall */
  public void paint(Graphics g) {
    g.drawImage(myImage, (int)(positionX - width/2),
        (int)(positionY - height/2), null);
  }
```

One sprite alone is not that much fun. But this next class, the SpriteDemo applet, uses sprites to create a little excitement.

```
import java.awt.*;
import java.applet.*;
import java.lang.*;
/**
 * This applet demonstrates Sprite objects
   @version 1.2, 5/29/98
   @author <a href="mailto:anatoly@isc.com">Anatoly Goroshnik</a>
 */
public class SpriteDemo extends Applet implements Runnable {
    final int quantum = 10;
    final int numSprites = 11;
    final boolean showTraces = false;

    Image offScreenImage = null;
    Graphics offScreenGraphics = null;
    Dimension offScreenSize = null;
```

(continued)

(continued)

```
Thread demo;
Sprite demoSprites[] = new Sprite[numSprites];

private boolean run = true;

public void init() {
    Image img = null;

    showStatus("loading images...");

    /* load the first Sprite image */
    img = getImage(getDocumentBase(), "dan.gif");
    demoSprites[0] = new Sprite(img, 100, getSize().height - 100);
    demoSprites[0].heading(150);
    demoSprites[0].setSpeed(9);
    demoSprites[0].startMovement();

    /* load the rest of the Sprite images */
    for (int i = 1; i < numSprites; i++) {
        img = getImage(getDocumentBase(), "image" + i + ".gif");
        demoSprites[i] = new Sprite(img, 10, 10);
        demoSprites[i].heading(Sprite.EAST - i * 5);
        demoSprites[i].setSpeed(3+i*0.9);
        demoSprites[i].startMovement();
    }

    showStatus("");
}

public void run() {
    while (run) {

        for (int i = 0; i < numSprites; i++) {
            demoSprites[i].tick();
            // check for boundary bounce conditions
            if (contains ((int)demoSprites[i].positionX,
                    (int)demoSprites[i].positionY)) {
                if (((demoSprites[i].positionX -
                    demoSprites[i].width/2) <= 0) ||
                    ((demoSprites[i].positionX +
                    demoSprites[i].width/2) >= getSize().width))
                    demoSprites[i].bounceVertical();
```

```
                    if (((demoSprites[i].positionY -
                        demoSprites[i].height/2) <= 0) ||
                        ((demoSprites[i].positionY +
                        demoSprites[i].height/2) >= getSize().height))
                        demoSprites[i].bounceHorizontal();
                }
            }

        update(getGraphics());
        try {
            Thread.sleep(quantum);
        } catch (InterruptedException e) {
            break;
        }
    }
}

public void start() {
    demo = new Thread(this); // create a new thread
    run = true;   // make sure the thread will loop until we want to stop it
    demo.start(); // start demo thread, run() will be called
}

public void stop() {
    run = false; // stop demo thread
    demo = null; // make demo thread a candidate for garbage collection
}

public final void update(Graphics g) {
  //implements no-flicker graphics
    Dimension dim = getSize();
    if ((offScreenImage==null) ||
      (dim.width != offScreenSize.width) ||
      (dim.height != offScreenSize.height)) {
        offScreenImage = createImage(dim.width, dim.height);
        offScreenSize = dim;
        offScreenGraphics = offScreenImage.getGraphics();
        if (showTraces)
            offScreenGraphics.clearRect(0, 0, offScreenSize.width,
                                    offScreenSize.height);
    }
    if (!showTraces)
        offScreenGraphics.clearRect(0, 0, offScreenSize.width,
```

(continued)

(continued)

```
                                                 offScreenSize.height);
        paint(offScreenGraphics);
        g.drawImage(offScreenImage,0,0,null);
    }


    public void paint(Graphics g) {
       for (int i = 0; i < numSprites; i++) {
          demoSprites[i].paint(g);
       }
    }

}import java.awt.*;
import java.applet.*;
import java.lang.*;
/**
 */
images...");
emoSprites[0].startMovement();
        /* load the rest of the Sprite images */
    for (int i = 1; i < numSprites; i++) {
       img = getImage(getDocumentBase(), "image" + i + ".gif");
       demoSprites[i] = new Sprite(img, 10, 10);
       demoSprites[i].heading(Sprite.EAST - i * 5);
       demoSprites[i].setSpeed(3+i*0.9);
       demoSprites[i].startMovement();
    }
    showStatus("");
}
  public void run() {
    while (true) {
      for (int i = 0; i < numSprites; i++) {
        demoSprites[i].tick();
        // check for boundary bounce conditions
        if (contains ((int)demoSprites[i].positionX,
            (int)demoSprites[i].positionY)) {
          if (((demoSprites[i].positionX -
             demoSprites[i].width/2) <= 0) ||
             ((demoSprites[i].positionX +
             demoSprites[i].width/2) >= getSize().width))
             demoSprites[i].bounceVertical();
          if (((demoSprites[i].positionY -
             demoSprites[i].height/2) <= 0) ||
             ((demoSprites[i].positionY +
             demoSprites[i].height/2) >= getSize().height))
```

```
            demoSprites[i].bounceHorizontal();
        }
    }
    update(getGraphics());
    try {
        Thread.sleep(quantum);
    } catch (InterruptedException e) {
        break;
    }
  }
}
public void start() {

(continued)
    demo = new Thread(this);
    demo.start();
}
public void stop() {
    demo.stop();
    demo = null;
}
public final void update(Graphics theG) {
    //implements no-flicker graphis
        Dimension dim = getSize();
        if((offScreenImage==null) ||
    (dim.width != offScreenSize.width) ||
    (dim.height != offScreenSize.height)) {
        offScreenImage = createImage(dim.width,
            dim.height);
        offScreenSize = dim;
        offScreenGraphics = offScreenImage.getGraphics();
        if (showTraces)
        offScreenGraphics.clearRect(0. 0.
            offScreenSize.width,offScreenSize.height);
        }
        if (!showTraces)
    offScreenGraphics.clearRect(0. 0.        offScreenSize.width.
            offScreenSize.height);
        paint(offScreenGraphics);
        theG.drawImage(offScreenImage,0,0,null);
}
public void paint(Graphics g) {
    for (int i = 0; i < numSprites; i++) {
        demoSprites[i].paint(g);
    }
  }
}
}
```

If You Want to Do It Yourself . . .

If you want to move your own pictures around on the screen, the preceding Sprite applet can do the trick for you. You need to change the `getImage()` call in the applet's `init()` method to load your own image file.

The `showTraces` variable controls whether the image leaves behind a trail. (Figure 13-2 shows some sprites with trails.) What's happening, of course, is that turning on `showTraces` prevents the sprite from clearing the screen between each tick (or appearance of onscreen movement).

You may also want to change the variable `quantum`, which controls the frequency of ticks (you can think of this frequency as a measure of frames-per-second). The `heading()` method enables you to set the sprite's direction. We build on the `Sprite` class in the JavaBots sample in Chapter 14.

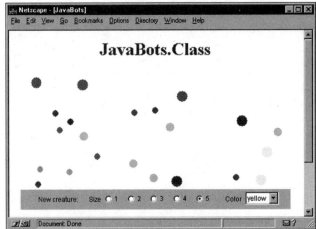

Figure 13-2:
Sprites
leaving
trails.

Chapter 14

JavaBots: Let the Wild Rumpus Begin!

In This Chapter

▶ Tracking your objects with vectors

▶ Holding your objects with arrays

▶ Guiding your objects' behavior with a random number generator

▶ Supporting the JavaBots with the `Runnable` interface

*T*his is a meaty chapter. In this chapter, we show you examples of many of the techniques that you've seen so far — and you'll see a few new tricks! A lot is in here, so you may want go over the examples in this chapter more than once.

We use the simple `Sprite` class that's explained in Chapter 13 to create a virtual world in which colorful little creatures multiply, move about, and devour each other. We use some old friends along the way, including `if`, `for`, `while`, `switch`, threads, exceptions, and double buffering. If you can master this chapter, you are well on your way to becoming a bona fide Java nerd. If you feel a sudden craving for strong coffee and pizza, don't worry — it's only natural.

The Wild Rumpus

This applet creates a game of life. The world of the applet is populated with sprites like our mutual friends from Chapter 13. But now, we extend the sprites to give them a life of their own.

The behavior of *Creatures* is much more complex than the behavior of simple sprites.

🖍 These Creature sprites come in a variety of sizes.

🖍 They come in five colors.

✔ There are two sexes.

✔ Creature sprites grow as they get older.

✔ Eventually, when their age becomes equal to their lifespan, the Creature sprites die.

✔ They may get hungry. A larger, hungry Creature sprite that bumps into a smaller sprite will eat it.

✔ If two Creature sprites of different sexes above the age of puberty bump into each other, a new sprite may be born (randomly).

✔ If both Creature sprites survive an encounter, the speed of the bouncing sprites is related to their relative size.

To give users a chance to participate in the fun, they can add a creature of any given color and size to the rumpus by clicking on the applet in the area of the sprite world.

This is not a fully finished game. We would be very interested to see how you complete and polish this game. If you send us a version that really impresses us, we'll post it on the *Java Programming For Dummies* resource page at www.isc.com.

Figure 14-1 shows what our version looks like onscreen.

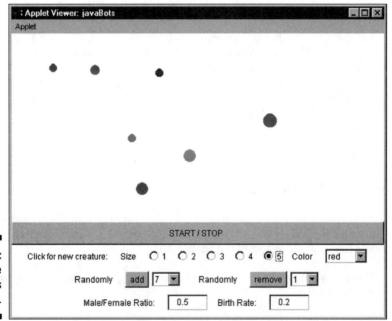

Figure 14-1:
The
JavaBots
have a riot.

The Man behind the Screen

Most of the tricks used to make this applet work were also used in earlier chapters. The `Runnable` interface, arrays, and `Math.random` appear in those chapters, but a word or two (or even three) of review is in order. *Vectors* are a new programming tool that you may not have heard of before. Vectors enable you to keep track of large and variable collections of objects (such as the creatures of this applet).

Up and running JavaBots

Like the sprite demo in Chapter 13, the applet that you examine in this chapter, JavaBots, implements the `Runnable` interface to make a class that can perform work in its own thread. Usually, you use a thread when your class is performing some ongoing, noncritical work, such as playing an animation or displaying the current time. In JavaBots, you continuously paint colorful circles that move around the playing area. You don't need to monopolize all the power of the computer to perform this work, so you run it in a thread.

A `Runnable` class must have a `run()` method, which is usually where the action takes place. JavaBots is no exception. We take a look at the JavaBots `run()` method later in this chapter. For now, review the basic structure of a typical implementation:

```
final static int PAUSE_LENGTH = 100;
public void run() {
    while (true) {
        myDoTheWorkMethod(); // do your work here
        try {
            Thread.sleep(PAUSE_LENGTH);
        } catch (InterruptedException e) {
            break;
        }
    }
}
```

The system calls `run()` whenever this class's thread can perform its work. `run()` calls `myDoTheWorkMethod()` — an arbitrary method that we made up, which does whatever work you need to do — and pauses for `PAUSE_LENGTH` milliseconds. To pass control to another thread, the system may interrupt the thread, causing an `InterruptedException`, which breaks out of the `while(true)` loop.

Give that programmer arrays!

In Chapter 9, we discuss *arrays,* which are handy data structures for holding a predetermined number of similar objects. Instead of making 100 string variables — `myString1`, `myString2`, and so on — arrays let you write the following:

```
final int MAX_STRINGS = 100;
// get space for MAX_STRINGS strings
String[] myStrings = new String[MAX_STRINGS];
// fill the array with MAX_STRINGS strings
for (int i=0; i < MAX_STRINGS; i++) {
    myStrings[i] = new String("string #" + i);
}
// now myStrings[0] is "string #0", myStrings[1] is
// "string #1", and so on.
```

Arrays are so convenient that they are a standard feature of nearly every programming language. Java arrays are a special kind of object (though this is not apparent) and are endowed with more smarts than you may think. Consider what would happen if the user entered 250 in the following code snippet:

```
String[] myStrings = new String[100];
// get space for 100 strings
int index = getNumberFromUser();
// get a number from the user
myNewString = myStrings[index];
```

Because `myStrings` has 100 elements, the valid values for `index` are the numbers from 0 to 99. If the user enters 250, a Java array throws an `ArrayIndexOutOfBoundsException`, which you can catch like any other exception:

```
try {
    myNewString = myStrings[index];
}
catch (ArrayIndexOutOfBoundsException e) {
    // do something about the invalid index;
    // for example, display an error message
}
```

Arrays also have a single variable, `length`, which you can inspect but not change:

```
/* get space for 100 strings */
String[] myStrings = new String[100];
/* the following line displays:
 "myStrings can hold up to 100 strings" */
showStatus("myStrings can hold up to " + myStrings.length +  "strings");
```

Vectors

Arrays are the ideal tool when you need to store a known number of similar objects. As you tackle complex Java applets, however, you sometimes don't know ahead of time how many objects you have to store.

Suppose that you've written a custom Web browser. Whenever you load a Web page, you want to create a list of all the URLs found on that Web page. A Web page can hold any number of URLs. You can construct an array to hold, say, 100 URLs, but preparing for the maximum case that you rarely, if ever, encounter is inefficient. It's the programming equivalent of cooking dinner for 30 people on the off chance that all your friends drop by for dinner. Inevitably, you run into a Web page with more than 100 URLs, and a number of your friends bring along close companions that you didn't know about.

You need more flexibility. Java provides a close cousin of the array, which gives you more flexibility — this cousin is the *vector*.

The Vector class, found in the java.util package, is a turbo-charged array. Vectors can hold any kind of Java object. (Remember, every class in Java is ultimately descended from the Object class.) Unlike arrays, vectors can grow to accommodate your requirements. This code snippet adds an arbitrary number of strings to a Vector object:

```
// Vector is in the java.util package
import java.util.*;
Vector myStrings = new Vector();
//get some unknown number of strings from the user...
while ((inputString = myGetStringMethod()) != null) {
    // add the string to the vector
    myStrings.addElement(inputString);
}
```

You don't need to worry about the size of the vector. You simply call addElement() for each string that the user enters. Table 14-1 lists some important methods of the Vector class:

Table 14-1	Vector Methods
Method	*Purpose*
`addElement (Object)`	Adds the specified object as the last element of the vector
`setElementAt(Object, int)`	Sets the element at the specified index to be the specified object
`elementAt(int)`	Returns the element at the specified index
`indexOf(Object)`	Searches for the specified object, starting from the first position, and returns an index to it
`contains(Object)`	Returns `true` if the specified object is a value of the collection
`removeAllElements()`	Removes all elements of the vector
`size()`	Returns the number of elements that you have stored in the vector
`elements()`	Returns an enumeration of the elements; use the `Enumeration` methods on the returned object to fetch the elements sequentially

The `elements()` method is worth looking at closely. Whenever you need to do something with every element in the class, you should use the `elements()` method. The `elements()` method returns an enumeration, whose sole purpose is to simplify working with items in a vector. The `Enumeration` interface has just two methods: `hasMoreElements()`, which returns `true` or `false`, and `nextElement()`, which returns a generic `Object`. The enumeration is a very useful tool, but the code to use it requires some unfamiliar forms.

The following code to print out all the strings in a vector is a model to follow when you use enumeration.

```
for (Enumeration e = myStrings.elements() ;
e.hasMoreElements() ;) {
    s = (String) e.nextElement();
    g.drawString(s);
}
```

Notice two special features about the preceding code snippet: the expression `(String) e.nextElement()`, which is called a *cast,* and the `for` loop, which has a nonstandard form.

- **The cast:** A structure that identifies the class of an object or converts it to a new type. A vector can contain objects of more than one class. Java doesn't know what subclass of `Object nextElement()` is unless *you* tell Java. By putting the class name in parentheses in front of the call to `nextElement()`, you tell Java what kind of object it's dealing with (see the second line of the code snippet).

- **The nonstandard `for` loop:** In the preceding code snippet, the nonstandard `for` loop has these characteristics:

   - The initialization statement `Enumeration e = myStrings.elements` is not a counter, it just instantiates the enumeration.

   - The loop contains a test — `e.hasMoreElements()`.

   - No increment statement at all is present inside the parentheses of the `for` statement.

What assures that the applet eventually exits from the loop is the `nextElement()` statement inside the loop. You see examples of this nonstandard `for` loop for enumerations in a variety of applets, in this book and elsewhere.

You can use arrays to store primitive types — `int`, `float`, `boolean`, and so on — or any kind of object. Vectors, on the other hand, can hold only Java objects. If you want to store primitive types in a vector, you must first wrap them in the appropriate object, such as this:

```
Integer myInt = new Integer (n)
```

Random behavior generating a color

In the beginning of this chapter, we said that you can create a virtual world in which colorful little creatures multiply, move about, and devour each other. How does that world look without a little random behavior? Chances are, it looks pretty dull. When programmers say *random,* they mean *unpredictable.* And a completely predictable world holds no surprises.

To add a little spice to things, the creatures in your virtual world have a random initial speed, a random initial color, and a random initial sex. If two compatible creatures meet, they may spawn children — or they may not; it's unpredictable.

The technique for producing each of these unpredictable behaviors is the same: You start with a random number. Coming up with good ways to generate random numbers is a fascinating and important area of computer science, you may be surprised to find out. It's a lot trickier than you may think. Fortunately, we are standing on the shoulders of giants. Java provides two ways to generate random numbers: the class `Random` in the `java.util` package, and the static method `random()` in the `java.lang.Math` package. In JavaBots, you use the static method `random()`, which is simple to use. The `random()` method returns a random number between 0.0 and 1.0.

To generate a random color, you can use the following code snippet:

```
Color(  (int)(Math.random() * 255),
        (int)(Math.random() * 255),
        (int)(Math.random() * 255))
```

The preceding `Color` constructor takes three parameters: the amount of red, the amount of green, and the amount of blue. By multiplying the random number by 255, you ensure that your values are between 0 and 255, which is what the `Color` constructor requires. (By the way, 255 is the highest number that can fit in 8 bits. That's why you often see 255 as an upper limit for a parameter.)

The Complete and Unexpurgated Code

Here is the complete code for the applet class and each of the other classes it uses that are not part of the standard Java Class Library. (By the way, you can find a copy of this applet on the CD-ROM at the back of the book. If you want to see it run or experiment with modifying it, you don't need to type all the code yourself. If you decide to write your own HTML page, use the tag `<applet code="JavaBots" width=550 height=400> </applet>` to start with.)

Notice that the code starts with some documentation.

```
/** Framework for artificial life simulations

        At present there is only one class for producing
    creatures. It is straightforward to derive new creature
    classes from it and change their behavior (handling
    of messages) and life patterns.
    The creature class is derived from the sprite class
```

which takes care of basic movement. The sprite class
has a static member object which handles output to the
screen. This is done in an object-oriented "model/view"
way, by using the Java mechanism of Observer and
Observable. To add new types of events to the system
more constants should be defined in sysEvent class and
corresponding handlers should be added to the
handleSysEvent function in the controller.
The controller handles interactions between creatures
when a collision occurs.

User Interface Instructions:
1. Add creatures to the system by either adding
   creatures randomly (select number of new creatures
   and press "add" button) or manually by clicking mouse
   on ecosystem area (select size and color
   beforehand).
2. Select Male/Female ratio and birth rate
   (between 0 and 1).
3. Press "START/STOP" button.

Creatures can be randomly removed while the simulation
is running. To randomly remove creatures select number
and press the "remove" button.

The Male/Female ratio and birth rate can only be changed
when the simulation is stopped.

At present creatures follow these rules:
1. Bounce off the walls of ecoSystem
2. Periodically grow
3. Die when too old
4. Get hungry from time to time
5. When hungry, bigger creature eats smaller one whenever
   there is a collision
6. Otherwise, creatures bounce off each other when there
   is a collision
7. When adults of different genders collide they might
   (randomly) give birth to a new creature

@version 1.2, 5/30/98
@author <A HREF="mailto:anatoly@isc.com">Anatoly Goroshnik</A>
*/

The first chunk of code declares a number of variables. If you look closely, you see three arrays: sizes[], stringColors[], and colorColors[]. You also see two vectors: creatureList and sysEventList.

```java
import java.awt.*;
import java.awt.event.*;
import java.applet.*;
import java.lang.*;
import java.util.*;

public class JavaBots extends Applet
            implements Runnable, ActionListener {
    // millisecs to pause between ticks
    final int PAUSE_LENGTH = 10;
    // do sprites show trail?
    final boolean SHOW_TRAIL = false;

    //variables for double-buffered painting...
    Image offScreenImage = null;
    Graphics offScreenGraphics = null;
    Dimension offScreenSize = null;

    //user interface objects
    Panel controlPanel = new Panel();
    Panel ecoSystem = new Panel();
    CheckboxGroup creatureSize = new CheckboxGroup();
    Checkbox sizes[] = new Checkbox[Creature.MAXSIZE];
    Choice creatureColor = new Choice();
    Button startStop = new Button("START / STOP");
    Button addButton = new Button("add");
    Button removeButton = new Button("remove");
    Choice addChoice = new Choice();
    Choice removeChoice = new Choice();
    TextField mfRatField =
        new TextField(" " + Creature.MFRAT + " ");
    TextField bRatField =
        new TextField(" " + Creature.BIRTH_RATE + " ");

    //array of color choices
    String stringColors[] =
        {"red", "green", "blue", "yellow", "black"};
    Color colorColors[] =
        {Color.red, Color.green, Color.blue,
         Color.yellow, Color.black};
```

```
Vector creatureList =
    new Vector(); //a dynamic array of creatures
Vector sysEventList =
    new Vector(); //a dynamic array of future events
Thread mainThread; //main thread
int males = 0;
int females = 0;
boolean isRunning = false;
```

An inner class is a class that lives inside another class, so that it becomes the private tool of the class that contains it. The BotMouseAdapter class you see here is an inner class defined inside of the JavaBots applet class. It appears inside the braces that begin and end the code for the applet. When you compile your code, you find that a class file named JavaBots1$Bot1MouseAdapter has been created. If you were to paste the same code inside of another class, for example, a class named Wiz, you would find another class file, Wiz$BotMouseAdapter. Each inner class works only for its particular owner.

An Adapter is a programmers' shortcut tool for writing a Listener. An Adapter is an abstract class that consists of empty versions of all the methods necessary to meet the requirements of a given Listener interface. MouseAdapter has methods to meet all the requirements of the MouseListener interface. If you want to save the trouble of writing empty methods for situations that are not of interest to your program, you can say extends MouseAdapter, instead of implements MouseListener. Then you are excused from the need to write methods for mouseEntered, mouseExited, and so on when you only need a mouseClicked method for your purposes. Here, the programmer decided to save a few lines of typing and used a MouseAdapter.

```
class BotMouseAdapter extends MouseAdapter {
    public void mouseClicked (MouseEvent e) {
        int size = Integer.parseInt(
            creatureSize.getSelectedCheckbox().getLabel(),
            10);
        Color col =
            colorColors[creatureColor.getSelectedIndex()];
        sysEventList.addElement(
            new sysEvent(sysEvent.GIVE_BIRTH,
            new Creature(ecoSystem, size, col,
            e.getX(), e.getY())));
        handleSysEvents();
        //update screen
        update(ecoSystem.getGraphics());
    }
```

In the `init` method, you create the user interface controls and fill the `ecoSystem` with an initial population of creatures. Note how the creatures are tracked in the vector `creatureList`.

```
public void init() {
        //create user interface
        setLayout(new BorderLayout());

        Panel newCreature = new Panel();
        newCreature.add(
            new Label("Click for new creature:"));
        newCreature.add(new Label("Size"));
        for (int i = 0; i < Creature.MAXSIZE; i++)
            if (i == 0)
                newCreature.add(new Checkbox ((i+1) + "",
                            creatureSize, true));
            else
                newCreature.add(new Checkbox ((i+1) + "",
                            creatureSize, false));
        for (int i = 0; i < stringColors.length; i++)
            creatureColor.addItem(stringColors[i]);
        newCreature.add(new Label("Color"));
        newCreature.add(creatureColor);

        Panel moreControls = new Panel();
        moreControls.add(new Label("Randomly"));
        moreControls.add(addButton);
        for (int i = 1; i <= 10; i++)
            addChoice.addItem("" + i);
        moreControls.add(addChoice);
        moreControls.add(new Label("        Randomly"));
        moreControls.add(removeButton);
        for (int i = 1; i <= 10; i++)
            removeChoice.addItem("" + i);
        moreControls.add(removeChoice);

        mfRatField.setEditable(true);
        bRatField.setEditable(true);
        Panel lifeControls = new Panel();
        lifeControls.add(new Label("Male/Female Ratio:"));
        lifeControls.add(mfRatField);
        lifeControls.add(new Label("   Birth Rate:"));
        lifeControls.add(bRatField);
```

```
controlPanel.setLayout(new GridLayout(4, 1));
controlPanel.add(startStop);
controlPanel.add(newCreature);
controlPanel.add(moreControls);
controlPanel.add(lifeControls);

add("South", controlPanel);
add("Center", ecoSystem);
Creature.sysEventList = sysEventList;

ecoSystem.addMouseListener (new BotMouseAdapter());
startStop.addActionListener (this);
addButton.addActionListener (this);
removeButton.addActionListener (this);

update(ecoSystem.getGraphics()); //update screen
}
```

The `run` method is where you check regularly for collisions and their consequences in the form of `sysEvents`. It's also where you update the display.

In this code, we use an enumeration. You see `(Creature)` in front of references to the enumeration. This *cast*, as programmers refer to the naming structure, notifies the computer that the objects in this particular enumeration must be handled with the methods of the `Creature` class. Without the additional information provided by the cast, the computer would have available only generic `Object` class methods.

```
public void run() {
    while (isRunning) {
        handleSysEvents(); //process all events
        for (Enumeration e = creatureList.elements();
            e.hasMoreElements() ; ) {
            //let creature know that clock had ticked
            ((Creature)(e.nextElement())).tick();
        }
        //check for collisions
        for (int i = 0; i < creatureList.size() ; i++) {
            for (int j = i + 1; j < creatureList.size() ; j++) {
                checkCollision(
                    (Creature) creatureList.elementAt(i),
                    (Creature) creatureList.elementAt(j));
            }
```

(continued)

(continued)

```
        }
        update(ecoSystem.getGraphics()); //update screen
        try {
            //wait for the next clock tick
            Thread.sleep(PAUSE_LENGTH);
        } catch (InterruptedException e) {
            break;
        }
    }
}


public void stop() {
    if (mainThread != null) {
        //mainThread.stop();
        isRunning = false;
        mainThread = null;
    }
}
```

The update method implements double buffering, which we talk about in Chapter 13.

```
public final void update(Graphics g){
    //implements no-flicker graphics using double buffering
    Dimension dim = getSize();
    if((offScreenImage == null) ||
        (dim.width != offScreenSize.width) ||
        (dim.height != offScreenSize.height)) {
        offScreenImage =
        createImage(dim.width, dim.height);
        offScreenSize = dim;
        offScreenGraphics = offScreenImage.getGraphics();
        if (SHOW_TRAIL)
            offScreenGraphics.clearRect(0, 0,
            offScreenSize.width, offScreenSize.height);
    }
    if (!SHOW_TRAIL)
    offScreenGraphics.clearRect(0, 0,
            offScreenSize.width, offScreenSize.height);
    paint(offScreenGraphics);
    g.drawImage(offScreenImage, 0, 0, null);
}
```

Here is an example of using the Enumeration interface to go through all the elements of a vector:

```
public void paint(Graphics g) {
//ask creature to paint itself on screen
for (Enumeration e = creatureList.elements();
            e.hasMoreElements() ; ) {
   ((Creature)(e.nextElement())).paint(g);
}
showStatus("Number of creatures: " + (males+females)
        + " Males: " + males
        + " Females: " + females
        + " Status: "
        + (isRunning?"running":"stopped"));
}
```

This is where the ActionListener interface is implemented.

```
public void actionPerformed (ActionEvent e) {
    String arg = e.getActionCommand();

    if ("START / STOP".equals (arg))
     startStop();
    else if ("add".equals (arg))
     addCreatures(Integer.parseInt(
        addChoice.getSelectedItem()));
    else if ("remove".equals(arg))
     removeCreatures(Integer.parseInt(
        removeChoice.getSelectedItem()));
 }
```

The handleSysEvents method is the place where you manage the life cycle of the creatures. This is very heavy stuff, fraught with philosophical implications, as you can see from even a brief glance at the code!

```
void handleSysEvents() {
    // handle ecoSystem events
    sysEvent evt = null;

    for (Enumeration e = sysEventList.elements();
                e.hasMoreElements() ; ) {
       evt = (sysEvent) e.nextElement();
       switch (evt.action) {
          case sysEvent.KILL:
```

(continued)

(continued)

```
                        //remove creature from the list
                        creatureList.removeElement(evt.subject);
                        if (evt.subject.gender == Creature.MALE)
                                males--;
                        else
                                females--;
                        break;
                    case sysEvent.GIVE_BIRTH:
                        //add creature to the list
                        creatureList.addElement(evt.subject);
                        if (evt.subject.gender == Creature.MALE)
                                males++;
                        else
                                females++;
                        break;
                    case sysEvent.GROW:
                        //increase creature size
                        evt.subject.grow();
                        break;
                    case sysEvent.BOUNCE:
                        //bounce creatures off each other
                        bounce(evt.subject, evt.subject2);
                        break;
                    case sysEvent.EAT:
                        //satisfy the hunger
                        evt.subject.eat(evt.subject2);
                        break;
                    /* handle new actions here */
            }
        }
    sysEventList.removeAllElements();
}


void addCreatures(int num) {
    //populate our ecoSystem
    for (int i = 0; i < num; i++) {
        sysEventList.addElement(
            new sysEvent (sysEvent.GIVE_BIRTH,
                new Creature (ecoSystem,
                    (int) (Math.random() *
                            (Creature.MAXSIZE - 1) + 1),
                new Color ((int)(Math.random() * 255),
```

```
                            (int) (Math.random() * 255),
                            (int) (Math.random() * 255)),
                    (int) (Math.random() * 500),
                    (int) (Math.random() * 250))));
        }
    handleSysEvents();
    update(ecoSystem.getGraphics()); //update screen
}


void removeCreatures(int num) {
    for (int i = 0; i < num; i++)
        if (creatureList.size() > 0) {
            sysEventList.addElement(
                new sysEvent(sysEvent.KILL,
                (Creature) creatureList.elementAt(
                    (int)(Math.random()*creatureList.size()))));
                handleSysEvents();
        }
    update(ecoSystem.getGraphics()); //update screen
}


void startStop() {
    if (isRunning) {
        //mainThread.stop();
        isRunning = false;
        mfRatField.setEditable(true);
        bRatField.setEditable(true);
        mainThread = null;
    }
    else {
        Creature.MFRAT =
            new Double(mfRatField.getText()).doubleValue();
        Creature.BIRTH_RATE =
            new Double(bRatField.getText()).doubleValue();
        mfRatField.setEditable(false);
        bRatField.setEditable(false);
        isRunning = true;
        mainThread = new Thread(this);
        mainThread.start();
    }
    update(ecoSystem.getGraphics()); //update screen
}
}
```

When two creatures meet, a little drama ensues. Does one creature perish? Is a new creature born, or does each creature just bounce away in its separate direction? Here is your opportunity to change the laws of nature.

```
void checkCollision(Creature firstCreature,
                    Creature secondCreature) {
    double  d = dist(secondCreature.positionX,
                    firstCreature.positionX,
                    secondCreature.positionY,
                    firstCreature.positionY);
    boolean allIsWell = true;

    if (d <= (secondCreature.radius + firstCreature.radius)) {
        if (secondCreature.size == firstCreature.size)
            sysEventList.addElement(
                new sysEvent(sysEvent.BOUNCE,
                    firstCreature, secondCreature));
        else { //is anybody hungry?
            if (secondCreature.size > firstCreature.size) {
                //secondCreature wins
                if (secondCreature.isHungry()) {
                    sysEventList.addElement(
                    new sysEvent(sysEvent.EAT,
                        secondCreature, firstCreature));
                    allIsWell = false;
                }
                else
                    sysEventList.addElement(
                    new sysEvent(sysEvent.BOUNCE,
                        firstCreature, secondCreature));
            }
            else { //firstCreature wins
                if (firstCreature.isHungry()) {
                    sysEventList.addElement(
                    new sysEvent(sysEvent.EAT,
                        firstCreature, secondCreature));
                    allIsWell = false;
                }
                else
                    sysEventList.addElement(
                    new sysEvent(sysEvent.BOUNCE,
                        firstCreature, secondCreature));
            }
        }
```

```
            //give birth?
            if ((secondCreature.gender != firstCreature.gender) &&
                (Math.random() < Creature.BIRTH_RATE) &&
                (secondCreature.isAdult()) &&
                (firstCreature.isAdult()) && allIsWell) {
                    // color of a new creature is a mixture of
                    // colors of its parents
                    Color col = new Color(
                        (int)((secondCreature.color.getRed() +
                            firstCreature.color.getRed()) / 2),
                        (int)((secondCreature.color.getGreen() +
                            firstCreature.color.getGreen()) / 2),
                        (int)((secondCreature.color.getBlue() +
                            firstCreature.color.getBlue()) / 2));
                    sysEventList.addElement(
                        new sysEvent(sysEvent.GIVE_BIRTH,
                        new Creature(ecoSystem, 1, col,
                            (int)(secondCreature.positionX +
                                secondCreature.radius),
                            (int)(secondCreature.positionY +
                                secondCreature.radius))));

                    secondCreature.justGaveBirth();
                    firstCreature.justGaveBirth();
                }
        }
    }
```

When creatures bounce, they obey Newton's laws of the conservation of mass and energy.

```
void bounce(Creature firstCreature,
            Creature secondCreature) {
    double massFirst =
        firstCreature.radius * firstCreature.radius;
    double massSecond =
        secondCreature.radius * secondCreature.radius;
    double speedFirst =
        (2 * massSecond * secondCreature.speed +
        (massFirst - massSecond) * firstCreature.speed) /
        (massSecond + massFirst);
    double speedSecond =
        (2 * massFirst * firstCreature.speed +
```

(continued)

(continued)

```
                (massSecond - massFirst) * secondCreature.speed) /
                (massSecond + massFirst);
        int combDir = (secondCreature.direction +
                        firstCreature.direction) / 2;
        double dist =
            dist(secondCreature.positionX,
                firstCreature.positionX,
                secondCreature.positionY,
                firstCreature.positionY);

        firstCreature.setSpeed(speedFirst);
        secondCreature.setSpeed(speedSecond);
        firstCreature.heading((combDir -
            (firstCreature.direction - combDir)) % 360);
        secondCreature.heading((combDir -
            (secondCreature.direction - combDir)) % 360);

        // remove firstCreature from zone of interference
        // with secondCreature
        firstCreature.positionX =
            (float)(secondCreature.positionX +
            ((secondCreature.radius + firstCreature.radius) *
            (firstCreature.positionX -
                secondCreature.positionX) / dist));
        firstCreature.positionY =
            (float)(secondCreature.positionY +
            ((secondCreature.radius + firstCreature.radius) *
            (firstCreature.positionY -
                secondCreature.positionY) / dist));
    }

    double dist(float x1, float x2, float y1, float y2) {
        return Math.sqrt((x1 - x2)*(x1 - x2) +
                    (y1 - y2)*(y1 - y2));
    }
}
```

The sprite class is an old friend of yours (we hope). The code is almost the same as in Chapter 13. We repeat it here to save some page-flipping, if you want to refer to it. To handle updates, we have made Sprite extend Observable and we have created a new class that implements the Observer interface. This separates the job of actually updating the onscreen image from that of calculating the sprite's behavior. As you read the code, you see that the Observable and Observed relationship are very similar to the relationship between a GUI object and a Listener.

```java
/** Sprite class allows to create moving objects
    on the screen.
*/
class Sprite extends Observable {
    //constants that can be used outside the class
    final static int NORTH = 180;
    final static int SOUTH = 0;
    final static int WEST = 270;
    final static int EAST = 90;
    final static int MAXSPEED = 12;

    protected final static int DELTA = 4;
    protected final static int DEFAULTSIZE = 10;
    private final static SpriteView view = new SpriteView();

    //some geometrical information
    float positionX = DEFAULTSIZE;
    float positionY = DEFAULTSIZE;
    protected double speed = 0;
    protected float radius = 0;
    protected int direction = SOUTH; //in degrees from SOUTH
    Color color = null;
    Panel environment = null;

    protected Sprite(Panel panel) {
        environment = panel;
        addObserver(view);
    }

    /** Sets the direction of sprite */
    public void heading (int dir) {
        direction = dir;
    }

    /** Sets the speed between 1 and MAXSPEED */
    public void setSpeed (double sp) {
        if ((sp >= 1) && (sp <= MAXSPEED))
            speed = sp;
    }
```

(continued)

(continued)

```
/** The tick method is called by our parent on every
    time tick. Here's where we it moves the sprite
    along its direction if necessary.
*/
public void tick () {
    if (speed > 0){
        positionX += ((float)speed / MAXSPEED) * DELTA *
            Math.sin((2 * Math.PI * direction) / 360);
        positionY += ((float)speed / MAXSPEED) * DELTA *
            Math.cos((2 * Math.PI * direction) / 360);
    }

    // check for boundary bounce conditions
    if ((positionX - radius) <= 0) {
        bounceVertical();
        positionX = radius;
    }
    if ((positionX + radius) >=
            environment.getSize().width) {
        bounceVertical();
        positionX = environment.getSize().width - radius;
    }
    if ((positionY - radius) <= 0) {
        bounceHorizontal();
        positionY = radius;
    }
    if ((positionY + radius) >=
            environment.getSize().height) {
        bounceHorizontal();
        positionY = environment.getSize().height - radius;
    }
}

/** Causes the sprite to bounce off the vertical wall */
public void bounceVertical() {
    direction = (0 - direction) % 360;
}

/** Causes the sprite to bounce off the horizontal wall */
public void bounceHorizontal() {
    direction = (180 - direction) % 360;
}
```

```
    public void paint(Graphics g) {
        setChanged();
        notifyObservers(g);
    }
}


/** a view class for sprite */
class SpriteView implements Observer {

    public void update(Observable o, Object arg) {
        Graphics g = (Graphics) arg;
        Sprite s = (Sprite) o;

        g.setColor(s.color);
        g.fillOval((int)(s.positionX - s.radius),
                   (int)(s.positionY - s.radius),
                   (int)(s.radius*2), (int)(s.radius*2));
    }
}
```

This next code builds on `Sprite` to add the new behaviors of creatures. Remember, creatures also inherit all the behavior of sprites. Experimenting with changing the constant values of BIRTH_RATE, PUBERTY_AGE, GROWTH_PERIOD, HAPPY_PERIOD, and LIFESPAN may be interesting. Or consider how you could set up several different species of creatures with different values for these constants. (***Hint:*** You could write one or more classes that inherit the behavior of `Creatures`.)

```
/** Creature class adds living organism properties to sprite. */
class Creature extends Sprite {
    final static int MAXSIZE = 5;
    final static int MALE = 2;
    final static int FEMALE = 3;
    final static int DEFAULTDIAMETER = 10;

    static double BIRTH_RATE = 0.2;
    static double MFRAT = 0.5;
    static int    PUBERTY_AGE = 100;
    // won't eat other creatures if happy
    static int    HAPPY_PERIOD = 200;
    static Vector sysEventList = null;

    int GROWTH_PERIOD = 2000;
    int LIFESPAN = 9999;
```

(continued)

(continued)

```
        int size = 0;
        int gender = (Math.random() > MFRAT) ? FEMALE : MALE;
        int age = 0;
        int last_happy = 0;

        Creature(Panel ecoSystem, int sz, Color col,
                                int posX, int posY) {
            super(ecoSystem);
            if ((sz >= 1) && (sz <= MAXSIZE))
                size = sz;
            else
                size = MAXSIZE;
            age = (size - 1) * GROWTH_PERIOD;
            feelingGood();
            radius = (DEFAULTDIAMETER + size*2) / 2;
            color = col;
            positionX = posX;
            positionY = posY;
            heading((int)(Math.random() * 359 + 1));
            setSpeed(MAXSPEED/size);
        }
```

Each time the clock ticks, the creatures grow older.

```
public void tick() {
        age++;

        //let sprite do whatever it finds useful first
        super.tick();

        //old creatures have to expire
        if (age > LIFESPAN) {
            sysEventList.addElement(
                new sysEvent(sysEvent.KILL, this));
        }

        //is it time to grow?
        if ((age % GROWTH_PERIOD) == 0)
            sysEventList.addElement(
                new sysEvent(sysEvent.GROW, this));
    }

public void paint(Graphics g) {
    super.paint(g);
    }
```

```
    public void grow() {
        Image img;

        if (size < MAXSIZE) {
            size++;
            radius = (DEFAULTDIAMETER + size*2) / 2;
//              setSpeed(MAXSPEED/size);
        }
    }
```

If you find violence disturbing, you may want to cover your eyes as you read this method.

```
public void eat(Creature victim) {
        // as we eat we acquire part of the victim color
        color = new Color(
            (int)((color.getRed() +
                victim.color.getRed()) / 2),
            (int)((color.getGreen() +
                victim.color.getGreen()) / 2),
            (int)((color.getBlue() +
                victim.color.getBlue()) / 2));
        sysEventList.addElement(new sysEvent(sysEvent.KILL, victim));
        feelingGood(); //food is good
    }

    public boolean isHungry() {
        //bigger creatures get hungry faster
        return ((age - last_happy) >
                (HAPPY_PERIOD * (MAXSIZE - size + 1)));
    }

    public boolean isAdult() {
        return (age > PUBERTY_AGE);
    }

    /**The following reason for feeling good is commented out, but you might want to
                remove the comment marking and see the effect*/
    public void justGaveBirth() {
        //feelingGood();

    }

    public void feelingGood() {
        last_happy = age;
    }
}
```

The following class is a good example of the way Java programmers package related bits of data into an object for safekeeping.

```java
/** sysEvent class, just a package to hold a
    creature-relevant event
*/
class sysEvent {
    final static int NOACTION    = 0;
    final static int KILL     = 1;
    final static int GIVE_BIRTH = 2;
    final static int GROW     = 3;
    final static int BOUNCE   = 4;
    final static int EAT      = 5;
    /* add new actions here */

    Creature subject = null;
    Creature subject2 = null;
    int action = 0;

    sysEvent(int a) {
        action = a;
    }

    sysEvent(int a, Creature firstCreature) {
        subject = firstCreature;
        action = a;
    }

    sysEvent(int a, Creature firstCreature,
                    Creature secondCreature) {
        subject = firstCreature;
        subject2 = secondCreature;
        action = a;
    }
```

Chapter 15

An Applet for Teacher

As every teacher knows, grading homework is a drag. The Java applet we explore in this chapter shows a way to let an applet do some of the work of providing constructive feedback to a self-directed learner. Our example is drawn from the world of business, but teachers and other academics reading this book can easily transpose this model to educational settings.

Learning from a Reference Document

Putting up some reference documentation on a Web site is easy. You can use a variety of tools to help convert word-processing text to HTML. With a little added effort and a modicum of graphic good taste, you can convert those tech manuals to a useful online reference, with an index and hypertext links to help the user navigate the document.

Imagine that you have such a document on your Web site. For example, suppose that you have a reference guide to HTML tags. As one component of a course to teach HTML, you want to make sure that the learners are familiar with the full range of HTML tags, including some of the less common ones. You want to administer a brief quiz to verify that they actually read and understand the documentation for all the tags. To keep things simple, you make the quiz multiple choice.

1. **Which tag should you use to embed a Java applet in an HTML document?**

    a. `<APP>`

    b. `<APPLET>`

    c. `<AREA>`

    d. `<UL>`

2. **Which HTML tag may be disabled by the user?**

    a. `<BLINK>`

    b. `<BGSOUND>`

    c. Both

    d. Neither

3. **Which of these items is NOT displayed onscreen?**

    a. `HEAD`

    b. `H1`

    c. `H6`

    d. `MARQUEE`

(Answers at the end of the chapter.)

Giving learners instant feedback is nice. That way, if someone already knows some of the information, he can check his knowledge with the quiz and skip reading the documentation. On the other hand, if he needs to check the other documentation for an answer, he can simply navigate the documentation with the browser and not lose his place in the quiz.

Oops! To make all this work, you need a way to keep your quiz applet onscreen even when the place where it's anchored in the HTML text moves off-screen. As you may suspect, you can put an applet in its own window so that it doesn't stop running when the user scrolls around in the document. See Figure 15-1 for a picture of the applet we have in mind.

```
┌ :: Quiz                                    _ □ ✕ ┐
│ Which of these items is NOT displayed on screen?  │
│  ⦿ HEAD                                           │
│  ○ H1                                             │
│  ○ H6                                             │
│  ○ MARQUEE                                        │
│                    ┌────┐┌─────┐┌────┐            │
│                    │Next││Score││Exit│            │
│                    └────┘└─────┘└────┘            │
│                                                   │
│                                                   │
│ Score: 3.0 of 3.0                                 │
│                                                   │
│ Score: 100%                                       │
└───────────────────────────────────────────────────┘
```

Figure 15-1:
The Quizem
applet.

The Secrets of Successful Quizzing

The main features of interest in this applet are all extremely useful extensions of techniques we've already introduced:

- ✔ How to put an applet in a frame
- ✔ How to read and parse a file
- ✔ How to calculate a score

I've been framed

All the applets we work with in previous chapters have a fixed location on the HTML page. Like an embedded image, their positions remained fixed next to a given bit of text. The Quizem applet requires putting an applet into a *frame,* which is an object that can be moved around the screen and resized. An applet in a frame can be closed by user choice, just like any other GUI window. A framed applet leads a pretty independent life, but it remains dependent on the browser. When the browser closes, so must the applet.

The catch to putting an applet in a frame is that a frame remains open until it is closed. And you must write the code to handle the closing. Otherwise, the frame just sits around cluttering up the screen until the user exits the browser — not a pretty sight! (And not endearing to users.)

Framing happens in two places — in your selection of parents and in the event handler. To make a frame, you must define a class that extends `Frame`. In the case of Quizem, that class is `QuizFrame`.

```
class QuizFrame extends Frame {
    ...
    the user interface is in the frame
    ...
}
```

By the way, because the applet's work is now done in the frame, the applet itself should take up very little browser real estate. When you put the applet into your Web page, you are required to give the frame a `WIDTH` and a `HEIGHT`. But you can give it zero width and zero height so that the frame doesn't introduce awkward blank space. The following HTML code shows you how to set up the frame space.

```
<APPLET CODE="Quizem.class" WIDTH=5 HEIGHT=5>
<PARAM NAME=QUIZFILE VALUE=htmquiz.data>
</APPLET>
```

After you have put the frame onscreen, you must arrange for a way to take it offscreen when the user clicks the Close button of the window or selects the Close option from the window control menu. You know that the Close button needs an `ActionListener`.

```
/* Implements ActionListener  */
    public void actionPerformed(ActionEvent e){
       if (e.getActionCommand()== "Exit") {
       dispose();
       System.exit(0);
       }
```

The window controls on your frame must be attended to by a `WindowListener`.

```
/*  Implements WindowListener  */
    public void windowClosing(WindowEvent e){
         dispose();
         System.exit(0);
      }
```

Teach me how to read

Being forced to edit the HTML page to insert all questions and answers for a quiz as `<PARAM>` tags would be a big nuisance. So the Quizem applet gets its list of questions and answers from a separate file. That way, you can install a Quizem in the HTML page, but write and update question lists separately. The only thing you need to code into the HTML page is the name of the file containing the quiz contents.

In order to supply your quiz with questions and answers from a file, you must teach the computer how to *parse* the file it reads. Parsing means dividing a file into its individual components and analyzing the components so that you can understand their meaning. In our example, we need to help the computer recognize the beginning of each new question, answer option, and so on.

In Chapter 12, we cover reading a data stream. In Chapter 14, we describe how to use a vector to keep track of a variable length collection of objects. These two techniques go together to help read and analyze the file of questions. The `QuizEngine` class reads an input stream and puts it into a vector. But to understand the `QuizEngine`, you first need to find out about a new player — `StringTokenizer`. `StringTokenizer` is the object that breaks up the data input stream into individual items made up of questions and answers.

A `StringTokenizer` breaks up a string into substrings by looking for special characters that are used as breaks. When we read English, we break sentences into words by looking for spaces. For the Quizem applet, we need to break the stream into chunks that are questions and chunks that are answer options. We arbitrarily decided to use $ as the symbol to indicate the breaks between chunks of a quiz item and \n (new line) to indicate the breaks between quiz items. So the layout of the file containing the quiz items looks like this:

```
Question$option 1$ option 2$ option 3$ option 4$answer\n
Question$option 1$ option 2$ option 3$ option 4$answer\n
Question$option 1$ option 2$ option 3$ option 4$answer\n
```

(You can use whatever symbols you want for indicating the breaks in your data.)

The `QuizItem` class is the object that embodies a single quiz item. Its constructor sets up a `StringTokenizer` object that breaks up the input from the file into chunks and passes the chunks on to the `QuizItem` object to organize them. Note the parameter of the constructor that says which characters are used to break up the item — $\n. And note the `toString()` method that's used to get back the question in the form of a text string.

When you use a `StringTokenizer`, you can select whatever character or group of characters is convenient as the break symbols. For example, $ may not be a good symbol to use as a divider if you expect to write questions and answers about financial matters.

```
class QuizItem {
    final static int ANSWERCOUNT = 4;
    String question = null;
    String[] answerList = new String[ANSWERCOUNT];
    int correctAnswer;
    /** Construct a QuizItem from a '$ 'delimitted input
        * line.
        * No error checking.  Expects exactly ANSWERCOUNT
        * candidate answers.
    */
```

(continued)

(continued)

```
public QuizItem(String s, URL url) {
    StringTokenizer t = new StringTokenizer(s,"$\n");
    question = t.nextToken();
    for (int i=0; i<answerList.length; i++){
        answerList[i] = t.nextToken();
        }
    correctAnswer = Integer.parseInt(t.nextToken());
    }


public String toString() {
    return question;
    }
}
```

Now that you understand how the individual quiz items are constructed, you can follow this next code to see how the input stream is broken up into `quizItemVector`, a vector structure containing a variable number of quiz items.

```
class QuizEngine {
    Vector quizItemVector = new Vector();
    Enumeration enum = null;
    int currentItem = 0;
    /** Construct a QuizEngine, loading quiz items
        *  (questions and answers) from the specified URL.
     */
    public QuizEngine(URL quizFileURL) {
        try {
            // open a stream to read the quiz file
            InputStream inStream = quizFileURL.openStream();
            BufferedReader dataStream = new BufferedReader(
                        new InputStreamReader(inStream));
            // load the quiz file into our quizItemVector
            String inLine = null;
            while ((inLine = dataStream.readLine()) != null)
            {
                quizItemVector.addElement(
                        new QuizItem(inLine,quizFileURL));
            }
            enum = quizItemVector.elements();
        }
        catch(IOException e) {
            // handle IO errors here
        }
    }
```

```
public QuizItem getNextQuizItem() {
    if ( enum.hasMoreElements() ) {
        QuizItem q = (QuizItem)enum.nextElement();
        currentItem++;
        return q;
    }
    else {
        return null;
    }
}
```

What's the score?

Quizem is going to give a score for self-evaluation. Of course, you could also arrange for the applet to send scores back to an administrative file to help evaluate the materials or the trainees, or just to keep records of participation. You see an example of how you can set up different data collection and distribution methods in Chapter 16.

You can do the actual scorekeeping in various ways. The applet keeps track of *possibleScore* (the number of questions) and *actualScore* (the number of correct answers). In the following code, you see a programmer's quick and dirty approach to scoring. We divide 100 by the number of possible answers (percentage points per item), multiply by the number of correct items (total points) and convert the result to an integer — (int) in front of the calculation tells Java to convert to an integer. Before you install this applet in your Web page, give some thought to what kind of feedback you would like to give and modify this section of the code to do what you want. For example, you may want to issue a report like "6 right out of 10." Or you may want to compare scores against some set of standards — if (actualScore > 23) {statusLabel.setText ("Top performer!")}

```
void displayScore() {
    statusLabel1.setText("Score: " + actualScore +
                         " of " + possibleScore);
    statusLabel2.setText("Score: " +
        ((int)((100/possibleScore)*actualScore)) + "%");
}
```

In Plain Javanese

We give you the complete code for Quizem.

As you see, we make good use of the Java Class Library! Aside from checking out the URL of the quiz file, the Quizem applet class does very little.

(continued)

```
import java.awt.*;
import java.awt.event.*;
import java.applet.*;
import java.io.*;
import java.util.*;
import java.net.*;

/** Quizem */
public class Quizem extends Applet {
    QuizFrame quizFrame = null;
    public void init() {
        try {
            // construct the URL of the quiz file String
            URL quizURL = new URL(getCodeBase(),
                          getParameter("QUIZFILE"));
            // construct a quizframe with a quizengine
            quizFrame =
                new QuizFrame(new QuizEngine(quizURL),this);
            // pop up the window
            quizFrame.show();
            quizFrame.displayNextQuizItem();
        }
        catch( MalformedURLException e) {
            showStatus( "Invalid Quiz URL: " +
                    getParameter("QUIZFILE"));
        }
    }
    public void start() {
        super.start();
        quizFrame. setVisible(true);
    }
    public void stop() {
        quizFrame.setVisible(false);
    }
}
```

`QuizEngine` reads the input file and puts the `QuizItems` into the `quizItemVector`. You can refer to Chapter 14 for more about this process.

```
class QuizEngine {
    Vector quizItemVector = new Vector();
    Enumeration enum = null;
    int currentItem = 0;
    /** Construct a QuizEngine, loading quiz items
     * (questions and answers) from the specified URL.
     */
```

```
public QuizEngine(URL quizFileURL) {
    try {
        // open a stream to read the quiz file
        InputStream inStream = quizFileURL.openStream();
        BufferedReader dataStream = new BufferedReader(
                    new InputStreamReader(inStream));
        // load the quiz file into our quizItemVector
        String inLine = null;
        while ((inLine = dataStream.readLine()) != null)
        {
            quizItemVector.addElement(
                    new QuizItem(inLine,quizFileURL));
        }
        enum = quizItemVector.elements();
    }
    catch(IOException e) {
        // handle IO errors here
    }
}

public QuizItem getNextQuizItem() {
    if ( enum.hasMoreElements() ) {
        QuizItem q = (QuizItem)enum.nextElement();
        currentItem++;
        return q;
    }
    else {
        return null;
    }
}

public String getStatusString() {
        return ("Question " + currentItem + " of " +
                quizItemVector.size());
    }
}
```

`QuizItem` is in charge of structuring individual items. Note the use of
`StringTokenizer` to break up each input line into a question, answer
options, and a correct answer reference.

```
class QuizItem {
    final static int ANSWERCOUNT = 4;
    String question = null;
    String[] answerList = new String[ANSWERCOUNT];
    int correctAnswer;
```

(continued)

(continued)

```
/** Construct a QuizItem from a '$ ' delimitted input
 *    line.
 *    No error checking.
 *    Expects exactly ANSWERCOUNT candidate answers.
 */
public QuizItem(String s, URL url) {
    StringTokenizer t = new StringTokenizer(s,"$\n");
    question = t.nextToken();
    for (int i=0; i<answerList.length; i++){
        answerList[i] = t.nextToken();
    }
    correctAnswer = Integer.parseInt(t.nextToken());
}


public String toString() {
    return question;

}
}
```

`QuizFrame` is the object that lives as a free window and is in charge of the GUI. By the way, if this window gets covered up by the browser window, as may happen in some circumstances, don't be alarmed. You can bring `QuizFrame` back to the top in the same way you would any open but temporarily covered window. For example, in an MS Windows environment, press Alt+Tab. Notice that this class implements all the necessary Listeners.

```
class QuizFrame extends Frame
    implements ItemListener, WindowListener, ActionListener
{
    QuizEngine quiz;
    Label questionLabel = new Label();
    Label statusLabel1 =
                    new Label("Pick your answer now.");
    Label statusLabel2 =
                    new Label("                    ");
    CheckboxGroup answers = new CheckboxGroup();
    Checkbox answerA;
    Checkbox answerB;
    Checkbox answerC;
    Checkbox answerD;
    Button nextButton = new Button("Next");
    Button scoreButton = new Button("Score");
    Button exitButton = new Button("Exit");
    boolean newItem = true;
    String lastAnswer = "";
```

```
float possibleScore = 0;
float actualScore = 0;

Panel ap = new Panel();
QuizItem item = null;
Applet applet;

QuizFrame(QuizEngine quiz, Applet a) {
    super("Quiz");
    this.quiz = quiz;
    setBounds(0,0,450,300);
    applet = a;

    setBackground(new Color(220,220,255));

    ap.setLayout(new GridLayout(5,1));
    ap.add(questionLabel);
    ap.add(answerA = new Checkbox("A",answers,false));
    ap.add(answerB = new Checkbox("B",answers,false));
    ap.add(answerC = new Checkbox("C",answers,false));
    ap.add(answerD = new Checkbox("D",answers,false));
    answerA.addItemListener(this);
    answerB.addItemListener(this);
    answerC.addItemListener(this);
    answerD.addItemListener(this);
    Panel bp = new Panel();
    bp.add(nextButton);
    bp.add(scoreButton);
    bp.add(exitButton);
    nextButton.addActionListener(this);
    scoreButton.addActionListener(this);
    exitButton.addActionListener(this);
    Panel cp = new Panel();
    cp.setLayout(new GridLayout(2,1,10,10));
    cp.add(statusLabel1);
    cp.add(statusLabel2);
    add("North",ap);
    add("Center",bp);
    add("South",cp);
    addWindowListener(this);
}

/*  Implements WindowListener  */
```

(continued)

(continued)

```java
    public void windowActivated(WindowEvent e){
    }
    public void windowClosed(WindowEvent e){
    }
    public void windowClosing(WindowEvent e){
        dispose();
        System.exit(0);
    }
    public void windowDeactivated(WindowEvent e){
    }
    public void windowDeiconified(WindowEvent e){
    }
    public void windowIconified(WindowEvent e){
    }
    public void windowOpened(WindowEvent e){
    }


    /* Implements ActionListener  */
    public void actionPerformed(ActionEvent e){
      if (e.getActionCommand()== "Exit") {
        dispose();
        System.exit(0);
      }
      else if (e.getActionCommand()== "Next") {
        displayNextQuizItem();
      }
      else if (e.getActionCommand()== "Score") {
        displayScore();
      }
    }
```

The following `itemStateChanged()` method captures the answers from the checkbox and compares the response for each item with the correct response. The `displayScore()` method gives a report to the user. The `displayNextQuizItem()` method does some useful housekeeping each time you move on to the next quiz item.

```java
/* Implements ItemListener */
    public void itemStateChanged(ItemEvent e) {
      if (newItem==true) {
        possibleScore++;
        switch (item.correctAnswer) {
          case 1:
            if (answers.getSelectedCheckbox() == answerA) {
```

```
                actualScore++;
         }
       break;
     case 2:
       if (answers.getSelectedCheckbox() == answerB) {
           actualScore++;
       }
       break;
     case 3:
       if (answers.getSelectedCheckbox() == answerC) {
           actualScore++;
       }
       break;
     case 4:
       if (answers.getSelectedCheckbox() == answerD) {
           actualScore++;
       }
       break;
     }
     lastAnswer =
             answers.getSelectedCheckbox().getLabel();
     statusLabel1.setText("You answered " + lastAnswer);
     newItem = false;
   }
   else{
      statusLabel1.setText("You already answered " +
                            lastAnswer);
   }
   statusLabel2.setText(quiz.getStatusString());
}

void displayScore() {
    statusLabel1.setText("Score: " + actualScore +
                         " of " + possibleScore);
    statusLabel2.setText("Score: " +
      ((int)((100/possibleScore)*actualScore)) + "%");
}

public void displayNextQuizItem() {
    // Remove the checkboxes from the checkbox group
    // to change their states
    answerA.setCheckboxGroup(null);
    answerB.setCheckboxGroup(null);
```

(continued)

(continued)

```
        answerC.setCheckboxGroup(null);
        answerD.setCheckboxGroup(null);
        answerA.setState(false);
        answerB.setState(false);
        answerC.setState(false);
        answerD.setState(false);
        //  And put them back afterwards
        answerA.setCheckboxGroup(answers);
        answerB.setCheckboxGroup(answers);
        answerC.setCheckboxGroup(answers);
        answerD.setCheckboxGroup(answers);
        lastAnswer="";
        if( (item = quiz.getNextQuizItem()) != null ) {
            questionLabel.setText(item.question);
            answerA.setLabel(item.answerList[0]);
            answerB.setLabel(item.answerList[1]);
            answerC.setLabel(item.answerList[2]);
            answerD.setLabel(item.answerList[3]);
            statusLabel1.setText("");
            newItem = true;
        }
        else {
            questionLabel.setText(
                        "This is the end of the quiz.");
            answerA.setLabel("");
            answerB.setLabel("");
            answerC.setLabel("");
            answerD.setLabel("");
        }
    }

}
```

And the Answers

Answers to quiz items from the first section of the chapter: b, a, a.

Chapter 16

Shopping Up a Storm

. . . .

. . . .

Several big retail operations in our home town make a business of buying up any kind of surplus merchandise they can find at a good buy. They pass along the savings to their customers. From one day to the next, you never know what they'll have in stock. Today, you may find power tools; tomorrow, apricot preserves. Or more likely, you find both on the same day and artificial ivory shirt buttons the next day.

Now, suppose they want to offer online shopping. . . .

Designing a Shopping Cart

To offer online shopping, you must first consider what an online store should contain. An online store must contain an inventory list; you can put together an HTML page with clever descriptions and maybe some photos of the items you have for sale. (Even though some prices are ridiculously low, this *is* merchandising.) Of course, you have to design the page so that you can update it easily as merchandise and prices change.

But how does the customer find his or her way around the store? Traditional, organized departments are not what this online type of store is all about. The idea is for the customer to pick up a *shopping cart* upon entering the Web site. The shopping cart is actually a Java applet that moves around the Web site with the shopper.

The applet is equipped with a complete inventory list. If you, the shopper, are looking for something specific, you can consult the inventory list that is part of the applet and use a hypertext link to retrieve the full description on the Web site. Or, if you like, you can just browse around on the page until you find something you want.

The applet is also equipped with a list of purchases — that's the shopping cart part of the applet. When you decide to buy something, you click a button to move it from the inventory list to your list of purchases (your cart). You can also change your mind and remove any item from your shopping cart by clicking another button. See Figure 16-1 for an example of the user interface.

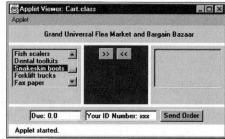

Figure 16-1:
A shopping
cart.

In the sample applet, we ask for just a shopper ID number. In a real business application, you may need to implement more elaborate security provisions. To save work for our Web server, we made the applet check that the shopper entered an ID number and that the shopping cart is not empty before sending the purchase list back to the server.

Specials of the Day

The Shopping Cart applet has some similarities to the Quizem applet explained in Chapter 15. Like Quizem, the Shopping Cart applet intends for users to browse various parts of the applet's host document while keeping the applet in view. Unlike Quizem, we implement this applet in a browser frame (because Netscape offers this option) instead of a Java Frame. Using the browser frame makes providing hypertext links between the applet and the rest of the document simpler.

Also like Quizem, Shopping Cart reads a file and puts information into an object that is a collection of other objects. In the case of Shopping Cart, the list the applet reads is a list of items for sale and their prices, and the collection is not a Vector, but something similar — a Hashtable.

However, you find some new wrinkles with this applet:

✔ Shopping Cart uses the Hashtable of items for sale to fill a List object onscreen so that the user can pick items from the list. Also, Shopping Cart must send a list of selected items back to the server.

✔ Shopping Cart is designed to let the applet control hypertext jumps by the browser. Clicking a link in the applet shifts the text in the browser.

Notice that many of the features of Shopping Cart may be useful in a revised and expanded Quizem. For example, you may want to send answer data back to the server, or you may want to implement hypertext links from the applet to the browser.

I've got a little list

When you keep your data in a vector structure, you identify individual objects in the vector by index number — item 1, item 7, and so on. When all you need to do is work your way from one end of the list to the other, identifying individual objects by number works very well. But the shopper may pick items out of the middle of the list in random order. In this case, keeping track of objects by name is easier. And that is what a Hashtable does.

Like a Vector, a Hashtable is a variable-length collection of objects. Unlike a Vector, a Hashtable gives each object a name.

In the applet's code, identify ShoppingItems to put into a Hashtable structure.

```
ShoppingItem (String n, URL u, double p) {
  itemName = n;
  itemURL = u;
  itemPrice = p;
  }
```

When the program reads the input file of items for sale, it uses a StringTokenizer object to parse the input into ShoppingItems and then puts the ShoppingItems into the offer Hashtable with name as the identifying key. The following code is part of the loadOffer method.

```
void loadOffer(URL u) {
  ...
  while ((inLine = dataStream.readLine()) != null) {
          StringTokenizer t =
                    new StringTokenizer(inLine,"$\n");
```

(continued)

(continued)

```
        String      name  = t.nextToken();
        URL         url   = new URL(u,t.nextToken());
        double      price =
            (new Double(t.nextToken())).doubleValue();
        ShoppingItem item =
                new ShoppingItem(name, url, price);


        offer.put(name, item);
    }


    ...
}
```

In the preceding code, `offer` is the name of the `Hashtable`. The key used to locate objects in the `Hashtable` is `name`. By using this hashtable structure, you can add, remove, or retrieve items by name. When you use a `Vector`, you keep track of items by number, a process that can become quite complicated as you add and remove items.

This next code puts the offered items into the list on the left side of the screen. `Enumeration` is used with `Hashtables` in exactly the same way as with `Vectors`. See Chapter 14 for other information about using these structures.

```
Panel ep = new Panel();

    for ( Enumeration e = offer.keys();
                    e.hasMoreElements(); ) {
      ShoppingItem s =
            (ShoppingItem)(offer.get(e.nextElement()));
      leftList.add(s.itemName);
    }
```

And I'm sending it to you

Sending information back to the server is very similar to receiving it from the server. Java takes care of a great many painful details with objects from the class libraries.

This list tells what happens when you send data out to the Web server:

✔ **Connect:** Use the Web server's URL to establish a connection to the Web server over the Internet.

   ✔ **Send header:** Send a string of magical incantations to the Web server to alert the server about what is coming.

   ✔ **Send data:** Send the data as a string.

We wrote this example with the assumption that you use a communications method called *CGI* (for Common Gateway Interface). At present, CGI is the most common standard for communicating from Web pages back to servers. Other methods are under development that give greater flexibility and security, but the sequence of events in the communication is similar.

The Socket class is the type of object that establishes a connection. Socket is a library class found in java.net. The following code sets up a number of strings with the various bits of information to go into the communication from the Web page to the server. Then it instantiates a Socket and a DataOutputStream and uses the writeBytes method of the DataOutputStream to send the information off to the Web server.

```java
    public void actionPerformed(
            java.awt.event.ActionEvent event) {
try {
// post the data to a cgi script on the web server...

    // your webserver goes here
    String webServer = "www.My-Web-Server.com";

    // the relative path, on your webserver,
    // to the CGI script
    String cgiScript = "/cgi-bin/MyScript.cgi";

    // For info on the CGI specification see:
    //        http://www.w3.org/pub/WWW/CGI/

    // build the argument string
    String dataString = "";
    for (Enumeration elems = take.elements();
                    elems.hasMoreElements(); ) {
        dataString += elems.nextElement();
        dataString += "&"; // provide a delimiter
    }
    dataString += (total + "&");
    dataString += idField.getText();

    // webservers are traditionally on port 80
```

(continued)

(continued)

```
        Socket sock = new Socket(webServer, 80);
        DataOutputStream outStream =
            new DataOutputStream(sock.getOutputStream());
        // send header
        outStream.writeBytes("POST " + cgiScript + "\n" +
                             "Content-type: plain/text\n");
        // tell the server how much data to expect
        outStream.writeBytes("Content-length: " +
                             dataString.length() + "\n\n");
        // send the data
        outStream.writeBytes(dataString);
    }
    catch (Exception exception) {
        System.out.println(exception);
    }
}
```

There's more than one way to frame an applet

The Netscape browser provides a feature called *frames* that enables you to view more than one document at the same time in an organized, tiled window display. See Figure 16-2.

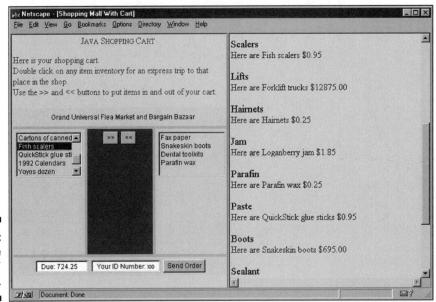

Figure 16-2:
A Netscape
FRAMESET
structure.

This display organization is formatted in a separate HTML document that uses the <FRAMESET> tag to set up a layout of columns and rows. The <FRAME> tag is then used to name the separate documents that can be displayed in the areas defined by <FRAMESET>. With the <FRAME> tag, you can also use several attributes to set some rules about the way you want the document displayed. For example, you may set a margin height and width (MARGINHEIGHT and MARGINWIDTH), turn SCROLLING on or off, and permit or prevent resizing (like NORESIZE).

Our Shopping Cart applet is in a <FRAMESET> structure that divides the browser screen into two equal columns. The left column contains the page that holds the applet. The right column contains the catalog descriptions and other promotional material that make up our online warehouse. This next HTML code is for the main Web page that sets up the frames.

```
<HTML>
<HEAD>
<TITLE>Shopping Mall With Cart </TITLE>
</HEAD>
<FRAMESET COLS="50%,50%">
<FRAME NAME=cart SRC=Cart4.html MARGINHEIGHT=2
MARGINWIDTH=2 SCROLLING="no" NORESIZE>
<FRAME NAME=store SRC=Store.html MARGINHEIGHT=2
MARGINWIDTH=2 SCROLLING="yes" NORESIZE>
</FRAMESET>
</HTML>
```

In the preceding code, Store.html is the catalog document and Cart4.html is the page that contains the Shopping Cart applet.

When I say "jump"

A Java applet can send messages to the browser that is currently displaying its Web page. An interface called AppletContext implements methods showDocument() and showStatus(), among others. These methods enable the applet programmer to give instructions to the browser.

First you must establish a connection to the AppletContext (also known as the browser) by using a method of the Applet class — getAppletContext(). Then you can send a message to the AppletContext, or browser, to show a document or to show a message in the status line.

The Shopping Cart applet follows this procedure. A double-click on one of the list items triggers a hypertext jump to a new location in the document. The lists are part of an object called a `DoubleList`. The Shopping Cart applet gets the `AppletContext` and passes it on to the `DoubleList` object in its constructor:

```
//Constructor for DoubleList
DoubleList(Cart c, Hashtable o, AppletContext ac) {
    offer = o;
    browser = ac;
    parent = c;
    }
//Instantiation of dl as a DoubleList by the applet Cart
dl = new DoubleList(this, offer, getAppletContext());
```

Double-clicking on a list item generates an `ActionEvent` that's handled by the `actionPerformed()` method.

```
else if (event.getSource() == rightList) {
getURL(rightList.getSelectedItem());
}
else if (event.getSource() == leftList) {
getURL(leftList.getSelectedItem());
}
```

The `getURL()` method is the one that speaks to the browser. Courage — a translation follows immediately!

```
void getURL(String item) {
browser.showDocument((((ShoppingItem)(offer.get(item))).itemURL),"store");
}
```

The following list is a breakdown of all the stuff in the preceding parentheses. (Just in case you lost track.)

- ✔ `offer.get(item)` — A message to the `offer` hashtable requesting the item identified by the string you clicked on.
- ✔ `(ShoppingItem)` — Puts the result of `offer.get` into the form of a `ShoppingItem`.
- ✔ `(a ShoppingItem).itemURL` — A message to the particular `ShoppingItem` selected, requesting it to tell us its URL.

So when the computer finishes digesting the parentheses, it ends up with a message to the browser that says `showDocument(URL of the selected item, "store")`. The first parameter, `URL of the selected item`, tells the browser where to go; the second parameter, `"store"`, tells it the name of the browser frame for displaying the document.

This communication technique works for Netscape browsers. The standards and software support for letting applets speak to the browser are still evolving. Test anything you do in this area. Don't count on one technique working for all browsers. And don't blame yourself if it doesn't work as expected. The possibilities are too exciting for us to ignore, but the methods are too new for us to give rock-solid instructions.

The price is right

Our Shopping Cart applet has a small problem that you may not expect. How do you track and add the prices? If you stop to think about it, dollars and cents are integers. We are in the habit of expecting prices to be accurate to the penny. For this reason, the correct way to handle the prices is to make them integer numbers of cents. (If you expect to be making extraordinarily large sales, you may want to use a `long` instead of an `int` type of number. See Chapter 10 for more on number types.)

As a practical matter, you wouldn't expect that using `floats` (the number type, that is) for your dollar values could make a difference. But in fact, because of some arcane details in the way the computer translates between its internal binary number system and our decimal system, using `floats` can sometimes lead to a cumulation of small rounding errors. As a result, adding to and then removing from the shopping cart a large number of items in random order may leave the shopper buying nothing but owing $0.01.

How, then, do you make a display that shows dollars and cents with a decimal point? You can use this next trick that takes advantage of the remainder operator (also known as the *modulus*, %) which is discussed in Chapter 10:

1. **Use `toString(num/100)` for the dollars portion of a price in string form.**

   For example, when using integer math, 1295/100 = 12, remember that you discard the remainder when you divide integers. The `toString` method then gives you the number 12 as a string you can display.

2. **Use `toString(num%100)` for the cents portion of the price.**

   The % operator gives you the remainder after a division of integers. So 1295%100 = 95, and `toString` then gives you the number 95 as a string.

3. **Put in the decimal point by combining strings.**

   ```
   ResultString = (toString(num/100)) + "." +
   (toString(num%100))
   ```

   The result is 12.95

Another name for the remainder operator is *modulus* or just *mod* for short.

A Shopping Cart Full of Code

Here is a complete listing of the applet code. The major components of this applet are the applet class, Cart, and a class called DoubleList that handles the two lists — the offered items and the taken items. We start the complete code for this applet by making all the necessary library classes available.

```
import java.awt.*;
import java.awt.event.*;
import java.applet.*;
import java.util.*;
import java.net.*;
import java.io.*;
```

This next code is the applet class.

```
/**
 * This is our MODEL object
 */
public class Cart extends Applet implements ActionListener
{
    Label titleLabel = new Label(
        "Grand Universal Flea Market and Bargain Bazaar");
    TextField idField = new TextField(
        "Your ID Number: xxx");
    TextField   amtField = new TextField("No Purchases");
    Button      sendButton = new Button("Send Order");
    long        total     = 0;
    String      amtString  = "Due: ";
    DoubleList  dl         = null;
    Hashtable   offer      = new Hashtable();
    Vector      take       = new Vector();
```

The following code for the init method sets up a BorderLayout with fields for amount owed and user ID number at the bottom of the screen, and a button to send in the order. The code also checks the URL (try).

Notice that this code includes some troubleshooting printouts like System.out.println(e); //this data will help to troubleshoot problems. These statements appear in the browser's Java console display and may help you to figure out what is going on if trouble strikes. (Check your browser's Help file or documentation for how to access the Java console.) Writing and keeping some test prints such as these is a good idea, especially when dealing with communications that may go wrong for reasons unrelated to your code.

```
public void init() {
      setLayout(new BorderLayout(5,5));
      Panel np = new Panel();
      np.add(titleLabel);
      add("North",np);
      np.setBackground(Color.cyan);
      np.setSize(300,50);

      Panel sp = new Panel();
      add("South",sp);
      sp.add(amtField);
      sp.add(idField);
        sendButton.addActionListener(this);
      sp.add(sendButton);
      sp.setSize(300,50);
      sp.setBackground(Color.cyan);

      try {
          // construct the URL of the data file String
          URL listURL = new URL(getCodeBase(),
                            getParameter("DATAFILE"));
          loadOffer(listURL);
      }
      catch(MalformedURLException e) {
          System.out.println(e);
          showStatus(e.toString()); // catch bad URL's
      }
      dl = new DoubleList(this, offer,
                              getAppletContext());
      add("Center", dl);

  }
```

The next code is where we call the method that does the trick to print dollars and cents. `AddToCart` and `removeFromCart` are similar packaged routines; you can spell them out fully in the body of the code. By putting the routines into their own separate methods, we make the code easier to read and easier to revise.

```
public void paint(Graphics g) {
    amtField.setText( amtString +
                    MoneyUtil.centsToDollars(total));
    dl.paint(g);
  }
```

(continued)

(continued)

```
public void addToCart(String item) {
  take.addElement(item);
  total += ((ShoppingItem)(offer.get(item))).itemPrice;
  repaint();
}


public void removeFromCart(String item) {
  take.removeElement(item);
  total -= ((ShoppingItem)(offer.get(item))).itemPrice;
  repaint();
}
```

The following code contains the loadOffer method that reads the input
stream and puts it into the offer Hashtable.

 When you write code to read a URL from an input stream, keep the two
exception tests you see at the end of this block of code in the order that you
see them here. (If you're reading from a local file on your computer, you
need to catch the FileNotFoundException and not the
MalformedURLException.)

```
void loadOffer(URL u) {
    try {
      // open a stream to read the data file
      InputStream inStream = u.openStream();

      BufferedReader dataStream = new BufferedReader(
                  new InputStreamReader(inStream));

      String inLine = null;

      // load the data file into our shopping items
      while ((inLine = dataStream.readLine()) != null) {
        StringTokenizer t =
                  new StringTokenizer(inLine,"$\n");
        String     name  = t.nextToken();
        URL        url   = new URL(u,t.nextToken());
        double     price =
            (new Double(t.nextToken())).doubleValue();
        ShoppingItem item  =
                  new ShoppingItem(name, url, price);

        offer.put(name, item);
```

```
    }
  }
  catch(MalformedURLException e) {
    // handle URL errors here
    System.out.println(e);
  }
  catch(IOException e) {
    // handle IO errors here
    System.out.println(e);
  }


}
```

Next is the `actionPerformed` method of the applet. The `DoubleList` object is its own Listener. The applet is responsible for sending data back to the server when the user clicks the Send button.

```
    public void actionPerformed(
            java.awt.event.ActionEvent event) {
  try {
  // post the data to a cgi script on the web server...

    // your webserver goes here
    String webServer = "www.My-Web-Server.com";

    // the relative path, on your webserver,
    // to the CGI script
    String cgiScript = "/cgi-bin/MyScript.cgi";

    // For info on the CGI specification see:
    //      http://www.w3.org/pub/WWW/CGI/

    // build the argument string
    String dataString = "";
    for (Enumeration elems = take.elements();
                 elems.hasMoreElements(); ) {
       dataString += elems.nextElement();
       dataString += "&"; // provide a delimiter
    }
    dataString += (total + "&");
    dataString += idField.toString();

    Socket sock = new Socket(webServer, 80);
```

(continued)

(continued)

```
        DataOutputStream outStream =
            new DataOutputStream(sock.getOutputStream());
        // send header
        outStream.writeBytes("POST " + cgiScript + "\n" +
                            "Content-type: plain/text\n");
        // tell the server how much data to expect
        outStream.writeBytes("Content-length: " +
                            dataString.length() + "\n\n");
        // send the data
        outStream.writeBytes(dataString);
      }
    catch (Exception exception) {
      System.out.println(exception);
      }
    }
```

The DoubleList class is a container for the two lists objects. You may find this class useful in other situations where you want to be able to move information back and forth between two lists. In fact, you might find this kind of code available as a JavaBean.

By the way, notice that this code refers to the AWT library List class by its full name, java.awt.List. This code imports and uses the java.util library package as well as the java.awt package. And java.util includes an interface named List that has nothing to do with the AWT component we are using. To avoid confusion, we need to spell out which List we have in mind.

```
/** A DoubleList (for lack of a better name) is two lists
 *  with buttons to transfer stuff between them.
 *  This is our VIEW object
 */
class DoubleList extends Panel implements ActionListener {
    Button      toRightButton = new Button(">>");
    Button      toLeftButton  = new Button("<<");
    java.awt.List leftList     = new java.awt.List(5,false);
    java.awt.List rightList    = new java.awt.List(5,false);
    Cart          parent       = null;
    Hashtable     offer        = null;
    AppletContext browser      = null;

    DoubleList(Cart c, Hashtable o, AppletContext ac) {
      offer = o;
      browser = ac;
      parent = c;
```

```
      setLayout(new BorderLayout(5,5));

      Panel ep = new Panel();

      for ( Enumeration e = offer.keys();
                    e.hasMoreElements(); ) {
        ShoppingItem s =
             (ShoppingItem)(offer.get(e.nextElement()));
        leftList.add(s.itemName);
      }
      rightList.addActionListener(this);
      leftList.addActionListener(this);
      toLeftButton.addActionListener(this);
      toRightButton.addActionListener(this);

      ep.add(rightList);
      add("East",ep);
      ep.setSize(125,200);
      ep.setBackground(Color.cyan);

      Panel wp = new Panel();
      wp.add(leftList);
      add("West",wp);
      wp.setSize(125,200);
      wp.setBackground(Color.cyan);

      Panel cp = new Panel();
      add("Center",cp);
      cp.setBackground(Color.blue);
      cp.setSize(50,200);
      cp.setLayout(new FlowLayout());
      cp.add(toRightButton);
      cp.add(toLeftButton);
    }
```

Next we show code for the `actionPerformed` method for `DoublePanel`. This code handles shifting items from the offered list to the taken list, and back. Also in this code, `DoublePanel` responds to double-clicks on the lists by sending a message to the browser.

```
public void actionPerformed(
              java.awt.event.ActionEvent event) {
    if (event.getSource() == toRightButton) {
      parent.addToCart(leftList.getSelectedItem());
      rightList.add(leftList.getSelectedItem());
```

(continued)

(continued)

```
        leftList.remove(leftList.getSelectedIndex());
    }
    else if (event.getSource() == toLeftButton) {
      parent.removeFromCart(rightList.getSelectedItem());
      leftList.add(rightList.getSelectedItem());
      rightList.remove(rightList.getSelectedIndex());
    }
    else if (event.getSource() == rightList) {
      getURL(rightList.getSelectedItem());
    }
    else if (event.getSource() == leftList) {
      getURL(leftList.getSelectedItem());
    }
  }


  void getURL(String item) {
    browser.showDocument(
    (((ShoppingItem)(offer.get(item))).itemURL),"store");
  }

}
```

`ShoppingItem` is a convenience class that wraps a few items of data into a class.

```
class ShoppingItem {
    String  itemName;
    URL     itemURL;
    double  itemPrice;

    ShoppingItem (String n, URL u, double p) {
        itemName = n;
        itemURL = u;
        itemPrice = p;
    }
}
```

`MoneyUtil` is a convenience class that enables us to convert cents to dollars. You ought to find this class useful in lots of places!

```
class MoneyUtil {
        static public String centsToDollars(long cents) {
          return ((cents/100) + "." + (cents%100));
    }
}
```

Chapter 17

Fun with Fractals

● ●

In This Chapter

▶ Fishing for fractals

▶ Comparing methods of animation

● ●

A *fractal* is a geometric shape that is self-similar and has fractional dimensions. *Self-similar* means that no matter how much you magnify a fractal, you end up with something that looks very much like that with which you started. Fractals can describe the shape of clouds, mountains, coastlines, and other naturally occurring forms. More important, for our purposes, fractals are interesting to look at and explore. (We provide some good starting points for exploring fractals at the end of this chapter.) Figure 17-1 is one snapshot of a particularly famous fractal, called the Julia set, after its discoverer, Gaston Julia.

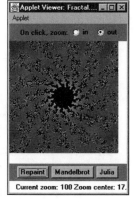

Figure 17-1:
A view of
the world-
famous
Julia set.

Give a Friend a Fractal . . .

Here already? Well, I don't expect one snapshot of a Julia fractal to hold your attention very long. Give a friend a fractal, and you entertain that friend for a day; teach a friend to make fractals, and you entertain your friend for a lifetime. With the fractal applet in this chapter and the power of your computer, you can generate an infinite number of fractal images. You can view these images in full color, play with the source code, and alter and improve this applet to your heart's content. (If you tell us about your experiments, we'll be happy to include a link to your work on the resource Web page for this book!)

An Explanation of Animation

The fractal applet isn't exactly an animation — it's more like a picture generator. Although we make this distinction, you should understand some useful points about Java applets and animations.

If you're an experienced Web developer, you may know the technique of building small animations using GIF89 images. (If you haven't heard of these techniques and are interested, we refer you to the Netscape Web site — www.netscape.com — where you can search for the word *animation*. We also provide references on the resource page for this book at www.isc.com/JPFD.)

Comparing Java animation to GIF

We are often asked how Java animation compares to these other techniques. A quick comparison follows.

Most image files on the Web are stored in Graphics Interchange Format — *GIF* — a standard published by CompuServe and last revised in 1989.

Optimize your applet

It's only fair to warn you: Generating a complete fractal may take many minutes on an average computer. You probably want to tell the Java compiler to *optimize* your applet by using the *-O* flag, like so:

```
javac -O Fractal.java
```

It takes longer to compile with optimization, but notice that your resulting class files are smaller and your applets run faster.

Though you have seen hundreds of GIF pictures in Web pages, you may not have realized that GIF images can display a series of pictures sequentially, like a film strip. That's right — the GIF 1989 standard provides a way to include many images within a single file and to loop through these images.

Because browsers from Netscape and others support the GIF 1989 standard, you can create an animation using a multi-image GIF file.

Working on the same principle, one basic approach for using Java to do simple frame-by-frame animation is to download a series of images as well as a Java applet to play the images. This technique is used in the Animator demo, which is part of the Java Developer's Kit included on the CD-ROM accompanying this book.

The fact is, Java does not give you a lot of benefits for the kind of animation we've just described. In fact, Java 1.0 had a real handicap, because it was pretty slow at downloading multiple files. If your applet required, say, three class files and seven GIFs (animation frames), Java 1.0 would open a network connection, fetch a file, and close the connection *ten times!* This is the programming equivalent of hanging up the phone and redialing at the end of every paragraph. With Java 1.1, you can put all the needed files in a JAR (see Chapter 8) so that the file downloading is considerably faster, but you still need to download and display the GIFs, and Java offers no distinctive advantage for this process.

Using Java animation intelligently

On the other hand, if your animation is one in which a single image moves across a background — perhaps a fish moving through the water — Java may be just right for you. The fish moving through water is, of course, the perfect job for a `Sprite` class such as the one we work with in Chapters 13 and 14. A Java Sprite animation takes advantage of your computer's power to generate all the snapshots of your fish moving from Point A to Point B.

The fractal applet in this chapter is a similar example. Instead of downloading thousands of images to illustrate the beauty of fractals, you download a small applet that knows how to generate an infinite number of images.

Yet another compelling use of Java would be, for example, as a viewer for CAD (computer-aided design) files. CAD drawings are line drawings of the sort typically used by architects and engineers to display building plans, circuit diagrams, and similar pictures. With a CAD-viewing applet, users could download a single CAD picture and then view it at any angle or magnification they want. Again, the applet uses the power of the applet user's computer to generate thousands of possible images from a single description.

A Java animation also differs from a GIF animation in that it can have a lot more smarts. It can start playing or change images or jump to a URL or pop up a dialog box in response to a mouse click or because it was set to open at a certain time of day or in response to some other external input.

The Code

```
import java.awt.*;
import java.awt.event.*;
import java.applet.*;
import java.net.*;
/**
 * Fractal applet allows you to interractively explore
 * the infinite beauty of fractal world
 * @author Anatoly Goroshnik
 * @version 0.1, 5 Mar 96
 */
public class Fractal extends Applet implements
ActionListener {
    //constants
    final static double INIT_ZOOM_X_MANDELBROT = -50;
    final static double INIT_ZOOM_Y_MANDELBROT = 0;
    final static double INIT_ZOOM_X_JULIA = 0;
    final static double INIT_ZOOM_Y_JULIA = 0;
    // user interface objects
    Panel staticPanel1 = new Panel();
    Panel staticPanel2 = new Panel();
    Panel drawPanel = new Panel();
    CheckboxGroup zoomGroup;
    Checkbox zoomIn;
    Checkbox zoomOut;
```

Using numRows, numCols, and numColors

Following are a few of the more interesting parameters for you to experiment with. numRows and numCols set the image size in pixels. numColors indicates the maximum number of different colors. If you set numColors very small, you quickly generate a relatively dull fractal image. If you set numColors to the maximum — 255 — you slowly generate a relatively interesting fractal image.

```
// image generation parameters
  int numRows = 100;
  int numCols = 200;
  int numColors = 200;
  int colors[] = new int[256];
  // initial image parameters
  double zoom = 1;
  double zoomPointx = 0;
  double zoomPointy = 0;
  double priorZoomPointx = 0;
  double priorZoomPointy = 0;
  GenFractal genObject = null;
  int currentFractal;
  //image to draw on to keep memory of generated image
  Image    oImg = null;
  Graphics oGr = null;
```

The inner adapter class

An inner class is a class that lives inside another class, so that it becomes the private tool of the class that contains it. The `Fractal MouseAdapter` class you see here is defined inside of the `Fractal` class. When you compile your code, you find that a class file named `Fractal$FractalMouseAdapter` has been created. If you were to paste the same code inside of another class, for example a class named `Wiz`, you would find another class file, `Wiz$FractalMouseAdapter`. Each inner class works only for its particular owner.

An *Adapter* is simply a programmer's shortcut to writing a Listener. An Adapter is an abstract class that consists of empty versions of all the methods necessary to meet the requirements of a given Listener interface. If you want to save the trouble of writing some empty methods, you may say "extends `MouseAdapter`" instead of "implements `MouseListener`."

The `FractalMouseAdapter` is the only interactive part of this applet. If you click the current fractal image, you *zoom in* or *zoom out,* depending on which radio button is currently selected. To *zoom,* in this case, simply means to perform the same calculations we started with, using the current state and the position of the mouse click in order to generate a new state.

```
/* inner adapter class for catching mouse clicks on
   drawPanel */
   class FractalMouseAdapter extends MouseAdapter {
       public void mouseClicked (MouseEvent e) {
           int x = e.getX();
           int y = e.getY();
```

(continued)

(continued)

```
        // calculate zoom point in rows, columns coordinates
        zoomPointx = (double)(x - numCols) / zoom;
        zoomPointy = (double)(numRows - y) / zoom;
        zoomPointx = zoomPointx + priorZoomPointx;
        zoomPointy = zoomPointy + priorZoomPointy;
        priorZoomPointx = zoomPointx;
        priorZoomPointy = zoomPointy;
        if (zoomGroup.getSelectedCheckbox() == zoomIn)
            zoom = zoom * 10;
        else
            zoom = zoom / 10;
        generateFractal(currentFractal);
        }
    }
private void setRGBpalette(int c, int r, int g, int b) {
    colors[c] = r * 256 * 256 * 4 + g * 256 * 4 + b * 4;
}
```

Using `initColors`

You can also have some fun with this section. `initColors` loads your
crayon box with colors. You must experiment some to come up with color
combinations that are pleasing. In general, as you zoom in to the fractal, you
end up favoring the high end of the array. If all the colors in the top half of
your array are very similar, your fractal won't be very interesting. For this
reason, the following code puts a greater variety of colors at the higher end
of the array.

```
private void initcolors() {
    int j;
    int c = 0;
    for (j = 0; j < 1; j++, c++)
        setRGBpalette(c, 0, 0, 0);
    for (j = 0; j < 14; j++, c++)
        setRGBpalette(c, (14-j)*4, j*4, 0);
    for (j = 0; j < 14; j++, c++)
        setRGBpalette(c, 0, (14-j)*4, j*4);
    for (j = 0; j < 14; j++, c++)
        setRGBpalette(c, (14-j)*4, 0, j*4);
    for (j = 0; j < 14; j++, c++)
        setRGBpalette(c, (14-j)*4, j*4, j*4);
    for (j = 0; j < 60; j++, c++)
        setRGBpalette(c, 0, 60-j, j);
    for (j = 0; j < 60; j++, c++)
```

```
        setRGBpalette(c, j, 0, 60-j);
    for (j = 0; j < 60; j++, c++)
        setRGBpalette(c, 60-j, j, 0);
    setRGBpalette(255, 60, 60, 60);
}
private void generateFractal(int fractalType) {
    if (genObject!= null) {
        genObject.stop();
        genObject = null;
        System.gc();
    }
    if (fractalType == GenFractal.MANDELBROT) {
        genObject = new GenFractal(this, numRows, numCols,
                        numColors, colors, zoom,
                        zoomPointx, zoomPointy,
                        drawPanel, oGr, currentFractal);
        }
    else {
        genObject = new GenFractal(this, numRows, numCols,
                        numColors, colors, zoom,
                        zoomPointx, zoomPointy,
                        drawPanel, oGr, currentFractal);
    }
    genObject.start();
}
    public void update (Graphics g) {
        paint(g);
}
    public void paint (Graphics g) {
        Graphics drawPanelGraphics =
    drawPanel.getGraphics();
        drawPanelGraphics.drawImage(oImg, 0, 0, this);
}
```

Setting up the interface

In the code that follows, we set up the interface. A radio button is at the top, a panel on which the fractal is painted is in the middle, and three buttons are at the bottom.

```
public void init() {
    setBackground(Color.white);
    setLayout(new BorderLayout());
    drawPanel.addMouseListener (new
```

(continued)

(continued)

```
        FractalMouseAdapter());
        add("Center", drawPanel);
        staticPanel1.setBackground(Color.gray);
        staticPanel1.setLayout(new FlowLayout());
        Button b = new Button("Repaint");
        b.addActionListener (this);
        staticPanel1.add(b);
        b = new Button("Mandelbrot");
        b.addActionListener (this);
        staticPanel1.add(b);
        b = new Button("Julia");
        b.addActionListener (this);
        staticPanel1.add(b);
        add("South", staticPanel1);
        zoomGroup = new CheckboxGroup();
        zoomIn = new Checkbox("zoom in", zoomGroup, true);
        zoomOut = new Checkbox("zoom out", zoomGroup, false);
        staticPanel2.setBackground(Color.gray);
        staticPanel2.setLayout(new FlowLayout());
        staticPanel2.add(new Label("On Mouse Click:"));
        staticPanel2.add(zoomIn);
        staticPanel2.add(zoomOut);
        add("North", staticPanel2);
        //create off screen image
          oImg = drawPanel.createImage(numCols*2, numRows*2);
          oGr = oImg.getGraphics();
        //initialize graphics
          initcolors();
          repaint();
    }
```

Listening for buttons

As you may have noticed in the preceding section, this applet implements
ActionListener and is the registered Listener for the Repaint, Mandelbrot,
and Julia buttons. Here is the code that responds to button clicks:

```
public void actionPerformed (ActionEvent e) {
        String arg = e.getActionCommand();
    if ("Repaint".equals(arg)) {
      repaint();
    }
    else if ("Mandelbrot".equals(arg)) {
        currentFractal = GenFractal.MANDELBROT;
        zoom = 1;
```

```
            zoomPointx = INIT_ZOOM_X_MANDELBROT;
            zoomPointy = INIT_ZOOM_Y_MANDELBROT;
            priorZoomPointx = INIT_ZOOM_X_MANDELBROT;
            priorZoomPointy = INIT_ZOOM_Y_MANDELBROT;
        generateFractal(GenFractal.MANDELBROT);
    }
    else if ("Julia".equals(arg)) {
        currentFractal = GenFractal.JULIA;
        zoom = 1;
        zoomPointx = INIT_ZOOM_X_JULIA;
        zoomPointy = INIT_ZOOM_Y_JULIA;
        priorZoomPointx = INIT_ZOOM_X_JULIA;
        priorZoomPointy = INIT_ZOOM_Y_JULIA;
        generateFractal(GenFractal.JULIA);
    }
}
```

Julia and Mandelbrot

The GenFractal class knows how to generate two kinds of fractals: Julia
sets, as in Figure 17-1 at the beginning of this chapter, and Mandelbrot sets,
as in Figure 17-2.

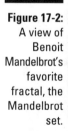

Figure 17-2:
A view of
Benoit
Mandelbrot's
favorite
fractal, the
Mandelbrot
set.

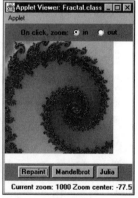

```
class GenFractal implements Runnable {
    final static int MANDELBROT = 0;
    final static int JULIA = 1;
    private Applet parent;
    int numRows;
    int numCols;
```

(continued)

(continued)

```
int numColors;
int colors[];
double zoom;
double zoomPointx;
double zoomPointy;
Graphics oGr;
Graphics gr;
int fractalType;
Thread me = null;
public GenFractal(Applet p, int rows, int cols,
int ncolors, int acolors[], double z,
double zpx, double zpy,Panel dp, Graphics g, int fType) {
  parent = p;
  numRows = rows;
  numCols = cols;
  numColors = ncolors;
  colors = acolors;
  zoom = z;
  zoomPointx = zpx;
  zoomPointy = zpy;
  oGr = g;
  gr = dp.getGraphics();
  fractalType = fType;
}
```

Using run( )

The run( ) method calculates colors and sets screen pixels accordingly. As you may expect, run( ) is where the action takes place.

```
public void run() {
    int     thresh = 4;
    double  cx;
    double  cy;
    double  x;
    double  y;
    double  tmp;
    double  fsq;
    int     count;
    Color   curColor;
    for (int path = 0; path < 4; path++) {
      for (int i = -numCols; i <= numCols; i += 4-path) {
        for (int j = -numRows; j <= numRows; j += 4-Æ path) {
            //the magic part
```

```
        x = cx = (zoomPointx*zoom+(double)i)/ ((double)numCols*zoom);
        y = cy = (zoomPointy*zoom+(double)j)/ ((double)numRows*zoom);
          fsq = x * x + y * y;
       for (count = 1; (count <= numColors) && (fsq <= thresh); count++) {
          tmp = x;
          if (fractalType == MANDELBROT) {
            x = x * x - y * y + cx;
            y = 2.0 * tmp * y + cy;
           }
           else { // JULIA
            x = x * x - y * y + 0.025;
            y = 2.0 * tmp * y - 0.65;
           }
       fsq = x * x + y * y;
       }


       /*
          parent.showStatus("Current zoom: "+(new Double(zoom)).toString()+
             " Zoom center: "+(new Double(zoomPointx))Æ      .toString()+
             ", "+(new Double(zoomPointy)).toString()+
             " Current color index: "+(new Integer(count)).toString());
          */


       curColor = new Color(colors[count]);
       // draw on screen as we go
       gr.setColor(curColor);
       gr.fillRect(i + numCols, numRows - j, 4 - path, 4 - path);
       // keep memory of image
       oGr.setColor(curColor);
       oGr.fillRect(i + numCols, numRows - j, 4 - path,
       4 - path);
       try { Thread.sleep(0); }
       catch (InterruptedException e) { return; }
      }
    }
  }
  parent.showStatus("Current zoom: "+(new
  Double(zoom)).toString()+" Zoom center: "+
     (new Double(zoomPointx)).toString()+
     ", "+(new Double(zoomPointy)).toString()+" Done!");
}
public void start() {
   if (me == null) {
      me = new Thread(this);
   }
```

(continued)

(continued)

```
    else {
        me.stop();
    }
    me.start();
}
public void stop() {
  if (me != null) {
    me.stop();
    me = null;
  }
 }
}
```

Part IV
Only Java

The 5th Wave   By Rich Tennant

You the guy writing all those interactive applets?

In this part . . .

What can we say about Part IV? It's only Java, and Java stands alone. We introduce you to the potential of Java programming for creating more than just applets for use on World Wide Web pages. Java is a programming language that can make secure, portable, platform-independent, multithreaded, and stand-alone applications. And we show you how to make the transition from applet to application.

In Part IV, we compare and contrast the relative merits of Java with other object-oriented programming languages. We point out how Java has become a rising star in the Internet community as every major vendor in the Internet-related world seeks to integrate support for Java into their own applications.

Chapter 18

Java Stands Alone

• •

• •

*Y*ou can use Java to write applications that run without the support of a browser. That is, you can create Java applications that run on their own (stand alone). A *stand-alone* Java application doesn't depend on a browser for its existence and isn't subject to the applet's security restrictions.

For example, although an applet isn't permitted to touch the contents of the user's hard drive, a stand-alone Java application may create a new translation of *War and Peace* and store it on the user's hard drive. Similarly, an applet may connect to data only in the same Internet location as the HTML page on which it lives, but a stand-alone Java application may access any address on the Internet.

In this chapter, we investigate the main differences between Java applets and applications, and we show you some code for making a stand-alone application. We also look at a bigger picture by comparing Java to C++ (another object-oriented programming language) and giving you a glimpse of the gathering support for Java.

Java without a Browser

When you run a Java applet in a browser, the applet depends on the browser for its existence. The browser provides for communications between the applet and the user's computer hardware and software. If you close the browser, the applet closes also.

Security is one of the special advantages of Java for creating applets that run over the Internet. By running the applet in a restricted *virtual machine* with limited capabilities, the browser enforces security restrictions on what an applet is permitted to do — especially restrictions on moving information in and out of the user's system. However, when you want to store information for future use, or to communicate with another computer or a printer, the security advantage turns into a disadvantage.

The *theoretical* design of the Java language enables users to indicate that certain applets are *trusted* and can be granted access to disks, printers, or other computers. At the time of this writing, the leading browsers from Netscape and Microsoft provide this capability. Moreover, you may simply want an application that runs in its own space without the overhead of running a browser. You're in luck! You can overcome these applet restrictions by making stand-alone Java applications.

The `main` *difference in standing alone*

We already presented all the hard stuff for figuring out how to write a Java applet. The difference between the code of an applet and the code of a stand-alone application is a class. That is, a stand-alone application must have one class that takes the place of the browser and HTML page. This *master class* speaks with the hardware and the Java bytecode interpreter and must include a method called `main`. The stand-alone application may take input parameters in exactly the same way that the applet takes parameters from the HTML page (see Chapter 3).

The following code is an example of the simplest of Java stand-alone applications:

```
public class StandAloneApp {
    public static void main (String args[]){
        System.out.println("This is an application.");
    }
}
```

As you no doubt suspect, running the application represented by the preceding code puts `This is an application.` on your screen. Not much different from the HelloWorld applet from Chapter 2, is it? See Figure 18-1.

When you run a stand-alone Java program, you run the Java interpreter (`java.exe`) by typing a command-line instruction such as the following one, where `java` calls out the interpreter and `StandAloneApp` is the name of your stand-alone program:

```
java StandAloneApp
```

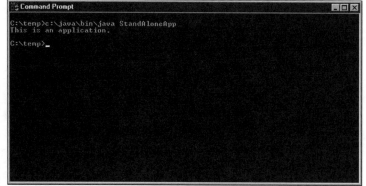

Figure 18-1:
This is a
stand-alone
Java
application.

Careful! Don't include .class in your command, as you would run the
compiler. And remember that the command is java, not javac.

Some code to play with

Take a look at the following code sample. You can save the code in a file
named MyApplet.java and compile it as usual, and it will work two ways. If
you invoke Java from the command line by keying java MyApplet, the
program runs as a stand-alone program. If you put an applet tag in an HTML
page, the code runs as an applet.

The code adds a main method to the applet. When you use the java command to run the applet class, the computer executes the main method. The
main method constructs a frame for the applet to run in (in place of the
browser) and constructs a new instance of the applet class that does its
thing inside the frame. When you run the applet from a browser, the browser
never calls the main method. Instead, it calls the init and start methods
of the applet, and the applet performs inside the browser.

When you copy this code, pay particular attention to the WindowAdapter
class and the way it's added to MyAppletFrame. This Listener is required so
that you can gracefully exit the application by clicking the close option of
the window. System.exit(0) is the instruction that stops running the Java
interpreter. If you make an error in this code or put it in the wrong place,
you may be unable to close the applet frame in a normal way. For example,
you may discover that you have to reboot to get the applet window off your
screen. If this happens, double-check that the WindowListener is correctly
registered with the Frame and that it includes the System.exit(0) instruction in the windowClosing() method.

```java
import java.awt.*;
import java.awt.event.*;
import java.applet.*;

/** This Java program can run as an applet or an application.  Wow! */

public class TwoWay2 extends Applet {

    Button button = new Button("Press Me");
    Label label = new Label("Go ahead, press the button!");
    ButtonListener press = new ButtonListener(label);

    public void init() {
        add(button);
        add(label);
      button.addActionListener(press);
     }

    //  main()called only when run as a stand-alone application
    public static void main(String args[])  {
        MyAppletFrame appletFrame= new MyAppletFrame ("My Applet");
        //The following makes a new instance of MyApplet
        TwoWay2 myNewApplet = new TwoWay2();
        WinListen off = new WinListen();
        myNewApplet.init();
        myNewApplet.start();
        appletFrame.addWindowListener(off);
        appletFrame.add("Center",myNewApplet);
        appletFrame.setSize(500,200);
        appletFrame.show();
    }
}


/** Appletframe takes the place of the browser run as
      a stand-alone application */

class MyAppletFrame extends Frame {
    //constructor - just instantiates a frame
    public MyAppletFrame(String s) {
        super(s);
    }
}


class ButtonListener implements ActionListener{
    private Label it = new Label("");
    private boolean toggle = true;
    //constructor
```

```
    ButtonListener(Label target){
          it=target;
      }
    //Methods required to implement ActionListener interface
    public void actionPerformed(ActionEvent e){
    if(toggle==true){
        it.setText("Button clicked!");
            toggle=false;
      }
    else{
          it.setText("Click the button!");
        toggle=true;
      }
      }
} //end buttonListener

class WinListen extends WindowAdapter {
    //necessary to avoid hanging the system when run stand alone
    public void windowClosing(WindowEvent e){
    System.exit(0);
    }
  }
```

Printing: At last

Applets have limited access to computer resources. Some browsers may
allow a Java applet access to a local printer, but this access depends on the
browser and the permissions the user has set up in the browser. For practical purposes, it's best to assume that applets can't print. But a stand-alone
program has the right to do whatever it wants with the resources available
to the computer it's running on. At last, you can print from Java.

Here's how. First, type and compile the following Print class.

```
import java.awt.*;
public class Print extends Frame{
  public Print(){     }
      public void doPrint(){
      PrintJob pjob=getToolkit().getPrintJob(null, "Job", null);
      if(pjob != null){
      Graphics pg = pjob.getGraphics();
          pg.setFont (new Font("Helvetica", Font.PLAIN, 23));
          pg.drawString("Hello, printer!", 100, 100);
```

(continued)

(continued)

```
            pg.dispose();
            pjob.end();
        }
    }
}
```

Then use the `Print` class in an application class, like the following `MyPrintingApplication.java`. and compile it.

```
import java.awt.*;
public class MyPrintingApplication extends Frame{
  public static void main(String args[]){
      Print printTester = new Print();
      printTester.doPrint();
      System.out.println("Hello, printer!");
  }
}
```

From the command line, run `MyPrintingApplication`.

Why Write in Java When I Could Learn C++?

Because you're reading this book, we assume that you're not fluent in C++. You're probably not interested in a deep technical discussion on the differences between C++ and Java. Nevertheless, a brief overview can help you recognize when you need a second opinion from your brother-in-law or some other trusted technical guru.

Java is easy to understand

One goal of the Java developers was to build on earlier languages like C++ and Smalltalk, but to fix what they saw as gaps and inconsistencies. The literature about Java devotes much attention to how it resembles and differs from C++. One key difference relates to the use of pointers.

C++ relies heavily on pointers, bits of code that are used to refer the computer from the class definition to the specific object that is an instance of the class. These pointers are hard to understand and hard to keep track of, even when you do understand them. As a result, many programming errors relate to the use of pointers.

In the C and C++ languages, responsibility for preventing errors related to the use of pointers rests almost exclusively with the programmer. Behind the scenes, Java organizes the connections between classes and their objects in a way similar to that of C++. But the Java compiler takes care of the complex clerical task of using pointers and leaves only the overall direction to the programmer. (Taking care of complex clerical tasks is what computers are for, isn't it?)

Java developers addressed a variety of other small and large issues. Speaking from personal experience, believe me: Java is easier to learn than C++!

Java helps to bug proof and virus proof

Just as the Java compiler takes care of pointers without bothering the programmer about the messy details, Java also handles a number of similar tiresome and trouble-prone housekeeping tasks.

✔ The programmer can rely on the Java system to make sure that the program doesn't keep reading past the end of a string of data and accidentally wander off into some other program's data or instructions. This accounting process shuts off one of the common entry points for bugs and viruses.

✔ As a program instantiates objects, it sets aside computer memory to keep track of the objects' data and methods.

✔ When the object is no longer needed by the program, the computer must somehow be notified that the related block of memory may be reused for something else. If the computer isn't notified and more objects are instantiated, you eventually encounter the dread `Out of Memory` message. Java has automatic *garbage collection* to help avoid this situation. That is, Java helps the computer clean up after the program, without the need for the programmer to write specific clean-up code.

✔ Java also checks all code to make sure that instructions are legitimate program codes that perform legal steps. By doing this code checking, the Java interpreter can stop a virus that tries to revise the computer's operating system by sneaking in as bytecode.

Java supports new standards

The computing community relies on standards of various kinds to keep everyone's different software products and projects working together. Java comes fully equipped to recognize and work with the most recently adopted standards. These include not only the Internet standards for communication, file transfer, and so on, but also the CORBA standard for trading bundles of data and methods among programs and operating environments. ("Bundles of data and methods . . ." sounds like an object — and it is!) Java also supports standard ways of communicating with databases so that linking Java applets with server-based databases is easy.

Also, the use of *threads,* which is inherent in Java (see Chapter 12), enables the Java programmer to more easily work with modern hardware and operating system software to coax more productivity out of systems. That is, Java threads enable computer systems to be more productive by running multiple tasks at the same time. Although various operating systems and languages support threads, Java makes them easy for programmers to use.

Why Write in C++ When I Know Java?

The preceding heading voices a good question! For now, one good answer is that you may need the support tools available to a more mature development environment (such as C++). A commercial software product relies on a long list of support items — such as device drivers for printers and other peripherals and platform-specific code that enables programs to intercommunicate. The pool of these resources isn't as complete for Java as it is for languages that have been around longer.

But make no mistake: Java has inspired an unprecedented number of high-quality development tools in a very short time. Inprise's JBuilder, which is included on the CD for this book, is one example. If the resource or tool you want is not yet available, check again tomorrow!

Another consideration for Java programming is that Java isn't designed to provide low-level control of hardware. Unless the computer chip you're cooking up in your kitchen is designed to run Java bytecode, you need to write its operating system in some other language. (Sun has recently begun to market a chip that does run Java bytecode.)

For the same reason (lack of low-level control), don't plan to use Java to squeeze the maximum possible performance out of an application. If you're designing a graphics-based game that requires lightning-fast response in processing gigabytes of data, you need a programming language that stays very close to the hardware, such as C++. With such a language, you can use every little trick to save a tick of processor time.

Part V
The Part of Tens

The 5th Wave   **By Rich Tennant**

"Okay, gather around kids! You can each put one item in the shopping basket.

In this part . . .

Part V includes some top-ten lists for you. To help you troubleshoot, you find the top ten (or so) common mistakes. We include two chapters of URLs for Web sites that contain further Java lore or hot Java applets. Another top-ten list helps you out with programming in style. And, so as not to ignore the *other* Java, we've included ten interesting facts about that nation and its culture as well.

Chapter 19
Ten Common Mistakes

Missing ( ) {}

A missing parenthesis or brace causes the Java compiler to lose track of where one thing begins and another ends. Occasionally, the compiler is smart enough to know what's going on, but often it only knows that nothing seems to make sense anymore (it's a lot like people that way). When that happens, the compiler gives you a long series of error messages. Look for a missing grouping character somewhere on or shortly before the line that produced the first error message.

A good way to avoid missing grouping characters is to make a habit of putting both the open and the close character first, before you fill in the information that goes between parentheses or braces.

Lost or Forgotten Imports

You can easily forget to include an import statement at the top of your code file.

When writing applets, you must always import `java.applet.*`. Usually, you want to import `java.awt.*` and `java.lang.*`. You may also have a package of your own classes, or you may want to use a class from another part of the Java Class Library.

Remember to import everything to which your code refers.

Mistaking a Class for an Object

A class is just the blueprint for an object.

Even when the object is one of a kind, you must both define the class and then construct an instance of the class. Afterward, in methods that refer to the object, be sure to use the object name and not the class name.

You will be on the right track if you get in the habit of declaring and instantiating each object at the start of the class definition:

```
Thing myThing = new Thing (parameter1, parameter2);
```

Spellng Rong

Each Java Class Library is full of variable and class names that are extremely similar. Sometimes, only the capitalization distinguishes one thing from another.

Be careful not to create errors through misspelling or inattention to case.

Incorrect Signatures

Each constructor and method have specific signatures — the group or parameters that go within the parentheses. If the number and type of parameters don't match the signature of the specific constructor or method you have in mind, you may get an error message from the compiler. Worse yet, you may compile your code successfully and get behavior that is not what you intended.

Make it a habit to check the documentation to make sure that you have the right signature for each AWT method you use.

A Method That Gives Nothing in Return

Every method (except a constructor) must return something. If it has nothing else to return, it returns *void*.

The Wrong Kind of Equality

To test whether two objects are *equal* — for example, to test whether two strings contain the same series of characters — use the `Object.equals` method. You may compare two numbers using = = (double equal sign). If you want to assign a value to an object but *not* make a comparison, use = (just one equal sign). These usages are not interchangeable.

`a=b`; means "change *a* so that it becomes equal to *b*."

`(a==b)` is an expression (that may or may not be true) that says "*a* and *b* are in fact equal."

Use = = in `if`, `for`, and `while` statements.

Tight Loops

You want to be sure iteration statements always reach an exit from the loop, no matter what data is entered. If your program doesn't provide an exit, the computer happily continues looping as long as you leave the power on.

Step through your loop mentally to make sure that it always reaches an exit.

Going Public

Only one class in a file may be public — the class the file is named after. If a method or class is going to be used by classes from another file, you must declare that method or class public.

When you are working on a code file and want to save a copy of the old version, rename the old version so that the new, revised version keeps the name of the class you're working on.

Trusting Yourself Too Much

Suppose that you find only three small, obvious things wrong with your applet. You fix the errors, compile the code, and turn the applet over to be installed on your Web page. No need to check the thing for the umpteenth time. Right? Wrong!

Trivial revisions have a way of introducing unexpected consequences. Always test the last change you make.

Chapter 20

Ten Hot Pages to Peek At

In This Chapter

▶ Examples of what Java can do

▶ Sites that may have hot news

▶ Creations that we think are neat

*T*hings are changing rapidly in the world of Java programming. Sometimes Web sites are abandoned because the Webmaster got too busy doing other things. Sometimes they're abandoned because they became too successful and, hence, demanded too much work to support. Sometimes they're restructured and become just plain dull.

Of the sites listed in this chapter, some may go the way of those that looked promising and then faded away. But others are sure to still be there when you read this book. We listed these Java-related sites in no particular order.

Blue Skies for Java

Live weather data:

```
cirrus.sprl.umich.edu/javaweather/
```

Home Ideas Applet Area

How much wallpaper or paint or tile will it take for your home improvement project? A handful of simple applets answers these and similar questions.

```
www.homeideas.com/applets/
```

SmartMoney

Charts and financial analysis:

```
www.smartmoney.com/si/tools/chartcenter/
```

HotWired

A journal of Internet cultural frontiers:

```
www.hotwired.com
```

Interactive Physics and Math

Lots of applets that simulate applications of the laws of physics. The site has two URLs.

```
theory.uwinnipeg.ca/physics/java/index.html
kret.ifd.uni.wroc.pl/java/javapm/index.html
```

Fred

Fred is a prototype for a networked, 3-D, first-person game implemented entirely in Java.

```
langevin.usc.edu/Fred/
```

Eliza

Eliza is a Java applet that acts like a psychologist.

```
www.livingroom.org/eliza/
members.home.com/chayden/eliza/Eliza.html
```

Playsite

A Java-enabled site for interactive games (such as card games, backgammon, and go). You can compete with players from everywhere in the world.

```
www.playsite.com/
```

Coastiekids games

Links to dozens of Java games for kids. This site will keep you occupied for hours.

```
knsp.com/coastiekids/gamemenu.htm
```

Java Lobby

The Java Lobby is a group of people who share a common interest in Java software development and the advancement of Java standards and software. The main purpose of the Java Lobby is to represent the needs and concerns of the Java developer and user community to the companies and organizations who have influence in the evolution of Java. If you're interested in following the business and politics of Java, check out this site.

```
www.javalobby.org/
```

Chapter 21
Ten Web Sites for Java Lore

In This Chapter

▶ Places to find out more about Java

▶ Reference resources

▶ Places for moral support

*B*ecause we know that you're really intrigued and delighted by this Java programming stuff, we're using this chapter to give you an idea of where to look on the Web for more details.

JavaSoft

```
www.javasoft.com
```

The preceding is the home page of the JavaSoft business group within Sun Microsystems. This site contains links to Sun online documentation, among other useful things. You should make it a practice to check this site every once in a while for the latest news about the Java language, including updates to the JDK.

Sun Microsystems also has a general information page at

```
www.sun.com/java/
```

Big Blue

IBM has a major interest in Java. The site to check for programming tips and useful downloads is

```
ncc.hursley.ibm.com/javainfo/hurindex.html
```

You can also find an IBM general information site at

```
www.ibm.com/java/
```

Gamelan

```
www.developer.com/directories/pages/dir.java.html
```

Gamelan is an Internet directory and registry of Java-based programs and resources for developers and users of the Java programming language.

Java World

```
www.javaworld.com
```

This is the home page of *Java World* magazine. On this page, you get product announcements and other business news, tips and tricks, and articles from the magazine.

Java Report

```
www.sigs.com
```

This URL address takes you to the home page of *Java Report,* a technical journal for serious Java programmers.

Java Applet Rating Service

```
www.jars.com
```

The preceding represents the Academy Awards of applets. At this site, you find a collection of Java applets selected by a rating system with links to lots of good applets. Some are published with source code.

Java Newsgroup

```
comp.lang.java
```

This URL is for an Internet newsgroup for Java programmers featuring technical questions and answers and trade talk of all kinds related to Java programming. Java has stirred so much interest that you find a number of specialized subgroups in addition to the main group.

Java Woman

```
www.taxon.demon.nl/JW/javawoman.html
```

A lot of very handy information in a somewhat quirky personal compilation.

Java Users Groups

Java users groups are locally based groups of people interested in Java who meet periodically to exchange information and sometimes even socialize. Because users groups change officers and addresses from time to time, the best thing is to check the WWW for listings of groups in your area. To find them, ask your friendly neighborhood search engine to scan the Web for "java users group."

Java Programming For Dummies Resource Page

```
www.isc.com/JPFD
```

The authors have posted sample code from this book, update information, and links to other useful Internet resources on this resource page that is designed *especially* for you.

Chapter 22
Ten Tenets of Style

*W*e live in an uncertain and changing world, and so do our programs. Because of this, people as well as computers must read programs.

Good style makes a program easier for people to read. So far as we know, computers are not particularly sensitive to matters of style. That is, an ugly program can run just as well as a beautiful program. But a beautiful program is easier for a person to read and understand. When time comes to revise, debug, or adapt a piece of code, working with code that was written with attention to matters of style is easier.

Logically Group the Elements of Your Code

Group the elements of your code so that things that go together logically are near each other on your editing screen or the printed page. When unrelated methods are mixed randomly, the computer has no trouble finding the code it wants, but a human programmer may have trouble seeing the logic of the program.

If you find that making a small modification to a class requires you to jump to many different places in the code, something may be wrong with the way your code is organized.

Use Indentation and Alignment to Chunk Code

Braces {like these} mark off chunks of code. For humans to understand what is going on, quickly spotting the beginning and ending of each code chunk is important. Use a format that enables the eye to scan the code and identify the chunks of code without having to read every line.

For example, try putting the closing brace at the same distance from the margin as the keyword it closes for and indenting the contents of the code block.

```
for (n=1; n<= 10, n++){
      someCode();
      for (m=1; m<=25; m++){
        moreCode();
        yetMoreCode();
      }
      someMoreCode();
}
```

The following is an example of another style that we like:

```
for (n=1; n<= 10, n++)
    {
    someCode();
    for (m=1; m<=25; m++)
      {
      moreCode();
      yetMoreCode();
      }
    someMoreCode();
    }
```

Use White Space and Blank Lines to Group Code

White space is just what it sounds like, spaces, tabs, anything that puts empty space between two characters on the screen. The computer ignores white space and blank lines. But to human readers, white space is an important part of the information on a printed page.

Use spaces to make your expressions more readable. Use blank lines to flag breaks between chunks of code.

Use Short Comments to Clarify the Code

Use short comments to provide titles to sections of the code or to explain steps that may not be obvious to a reader of the code. A short comment guides the eye and saves the reader from trying to figure out the purpose of a calculator. For example:

```
//Center the bar chart
c += Math.max((size().width - (columns*(barWidth + (2 *
barSpace))))/2, 0);
```

Write Comments for Javadoc

Write comments that result in a useful Javadoc map of the code you have written. This is especially important if you're writing classes that may be reused in more than one applet and by more than one programmer. (See Chapter 11 for more information on Javadoc comments.)

Give Methods and Variables Meaningful Names

Giving meaningful names to variables makes your code much easier to read — and to write. Consider the difference between

```
for (n = 1; n <= 10; n ++){ ...
```

and

```
for (row = 1; row <= 10; row ++){ ...
```

Similarly, `intToString` is a more helpful method name than `iTS`.

Capitalize Constants

Constants are values that the program never changes. Occasionally, constants are numbers like pi. Often, they are choices that are arbitrarily coded as integers, for example, `LEFT`, `RIGHT`, `CENTER`. The custom among programmers is to give constants names in all caps.

Use Capitalization to Add Meaning to Names

Capitalization within a method name or class name can make the name more meaningful. For example, `setFrameNum()` is a more useful name than `frmnum()`.

Commit No Violence over Matters of Style

Layout and style of programming are tools that make it easier for programmers to communicate with each other. When collaborating programmers use a consistent style, each programmer saves time when reading the others' work. Conversely, being forced to decode a new style or — worse yet — coming to grips with the code of a programmer who has no consistent style is very irritating.

Some programmers defend to the death their style of indentation or their variable naming conventions. Let them live.

Write Code Like a Novel

The best code reads like a novel. It has well-defined characters, a clear plot line, and themes that can be appreciated at several levels of abstraction — all expressed in clear, yet elegant, language.

Chapter 23

Ten Facts about the Other Java

*J*ava, the programming language, is named for the invigorating brew that programmers use on occasion to keep themselves alert and creative when the demo is scheduled for tomorrow. Of course, another Java exists — it is the place where the coffee comes from.

As marketers searched for product names that carry associations with Java, some followed the coffee connection with names like *Latté* and *Café* and *Joe*. Others have honored the geographic connection.

Java Is a Large Island

Java is one of the thousands of islands that make up the nation of Indonesia, which is the fifth most populous country in the world. In addition to coffee, Java is known for batik fabrics, electronics, and the remains of *Java man,* a human ancestor that is one of the earliest specimens of *homo erectus*.

Jakarta Is a City

Jakarta is the largest city in Java and the capital of Indonesia. It is also the prerelease code name for a suite of Java development tools (now under development by Microsoft).

Wayang Kulit Are Shadow Puppets

Wayang Kulit are among the more famous cultural artifacts of Indonesia. Beautifully intricate shadow puppets, they are cut from buffalo hide and painted in additional detail that is never seen by the audience; the audience sees only the shadow of the flat puppet projected through a translucent screen.

Hmm . . . let me see how I can code that class:

```
public class WayangKulit extends class BuffaloHide
    private Color faceColor . . .
```

As far as I know, no one has as yet developed this theme, but be prepared.

Gamelan Is an Orchestra

Gamelan is the percussion orchestra that accompanies Wayang Kulit performances and other Javanese theatrical events. The orchestra consists of gongs, bells, and chimes — a description doesn't do it justice. You have to hear it.

Gamelan is also a Web site that contains postings of Java applets and other Java-related data.

The Dalang Is the Puppet Master

The Dalang is the puppet master who performs the Wayang Kulit shadow puppet plays. Similarly, the Dalang is also the Webmaster of the Gamelan Web site.

Garuda Is a God

Garuda is a god who takes the form of a bird and whose statues appear quite ferocious. Garuda is also the name of the Indonesian national airline. (This fact has no connection with programming; I just thought you might like to know.)

The Kris Is a Weapon

The kris is an Indonesian dagger — a thrusting weapon held not like a sword but like a pistol. Myth and mysticism accompany tales of this instrument. Some say that certain kris can fly; others say that once removed from its case, a kris will not return until it has drawn blood. The most popularly held belief is that a kris's blade holds the soul of its first or most courageous owner. The earliest known kris dates to 1342.

Although I have no inside information, I am ready to bet that we'll see Kris as a Java development tool real soon now.

Batik Is an Art Form

Batik is the process of printing a length of cloth with a wax-and-dye procedure. Beeswax is applied to both sides of the cloth in the areas that do not require color. The cloth is then dipped in dye until the correct color is achieved; then the wax is removed. A new pattern of wax is then applied, and a second color is applied. This process is repeated with as many as five different colors to build up an intricate pattern. Batik is usually printed on fine cotton or linen (sometimes silk is used). Traditional batik is still done by hand, but modernity has brought machinery to do much of the work.

Java Is a Land of Volcanoes

More than a hundred volcanic cones and craters dot Java's mountainous borders. Thirty-five of the volcanoes are active, and seven of them are under constant watch.

Yes, They Write Java in Java

For example, at the following URL, you will find an applet called Pujangga that composes poetry in Bahasa Indonesia, the native language of Indonesia.

```
http://sunsite.ui.ac.id/SunSITE/java/pujangga/index.html
```

Part VI
Appendixes

The 5th Wave   By Rich Tennant

How's that for interactivity?

In this part . . .

Part VI contains a helpful appendix that tells you what you find on the CD-ROM that comes with this book. We've enjoyed introducing you to the wonderful world of Java, and hope that your journeys onward in this remarkable program are both fun and fruitful.

Appendix

About the CD

The CD-ROM that comes with this book contains a bunch of useful goodies, including everything you need to compile, edit, debug, and document Java applets:

- The sample applets from this book
- Sample applets contributed by the Java Internet programming community
- JBuilder Professional V.2, a trial version professional-quality Java development environment for Windows 95 or Windows NT
- Java Developer Kit from Sun Microsystems
- MindSpring Internet Access trial
- Netscape Communicator 4.5, including Netscape's Navigator Web browser
- Internet Explorer 4.0, Microsoft's Web browser

Java Developer Kit

The Java Developer Kit (JDK) provides everything you need to compile, text, debug, and document Java applets and applications.

The CD includes Sun Microsystems development tools for the following platforms:

- Windows 98/95 (Java is not available for Windows 3.1)
- Windows NT

For JDK updates, or JDK versions for other platforms, check the JavaSoft Web site:

```
http://www.javasoft.com
```

The executable file is stored on the CD in the JDK folder. Before you run the executable to install the Java Developer Kit, close all of your applications (you have to restart your system to finish the installation). Follow the on-screen instructions during the installation process. Allow at least 50MB of disk space to install the Java Developer Kit.

When the installer asks you where to install the Java Developer Kit, be sure to write down the directory names. That's where you'll go when you want to run the JDK.

Java 2 was codenamed "1.2" during development, and a lot of official Sun Microsystems material for Java 2 still says "1.2." Wherever you see "Java 1.2" in the development tools, they mean "Java 2." It's the same thing.

Sample Applets

The JDK also contains many sample applets that you may find interesting and useful. To see these applets in action, start your Web browser, and then open the file Start.htm on the CD. Follow the link to Code Samples from Java Programming For Dummies. You find links to the sample applets in each chapter, as well as links to other useful resources.

Not all browsers support all Java 2 features on all computer systems. Some applets may not run on your system because of these glitches.

You can find the Java source code, HTML test pages, and other necessary files for these applets in the JPFD folder on the CD.

Other applets were created by Java developers throughout the world. To see these applets do their thing, start your Web browser and then open the Start.html file on the CD. Follow the link to Sample Applets from the Internet Community. You find links to each of the applets.

You can find the source code for these applets in the Applets folder on the CD.

- ✔ CrazyText — fancy text effects by Patrick Taylor in the United States
- ✔ Cube — a 3-D puzzle by Karl Hörnell in Sweden

- Fifteen — a 15-square puzzle by Anatoly Goroshnik in the United States (NY)
- Fireworks — animated fireworks by Tzu-Tai Liu in Taiwan
- FishTank — swimming fish by Leyth Keididi in the United States
- Frog — a hungry game by Karl Hörnell in Sweden
- Hands — a sophisticated finger counting game by Lee Oades in England
- Iceblox — a game by Karl Hörnell in Sweden
- Invaders — a game by Michael Girdley in the United States
- Mankala — the ancient game of Mankala by Roger E. Critchlow Jr. in the United States (CA)
- Mortgage — a mortgage calculator by Karl Jeacle in Ireland
- Puzzle — a 15-square puzzle using an image by Rick Field in Australia
- Skip — for experimenting with circuit diagrams by Jean-Claude Dufourd in France
- Tile — by John F. Cottrell in the United States
- Travel — the classic traveling salesman problem by Martin Hagerup in Denmark

Software

The *Java Programming For Dummies* CD has lots of the latest software for you to try. Here's how to use it

Microsoft Internet Explorer

Internet Explorer includes a web browser and a newsreader.

To install Internet Explorer, start in the CD's Software folder. In the CD's Software folder, look for the Ie40 folder. From the Ie40 folder, run IE4SETUP.EXE.

To avoid losing your work, shut down other applications before you install Internet Explorer.

Netscape Communicator

Communicator is a complete groupware suite, with a Web browser, e-mail, newsreader, and more.

To install Communicator, start in the CD's Software folder. In the CD's Software folder, look for the Netscape folder. In the Netscape folder, open the W95 folder for your Windows NT, Windows 98, or Windows 95 system. From the W95 folder, run cc32d45.exe to install Netscape Communicator.

To avoid losing your work, shut down other applications before you install Netscape Communicator.

JBuilder 2 Trial Version

JBuilder is a visual development tool for Java from Inprise. It includes a compiler and an object-oriented development environment.

The version of JBuilder on the *Java Programming For Dummies* CD is a trial version. Check the license agreement for conditions.

To install JBuilder, start in the CD's Software folder. In the CD's Software folder, look for the JBuilder folder. In the JBuilder folder, open the jbuilder folder and run setup.exe.

To avoid losing your work, shut down other applications before you install JBuilder.

Updates

If you have a problem during the installation of files or programs from the CD, please call the IDG Books Worldwide Customer Service phone number: 1-800-762-2974. Outside the United States, you can call 317-572-3000; extension 3993 for customer support, extension 3994 for technical support.

Index

• G •

•1•

• *X* •

• *Y* •

• *Z* •

Notes

Notes

Notes

Notes

To redeem this offer, mail this original coupon (no photocopies, please) along with payment and shipping information to:

Inprise Corporation
Order Processing
P.O. Box 660005
Scotts Valley, CA 95067-0005

Or call 1-800-932-9994, offer code 1543.

Name _____

Address _____

City _____

State/Province _____ Zip/Postal Code _____

Phone (_____) _____ Fax (_____) _____

Select one:

❏ JBuilder 2 Standard for Windows 95 & Windows NT	CD-ROM	$99.95
❏ JBuilder 2 Professional for Windows 95 & Windows NT (Reg. $799)	CD-ROM	$249.95
❏ JBuilder 2 Client/Server Suite for Windows 95 & Windows NT (Reg. $2,499)	CD-ROM	$1,999.00

Subtotal $ _____

State sales tax* $ _____

Freight ($10.00 per item) $ _____

Total order $ _____

Method of payment:

❏ Check enclosed (Make checks payable to Inprise Corporation)

❏ VISA ❏ MasterCard ❏ American Express

Card number: __ __ __ __ - __ __ __ __ - __ __ __ __ - __ __ __ __

Expiration date: __ __ / __ __

Offer Code 1543

Offer expires September 30, 1999.

This offer good in the U.S.A. and Canada only. International customers, please contact your local Inprise office for the offer in your country. Corporate Headquarters: 100 Enterprise Way, Scotts Valley, California 95066-3249, (831) 431-1000. **Internet: http://www.inprise.com** Offices in Australia (61-2-9248-0900), Canada (905-477-4344), Chile (56-2-233-7113), France (33-1-55-23-55-00), Germany (49-6103-9790), Hong Kong (852-2572-3238), Japan (81-3-5350-9380), Latin American Headquarters in U.S.A. (831-431-1126), Mexico (525-543-1413), The Netherlands (+31 [0] 20-503-5100), Taiwan (886-2-718-6627), and United Kingdom ([0800] 973139)

INPRISE™
Integrating the Enterprise

Exhibit A
Sun Microsystems, Inc.
Binary Code License Agreement

READ THE TERMS OF THIS AGREEMENT AND ANY PROVIDED SUPPLEMENTAL LICENSE
TERMS (COLLECTIVELY "AGREEMENT") CAREFULLY BEFORE OPENING THE SOFTWARE
MEDIA PACKAGE. BY OPENING THE SOFTWARE MEDIA PACKAGE, YOU AGREE TO THE
TERMS OF THIS AGREEMENT. IF YOU ARE ACCESSING THE SOFTWARE ELECTRONICALLY,
INDICATE YOUR ACCEPTANCE OF THESE TERMS BY SELECTING THE "ACCEPT" BUTTON AT
THE END OF THIS AGREEMENT. IF YOU DO NOT AGREE TO ALL THESE TERMS, PROMPTLY
RETURN THE UNUSED SOFTWARE TO YOUR PLACE OF PURCHASE FOR A REFUND OR, IF
THE SOFTWARE IS ACCESSED ELECTRONICALLY, SELECT THE "DECLINE" BUTTON AT THE
END OF THIS AGREEMENT.

1. LICENSE TO USE. Sun grants you a non-exclusive and non-transferable license for the
internal use only of the accompanying software and documentation and any error correc-
tions provided by Sun (collectively "Software"), by the number of users and the class of
computer hardware for which the corresponding fee has been paid.

2. RESTRICTIONS. Software is confidential and copyrighted. Title to Software and all
associated intellectual property rights is retained by Sun and/or its licensors. Except as
specifically authorized in any Supplemental License Terms, you may not make copies of
Software, other than a single copy of Software for archival purposes. Unless enforcement is
prohibited by applicable law, you may not modify, decompile, reverse engineer Software.
You acknowledge that Software is not designed or licensed for use in on-line control of
aircraft, air traffic, aircraft navigation or aircraft communications; or in the design, construction, operation or maintenance of any nuclear facility. Sun disclaims any express or
implied warranty of fitness for such uses. No right, title or interest in or to any trademark,
service mark, logo or trade name of Sun or its licensors is granted under this Agreement.

3. LIMITED WARRANTY. Sun warrants to you that for a period of ninety (90) days from the
date of purchase, as evidenced by a copy of the receipt, the media on which Software is
furnished (if any) will be free of defects in materials and workmanship under normal use.
Except for the foregoing, Software is provided "AS IS". Your exclusive remedy and Sun's
entire liability under this limited warranty will be at Sun's option to replace Software media
or refund the fee paid for Software.

4. DISCLAIMER OF WARRANTY. UNLESS SPECIFIED IN THIS AGREEMENT, ALL EXPRESS OR
IMPLIED CONDITIONS, REPRESENTATIONS AND WARRANTIES, INCLUDING ANY IMPLIED
WARRANTY OF MERCHANTABILITY, FITNESS FOR A PARTICULAR PURPOSE, OR NON-
INFRINGEMENT, ARE DISCLAIMED, EXCEPT TO THE EXTENT THAT THESE DISCLAIMERS
ARE HELD TO BE LEGALLY INVALID.**5. LIMITATION OF LIABILITY.** TO THE EXTENT NOT
PROHIBITED BY LAW, IN NO EVENT WILL SUN OR ITS LICENSORS BE LIABLE FOR ANY LOST
REVENUE, PROFIT OR DATA, OR FOR SPECIAL, INDIRECT, CONSEQUENTIAL, INCIDENTAL OR
PUNITIVE DAMAGES, HOWEVER CAUSED REGARDLESS OF THE THEORY OF LIABILITY,
liability to you, whether in contract, tort (including negligence), or otherwise, exceed the
amount paid by you for Software under this Agreement. The foregoing limitations will apply
even if the above stated warranty fails of its essential purpose.

6. Termination. This Agreement is effective until terminated. You may terminate this Agreement at any time by destroying all copies of Software. This Agreement will terminate immediately without notice from Sun if you fail to comply with any provision of this Agreement. Upon Termination, you must destroy all copies of Software.

7. Export Regulations. All Software and technical data delivered under this Agreement are subject to US export control laws and may be subject to export or import regulations in other countries. You agree to comply strictly with all such laws and regulations and acknowledge that you have the responsibility to obtain such licenses to export, re-export, or import as may be required after delivery to you.

8. U.S. Government Rights. If Software is being acquired by or on behalf of the U.S. Government or by a U.S. Government prime contractor or subcontractor (at any tier), then the Government's rights in Software will be only as set forth in this Agreement; this is in accordance with 48 CFR 227.7201 through 227.7202-4 (for Department of Defense (DOD) acquisitions) and with 48 CFR 2.101 and 12.212 (for non-DOD acquisitions).

9. Governing Law. Any action related to this Agreement will be governed by California law and controlling U.S. federal law. No choice of law rules of any jurisdiction will apply.

10. Severability. If any provision of this Agreement is held to be unenforceable, this Agreement will remain in effect with the provision omitted, unless omission would frustrate the intent of the parties, in which case this Agreement will immediately terminate.

11. Integration. This Agreement is the entire agreement between you and Sun relating to its subject matter. It supersedes all prior or contemporaneous oral or written communications, proposals, representations and warranties and prevails over any conflicting or additional terms of any quote, order, acknowledgment, or other communication between the parties relating to its subject matter during the term of this Agreement. No modification of this Agreement will be binding, unless in writing and signed by an authorized representative of each party.

For inquiries please contact: Sun Microsystems, Inc. 901 San Antonio Road, Palo Alto, California 94303

JAVA' 2 SDK, STANDARD EDITION, V 1.2.1
SUPPLEMENTAL LICENSE TERMS

These supplemental terms ("Supplement") add to the terms of the Binary Code License Agreement (collectively the "Agreement"). Capitalized terms not defined herein shall have the same meanings ascribed to them in the Agreement. The Supplement terms shall supersede any inconsistent or conflicting terms in the Agreement above, or in any license contained within the Software.

1. Limited License Grant. Sun grants to you a non-exclusive, non-transferable limited license to use the Software without fee for evaluation of the Software and for development of Java' applets and applications provided that you: (i) may not re-distribute the Software in whole or in part, either separately or included with a product; and (ii) may not create, or authorize your licensees to create additional classes, interfaces, or subpackages that are contained in the "java" or "sun" packages or similar as specified by Sun in any class file naming convention. Refer to the Java Runtime Environment Version 1.2.1 binary code license (http://java.sun.com/products/jdk/1.2/jre/index.html) for the availability of runtime code which may be distributed with Java applets and applications.

2. Java Platform Interface. In the event that Licensee creates an additional API(s) which: (i) extends the functionality of a Java Environment; and, (ii) is exposed to third party software developers for the purpose of developing additional software which invokes such additional API, Licensee must promptly publish broadly an accurate specification for such API for free use by all developers.

3. Trademarks and Logos. Licensee acknowledges as between it and Sun that Sun owns the Java trademark and all Java-related trademarks, logos and icons including the Coffee Cup and Duke ("Java Marks") and agrees to comply with the Java Trademark Guidelines at http://www.sun.com/policies/trademarks.

4. Source Code. Software may contain source code that is provided solely for reference purposes pursuant to the terms of this Agreement.

IDG Books Worldwide, Inc., End-User License Agreement

READ THIS. You should carefully read these terms and conditions before opening the software packet(s) included with this book ("Book"). This is a license agreement ("Agreement") between you and IDG Books Worldwide, Inc. ("IDGB"). By opening the accompanying software packet(s), you acknowledge that you have read and accept the following terms and conditions. If you do not agree and do not want to be bound by such terms and conditions, promptly return the Book and the unopened software packet(s) to the place you obtained them for a full refund.

1. **License Grant.** IDGB grants to you (either an individual or entity) a nonexclusive license to use one copy of the enclosed software program(s) (collectively, the "Software") solely for your own personal or business purposes on a single computer (whether a standard computer or a workstation component of a multiuser network). The Software is in use on a computer when it is loaded into temporary memory (RAM) or installed into permanent memory (hard disk, CD-ROM, or other storage device). IDGB reserves all rights not expressly granted herein.

2. **Ownership.** IDGB is the owner of all right, title, and interest, including copyright, in and to the compilation of the Software recorded on the disk(s) or CD-ROM ("Software Media"). Copyright to the individual programs recorded on the Software Media is owned by the author or other authorized copyright owner of each program. Ownership of the Software and all proprietary rights relating thereto remain with IDGB and its licensers.

3. **Restrictions on Use and Transfer.**

   (a) You may only (i) make one copy of the Software for backup or archival purposes, or (ii) transfer the Software to a single hard disk, provided that you keep the original for backup or archival purposes. You may not (i) rent or lease the Software, (ii) copy or reproduce the Software through a LAN or other network system or through any computer subscriber system or bulletin-board system, or (iii) modify, adapt, or create derivative works based on the Software.

   (b) You may not reverse engineer, decompile, or disassemble the Software. You may transfer the Software and user documentation on a permanent basis, provided that the transferee agrees to accept the terms and conditions of this Agreement and you retain no copies. If the Software is an update or has been updated, any transfer must include the most recent update and all prior versions.

4. **Restrictions on Use of Individual Programs.** You must follow the individual requirements and restrictions detailed for each individual program in the "About the CD" appendix of this Book. These limitations are also contained in the individual license agreements recorded on the Software Media. These limitations may include a requirement that after using the program for a specified period of time, the user must pay a registration fee or discontinue use. By opening the Software packet(s), you will be agreeing to abide by the licenses and restrictions for these individual programs that are detailed in the "About the CD" appendix and on the Software Media. None of the material on this Software Media or listed in this Book may ever be redistributed, in original or modified form, for commercial purposes.

5. Limited Warranty.

    (a) IDGB warrants that the Software and Software Media are free from defects in materials and workmanship under normal use for a period of sixty (60) days from the date of purchase of this Book. If IDGB receives notification within the warranty period of defects in materials or workmanship, IDGB will replace the defective Software Media.

    (b) IDGB AND THE AUTHOR OF THE BOOK DISCLAIM ALL OTHER WARRANTIES, EXPRESS OR IMPLIED, INCLUDING WITHOUT LIMITATION IMPLIED WARRANTIES OF MERCHANTABILITY AND FITNESS FOR A PARTICULAR PURPOSE, WITH RESPECT TO THE SOFTWARE, THE PROGRAMS, THE SOURCE CODE CONTAINED THEREIN, AND/OR THE TECHNIQUES DESCRIBED IN THIS BOOK. IDGB DOES NOT WARRANT THAT THE FUNCTIONS CONTAINED IN THE SOFTWARE WILL MEET YOUR REQUIREMENTS OR THAT THE OPERATION OF THE SOFTWARE WILL BE ERROR FREE.

    (c) This limited warranty gives you specific legal rights, and you may have other rights that vary from jurisdiction to jurisdiction.

6. Remedies.

    (a) IDGB's entire liability and your exclusive remedy for defects in materials and workmanship shall be limited to replacement of the Software Media, which may be returned to IDGB with a copy of your receipt at the following address: Software Media Fulfillment Department, Attn.: *Java Programming For Dummies,* 3rd Edition, IDG Books Worldwide, Inc., 10475 Crosspoint Blvd., Indianapolis, IN 46256, or call 800-762-2974. Please allow three to four weeks for delivery. This Limited Warranty is void if failure of the Software Media has resulted from accident, abuse, or misapplication. Any replacement Software Media will be warranted for the remainder of the original warranty period or thirty (30) days, whichever is longer.

    (b) In no event shall IDGB or the author be liable for any damages whatsoever (including without limitation damages for loss of business profits, business interruption, loss of business information, or any other pecuniary loss) arising from the use of or inability to use the Book or the Software, even if IDGB has been advised of the possibility of such damages.

    (c) Because some jurisdictions do not allow the exclusion or limitation of liability for consequential or incidental damages, the above limitation or exclusion may not apply to you.

7. U.S. Government Restricted Rights. Use, duplication, or disclosure of the Software by the U.S. Government is subject to restrictions stated in paragraph (c)(1)(ii) of the Rights in Technical Data and Computer Software clause of DFARS 252.227-7013, and in subparagraphs (a) through (d) of the Commercial Computer–Restricted Rights clause at FAR 52.227-19, and in similar clauses in the NASA FAR supplement, when applicable.

8. General. This Agreement constitutes the entire understanding of the parties and revokes and supersedes all prior agreements, oral or written, between them and may not be modified or amended except in a writing signed by both parties hereto that specifically refers to this Agreement. This Agreement shall take precedence over any other documents that may be in conflict herewith. If any one or more provisions contained in this Agreement are held by any court or tribunal to be invalid, illegal, or otherwise unenforceable, each and every other provision shall remain in full force and effect.

Using the CD

The CD-ROM that comes with this book contains a bunch of useful hgoodies, including everything you need to compile, edit, debug, and document Java applets:

- ✔ The sample applets from this book
- ✔ Sample applets contributed by the Java Internet programming community
- ✔ JBuilder Professional V.2, a trial version professional-quality Java development environment for Windows 95 or Windows NT
- ✔ Java Developer Kit from Sun Microsystems
- ✔ MindSpring Internet Access trial
- ✔ Netscape Communicator 4.5, including Netscape's Navigator Web browser
- ✔ Internet Explorer 4.0, Microsoft's Web browser

To use the samples or install the software, refer to Appendix A of this book.

Discover *Dummies*™ Online!

The *Dummies* Web Site is your fun and friendly online resource for the latest information about *...For Dummies*® books on all your favorite topics. From cars to computers, wine to Windows, and investing to the Internet, we've got a shelf full of *...For Dummies* books waiting for you!

Ten Fun and Useful Things You Can Do at www.dummies.com

1. Register this book and win!
2. Find and buy the *...For Dummies* books you want online.
3. Get ten great *Dummies Tips*™ every week.
4. Chat with your favorite *...For Dummies* authors.
5. Subscribe free to *The Dummies Dispatch*™ newsletter.
6. Enter our sweepstakes and win cool stuff.
7. Send a free cartoon postcard to a friend.
8. Download free software.
9. Sample a book before you buy.
10. Talk to us. Make comments, ask questions, and get answers!

Jump online to these ten fun and useful things at

http://www.dummies.com/10useful

For other technology titles from IDG Books Worldwide, go to
www.idgbooks.com

Not online yet? It's easy to get started with *The Internet For Dummies*® 5th Edition, or *Dummies 101*®: *The Internet For Windows*® *98*, available at local retailers everywhere.

Find other *...For Dummies* books on these topics:

Business • Careers • Databases • Food & Beverages • Games • Gardening • Graphics • Hardware
Health & Fitness • Internet and the World Wide Web • Networking • Office Suites
Operating Systems • Personal Finance • Pets • Programming • Recreation • Sports
Spreadsheets • Teacher Resources • Test Prep • Word Processing

IDG BOOKS WORLDWIDE BOOK REGISTRATION

Register This Book and Win!

We want to hear from you!

Visit **http://my2cents.dummies.com** to register this book and tell us how you liked it!

✔ Get entered in our monthly prize giveaway.

✔ Give us feedback about this book — tell us what you like best, what you like least, or maybe what you'd like to ask the author and us to change!

✔ Let us know any other ...*For Dummies*® topics that interest you.

Your feedback helps us determine what books to publish, tells us what coverage to add as we revise our books, and lets us know whether we're meeting your needs as a ...*For Dummies* reader. You're our most valuable resource, and what you have to say is important to us!

Not on the Web yet? It's easy to get started with *Dummies 101*®: *The Internet For Windows*® *98* or *The Internet For Dummies*,® 5th Edition, at local retailers everywhere.

Or let us know what you think by sending us a letter at the following address:

...*For Dummies* Book Registration
Dummies Press
7260 Shadeland Station, Suite 100
Indianapolis, IN 46256-3917
Fax 317-596-5498

...FOR DUMMIES™

BESTSELLING BOOK SERIES